Sustainable Infrastructure for Cities and Societies

The central role of infrastructure to cities, and in particular their sustainability, is essential for proper planning and design since most energy and materials are themselves consumed by or through infrastructures. Moreover, infrastructures of all types affect matters of economic and social equity, due to access that they provide or prevent. *Sustainable Infrastructure for Cities and Societies* shows how fundamental planning, design, finance, and governance principles can be adapted for sustainable infrastructure to provide solutions to make cities significantly more sustainable. By providing a contemporary overview on infrastructure, cities, planning, economies, and sustainability, the book addresses how to plan, design, finance, and manage infrastructure in ways that reduce consumption and harmful impacts while maintaining and improving life quality. It considers the interrelationships between the economic, political, societal, and institutional frameworks, providing an integrative approach including livability and sustainability, principles and practice, and planning and design. It further translates these approaches that professionals, policymakers, and leaders can use. This approach gives the book wide appeal for students, researchers, and practitioners hoping to build a more sustainable world.

Michael Neuman is Professor of Sustainable Urbanism at the University of Westminster and principal of the Michael Neuman Consultancy. He is the multi-award-winning author of numerous books, articles, chapters, reports, and plans that have been translated into ten languages. His research and practice span urbanism, planning, design, engineering, sustainability, infrastructure, and governance. He has advised mayors in Europe, the United States, and Australia, the Regional Plan Association of New York, the Barcelona Metropolitan Plan, and other governments and private clients around the world.

Sustainable Infrastructure for Cities and Societies

Michael Neuman

Routledge
Taylor & Francis Group
NEW YORK AND LONDON

Cover image: Getty Images

First published 2022
by Routledge
605 Third Avenue, New York, NY 10158

and by Routledge
4 Park Square, Milton Park, Abingdon, Oxon, OX14 4RN

Routledge is an imprint of the Taylor & Francis Group, an informa business

© 2022 Taylor & Francis

The right of Michael Neuman to be identified as author of this work has been asserted in accordance with sections 77 and 78 of the Copyright, Designs and Patents Act 1988.

All rights reserved. No part of this book may be reprinted or reproduced or utilised in any form or by any electronic, mechanical, or other means, now known or hereafter invented, including photocopying and recording, or in any information storage or retrieval system, without permission in writing from the publishers.

Trademark notice: Product or corporate names may be trademarks or registered trademarks, and are used only for identification and explanation without intent to infringe.

Library of Congress Cataloging-in-Publication Data
A catalog record for this title has been requested

ISBN: 978-0-367-34026-1 (hbk)
ISBN: 978-0-367-34024-7 (pbk)
ISBN: 978-0-429-32350-8 (ebk)

DOI: 10.4324/9780429323508

Typeset in Adobe Garamond Pro
by codeMantra

Contents

List of Figures vii
Preface ix
Acknowledgements xiii

PART I INFRASTRUCTURE, CITIES, AND SUSTAINABILITY 1

Introduction 3
1   Infrastructure Investments, Public and Private Gains 29
2   Infiltrating Infrastructure: Defining Infrastructure and its
    Role in Society 43
3   Sustainable Infrastructure Begets Sustainable Cities 63

PART II PLANNING FOR SUSTAINABLE INFRASTRUCTURES 83

4   City Planning and Infrastructure 85
Big Dig Project 111
5   Infrastructure Planning 115
Three Gorges Dam Project 145
6   Demand-Capacity Management 147

PART II MANAGEMENT 161

7   Governing Institutions 163
8   Financing and Budgeting 187
9   Future Directions 201

Appendix 1 209
Appendix 2 211
Appendix 3 219
Index 221

v

Figures

0.1	Atmospheric Carbon Dioxide Levels since 1957	4
0.2	Global Ecological Footprint Chart since 1961	12
0.3	Life Cycle of Infrastructure – Ideal versus Actual	13
0.4	Infrastructure Characteristics – Old versus New	19
3.1	Worldwide Annual Air Travel Passenger Miles Flown since 1950	73
5.1	Fifteen Stages in Life Cycle Infrastructure Planning	120
5.2	Comparison Chart of Assessments, Programs, and Budgets	132
5.3	Typical Expectations of Infrastructure Service Life in Years	134
6.1	Demand-Capacity Management	149
7.1	Infrastructure Institution Characteristics	172
7.2	The Life Cycle of Institutional Transformation	175
8.1	Life Cycle of Infrastructure – Ideal versus Actual	193

Preface

Infrastructure, seen and unseen, plays multiple roles in our lives on a daily basis. Roles often not noticed, under our radar, yet subliminally present. Until disruption or disaster, then how we wish it was working. This book is about infrastructures, the cities they build, the environments they improve or damage, the economies they buoy or sink, the activities and opportunities they afford or deny access to – in short, the work that infrastructure tirelessly performs for us as individuals, as societies, and every size of settlement and organization in-between. The book is also about how to plan and design infrastructure networks in concert with planning and designing cities, so that both are sustainable and mutually supportive. To the extent we are alive and well in contemporary society, it is largely due to life-supporting infrastructure and the cities in which we live, produce, consume, and thrive.

This has always been so. From Phoenician ports and Roman roads to Arab aqueducts and Mayan temples, each civilization based its prosperous trade and became enshrined in history through the infrastructures it invented and built. The eight wonders of the ancient world along with their modern equivalents are mostly infrastructures. They are such potent emblems that represent a populace that they are the first targets of destruction in war or rebellion, because not only do they serve vital functions, they symbolize society and rally solidarity.

Yet, writing as I am in the spring of 2021 in Marshall, California, overlooking Tomales Bay and my favorite place, Point Reyes National Seashore, I am in a bubble of several kinds. One is of wealth, where a two-bedroom, 1,000-square-foot home on a postage-stamp-sized lot just sold for $3 million. Of homogeneity, where each resident is white and the median age is 65. Of health, with no known cases of Covid-19, situated in Marin County, with one of the lowest case and death rates in the US of that disease in the midst of a global pandemic.

Why do I write this? Because this bubble reminds me of the stark contrast between a temporary place I have chosen, and the permanent places many humans live – billions around the globe – that do not have the basic provisions of a healthy, decent life. Lack of potable running water, lack of heat, lack of sanitary disposal of human waste, lack of food and housing, the list goes on. It is not just the so-called poor countries that harbor these conditions. We all see them every day in our cities and towns. In America today there are counties in Alabama where up to 90 percent of homes had no functioning septic systems (Coleman Flowers 2020; Fraser 2021, 17). These lacks denote the constant misery, unbridled poverty, degrees of despair, that are brought about by inferior infrastructure or an absence of it. It is clear that their situations can be changed for the better by the provision of adequate infrastructure. Infrastructure provided properly begets dignity in addition to opportunity. As such, infrastructure is a matter of human rights. Infrastructure is about equity and access, who has and who has not. It is the most ubiquitous yet often unseen and underrated public good.

Of the growing shelf of infrastructure books, four varieties can be discerned. One is technical, aimed at the engineer, utility foreman, or technician. Another is geared to the money people, the financiers, whether public, private, or mixed. In this group we also find infrastructure management and development guidance. The third group consists of coffee table books, those glossy, large picture books that display magnificent works in their glory, to inspire and embolden. The fourth group is made of historical texts that explore infrastructure and its relation to people and place over time, and endeavor to show its roles and consequences.

Then there are one-offs, such as those that signal new ways of thinking. Standing out is *Splintering Urbanism*. It illustrates what can be called the darker side of infrastructure, how it divides and splinters cities in addition to connecting them (Graham and Marvin 2001). In contrast, this book is about infrastructure planning, design, and governance. Its aim is to systematically link urban sustainability to all infrastructures, and to lay out a comprehensive life cycle method for infrastructure and its planning and financing. This book has a threefold emphasis:

- The reciprocal relations among infrastructures, cities, and sustainability
- The reciprocal relations of infrastructures with the sustainability of all forms of development: urban, societal, corporate, and economic
- The reciprocal relations between infrastructure and the practices of city planning and urban design, accounting and financing

These themes are inseparable. Cities, their growth, public health, environmental quality, economic vitality, social equity, and quality of life are inextricably bound with infrastructure networks and their proper operation. Because of this, a strong theme of integration runs throughout.

This book is an invitation to explore a new path on the way to attaining a more just and more sustainable society. The aim and hope is that the ultimate stewards of the infrastructure that makes the city possible – the people themselves – become acquainted with these sinews seen and unseen so that they may inspire our political leaders and city builders to do the right thing. It is to them, and to those professionals and their patrons, clients, benefactors, sponsors, and constituents this text is written. For it is they who dedicate themselves to the hidden bowels, the most profane structures. They are the unseen heroes of every day, without whom every act would be a struggle.

The solutions presented in this book are in the form of fundamental principles for planning, design, finance, and governance which can be adapted by any agent in any context. General principles are preferable to technologies, case examples, or best practices, which are specific to time, place, and fashion, and thus either quickly become out of date and / or are not applicable outside their context. Notwithstanding, a few selected case studies are presented to illustrate these principles.

This book is necessarily selective. Planning, design, finance, and governance are paid more attention to than technology and politics; as vital as the latter are. This is partly due to my experience and partly due to limits to knowledge and space constraints in such a book. One book and one person cannot do justice to as complex and big a topic as this.

References

Coleman Flowers, C. (2020). *Waste: One Woman's Fight Against America's Dirty Secret*. New York: The New Press.

Fraser, C. (2021). The stench of American neglect. *New York Review of Books*, 68(3): 16–18.

Graham, S. and Marvin, S. (2001). *Splintering Urbanism: Networked Infrastructures, Technological Mobilities, and the Urban Condition*. London: Routledge.

Acknowledgements

Notwithstanding major work for the states of New Jersey and California in the 1990s, and research in Spain in the same decade, the redirection of my career to focus to infrastructure began during a year-long sabbatical in Barcelona in 2004–2005. It coincided with the derivation of what I immodestly yet hopefully called then a general theory of sustainability. In that theory, I linked thermodynamics and rate process theory with ecology and economics to find a way to quantify the "absolute" or "scientific" degree of sustainability of any process, whether social, economic, or environmental (Neuman and Churchill 2005, 2011, Churchill and Neuman 2005). The more I worked on sustainability and infrastructure simultaneously, the more I realized that infrastructure is the way to attain sustainability in cities and regions. This became even more apparent in practice, as the city of Barcelona, while coming to the end of its then two decade long global prominence regarding innovations in urban planning and design, continued to innovate in the realm of sustainable infrastructures. This led to an outpouring of articles and research reports in the latter half of that decade.

Being in Barcelona, a special place for me going back to my first visit in 1982, was the most substantial living classroom for the integration of planning, design, architecture, sustainability, and infrastructure as I could have imagined. Having lived there for five years, and visited for several full summers and many other multi-week stays, my intimacy and love affair with the city only grew, despite the onslaught of tourism. Barcelona, with its special light from the Mediterranean, along with its history, culture, and urban fabric, has always inspired me. Much of my best creative work and thinking occurred there. One of the many things ingrained in my design and planning is the intuitive and sensible way in which urban planning, urban design, infrastructure, environment, and social analysis have long (since Ildefons Cerdà in the 1860s) been truly integrated there. In that city, designers, planners, engineers, and others tend to collaborate closely in all phases of urban development. Yet my infrastructure journey started before Barcelona.

John Epling hired me to work with the New Jersey Office of State Planning in the mid-1980s, at the outset of drafting its first state plan, *Communities of Place*. There, the outsize role of infrastructure became evident. A cornerstone of the state plan was the Infrastructure Needs Assessment, whose preparation and basis for the plan was codified in the State Planning Act. Among my responsibilities as Planning

Manager was to develop, in collaboration with Robert Kull, the methodology and algorithms to prepare the needs assessment, which included a life cycle analysis of municipal, county, and state needs over the 20-year horizon of the plan, from 1990 to 2010. This, along with the roles of infrastructure as the backbone of the plan and its innovative regional design system, marked my understanding of the strategic power of infrastructure. This journey at state-level engagement in infrastructure continued in California, where I was commissioned to prepare a report on the state's infrastructure planning, budget, and financing that resulted in several reforms (Neuman and Whittington 2000).

I am fortunate to deal with cities from several perspectives: governance, politics, institutions, planning, design, engineering, and ecology. I've come to realize that they are all critical, and must be dealt with together, in an integrated way. Historically, city planning and especially city plans did just that – integrate. They focused on the public interest, which in large measure is brought to tangible life by infrastructure. Some of this has been lost to the decline of the plan and the focus on process, as well as the decline of the public interest. Nonetheless, the increase in interdisciplinary work, the rise of sustainability and resilience, and the return of infrastructure as a strategic component of cities and economies have all conferred immense importance on infrastructure. The scope of infrastructure is vast, and I am indebted to numerous people for guiding me.

Academic mentors along with way exerted key influences, to whom I am eternally grateful. They include Martin Meyerson, Ian McHarg, Chris Alexander, Hajo Neis, Peter Hall, Manuel Castells, Gary Hack, Mike Teitz, Judy Innes, Luigi Mazza, and Ed Blakely. Colleagues with whom I've had the good fortune of collaborating on projects – both research and professional – have also been instrumental in shaping my evolving ideas. They include John Epling, Bob Yaro, Fritz Steiner, Jan Whittington, Sheri Smith, Antonio Font, Eduardo Mangada, Félix Arias, Albert Serratosa, and Alfonso Vegara. Specifically, for infrastructure I am indebted to many students, post-docs, and research assistants. I need to specially thank Baoliang Liu, Zhu Qian, Hwan Yong Kim, Araz Taeihagh, Mireille Tchapi, Megan Sharkey, and Irena Itova. Other friends and colleagues who have upped my infrastructure game are David Amborski, David Dowall, Gabriel Dupuy, Andreas Faludi, Steven Graham, Franziska Hassellmann, Lewis Knight, and Camilla Perrone.

There are others I could name, as well as emblematic cities that have inspired me, most significantly ones where I have lived and worked: Sydney, Barcelona, Madrid, London, Berkeley, Los Angeles, Seattle, San Diego, and Philadelphia. In my view, intimate place knowledge is the baseline for any practice of design.

My editor at Routledge, Kate Schell, has been especially supportive. Without her inspiration and encouragement, this book would not exist. In addition to her, and the entire production team at Routledge, particularly Sean Speers, I also want to thank the publishers of the journals' articles on which several of this book's chapters are based, listed below.

Michael Neuman
May, 2021

References

Neuman, M., Churchill, S. (2005). The role of thermodynamics and rate processes with respect to alternative fuels. *Proceedings*, American Institute of Chemical Engineers Spring National Meeting, 2389, Atlanta, Georgia.

Churchill, S. and Neuman, M. (2005). A generalized mathematical model for sustainability. *Proceedings*, American Institute of Chemical Engineers Annual Meeting, 344–354, Cincinnati, Ohio.

Neuman, M. and Churchill, S. (2011). A general process model of sustainability. *Industrial and Engineering Chemistry Research*, 50: 8901–8904.

The Introduction is an updated and revised version of Neuman, M. (2020). Infrastructure is key to make cities sustainable. *Sustainability*, 12(8308): 1–17.

Parts of Chapter 1 are selected and updated excerpts from Neuman, M. (2011). Ildefons Cerdà and the future of spatial planning: The network urbanism of a city planning pioneer. *Town Planning Review*, 82(2): 117–143; and Neuman, M. (2005). Infrastructure. In Caves, R. W. (ed.), *Encyclopaedia of the City*. London and New York: Routledge, 261–264.

Chapter 2 is a revised and updated version of Neuman, M. (2006). Infiltrating infrastructures. *Journal of Urban Technology*, 13(1): 3–31.

Chapter 4 contains updated selections from Neuman, M. and Smith, S. (2010). Infrastructure and city planning: Once and future partners. *Journal of Planning History*, 9(1): 21–42.

Parts of Chapter 6 are amended and updated from Neuman, M. (2011). Infrastructure planning for sustainable cities. *Geographica Helvetica*, 15(2): 100–107.

INFRASTRUCTURE, CITIES, AND SUSTAINABILITY

Introduction

Infrastructure is Key to Make Cities Sustainable

The Power of Hidden, and Not so Hidden, Flows

Infrastructure is all around us: under, above, even inside our built and natural landscapes. Sometimes hidden, becoming "visible" when not working. Sometimes visible, whether beautiful like the Golden Gate Bridge, or not, like mobile phone towers. The flows that course through them make our cities, economies, and lives possible. Cities could not even exist without infrastructure. The more powerful their infrastructures and their flows, then the more powerful the city, the economy, and the people that populate them. Life is endowed with more possibilities by infrastructure.

The centrality of infrastructure is pervasive. Worldwide, cities embrace infrastructure for economic competitiveness and issues across the board: health and well-being, travel and leisure, education and welfare, environmental protection and public safety. As cities are crucibles that concentrate the human condition, infrastructures are conduits that enable that concentration and empower human achievement. A telling example of how cities concentrate is that 95 percent of all Covid-19 cases were recorded in cities in the first months (UN Habitat 2021). Even more telling, this Habitat report lists infrastructure first of four "key priorities".

As if we needed more motivation and urgency, an April 2021 National Oceanic and Atmospheric Administration (NOAA) report revealed that in 2020, the pandemic year, atmospheric CO_2 increased by nearly 3 ppm, the fifth highest year on NOAA records, even as pundits and policymakers alike expected a decrease.

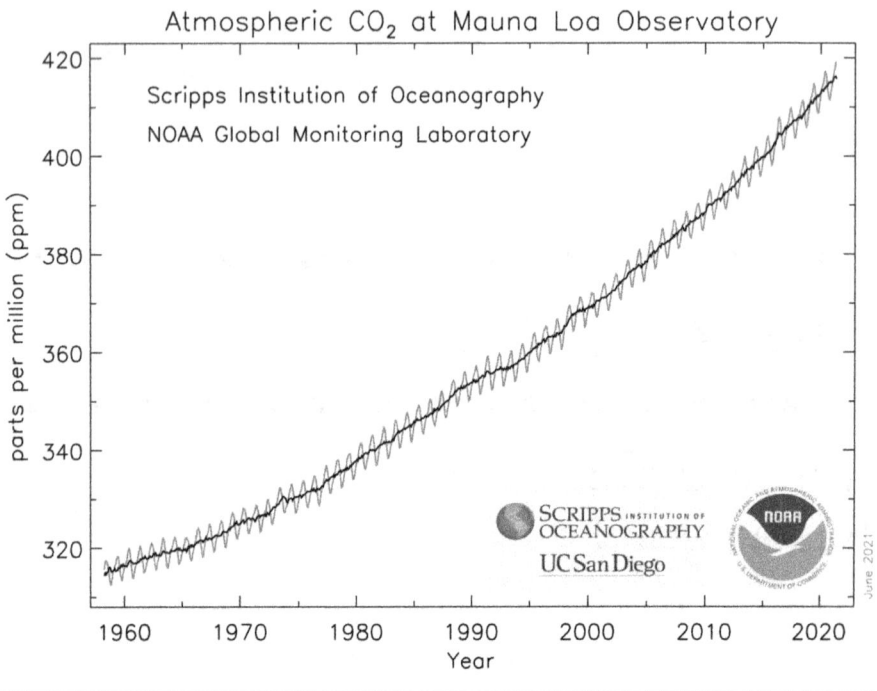

Figure 0.1 Atmospheric Carbon Dioxide Levels since 1957

The atmospheric burden of CO_2 is now comparable to where it was during the Mid-Pliocene Warm Period around 3.6 million years ago, when concentrations of carbon dioxide ranged from about 380 to 450 parts per million. During that time sea level was about 78 feet higher than today, the average temperature was 7 degrees Fahrenheit higher than in pre-industrial times (Stein 2021).[1]

See Figure 0.1. To compound the climate crisis, the rate of methane (CH_4) increase was equivalent, acknowledging that methane is 28 times more potent than CO_2 as a greenhouse gas.[2]

But it is not just the climate crisis that is shaped by, and can be abated or ended by, infrastructure. A similar logic applies to global pandemics. According to Steven Johnson,

> during the century since the end of the Great Influenza outbreak, the average human life span has doubled. There are few measures of human progress more astonishing than this.[3] One reason the [doubling of lifespan] was so egalitarian in scope is that it was propelled by *infrastructure advances* that benefited the entire population, not just the elites. Starting in the first decades of the 20th century, human beings in cities all around

the world began consuming microscopic amounts of chlorine in their drinking water … [and] it is lethal to bacteria that cause diseases like cholera (Johnson 2021a. emphasis added).

City water agencies did this using public waterworks infrastructure. Another example was the introduction of sewerage infrastructure to eradicate cholera and related epidemics in the 19th century. While this advance in life span was not due to infrastructure alone – science, advocacy, and policy played roles – even these three factors depend in large part on infrastructures both physical and administrative. Administrative (soft) infrastructures include institutions such as education and research, government, public health like local health agencies and hospitals, the WHO, the CDC, and others.

Infrastructures shape many aspects of daily life for all, not just humans. Consider their impacts on habitats far and wide, on the entire earth system, and on most if not all species. Our decisions and actions regarding infrastructure have long-term – at times millennial – and wide-ranging effects. The effects of infrastructure are multifold. They connect, enable, support, maintain, protect, enhance, and enrich. They also can destroy, divide, hamper, impinge, and make us dependent. After the sun, sea, and soil, infrastructures could be the most consequential factor in life on earth, as far as humans are concerned.

In cities and towns, infrastructure gets built first, shapes growth most, and lasts longest. Infrastructure provides opportunity and access. Infrastructure can remain in use for centuries and even millennia. Such longevity evokes the power of infrastructure. Infrastructure leads because it is first, provides the foundation, and has staying power.

The same is true for rural areas. For example, trains in the 19th century and rural electrification in the 20th, while dams, reservoirs, and canals permitted irrigation and development, opening up the Great Plains and the West of the United States to settlement. In country and city alike, infrastructure affords advantages.

This is especially true for contemporary global cities and urban megaregions. When the biggest urban conglomerations extend across tens of thousands of square kilometers and tens of millions of persons, the most strategic and robust opportunities for their planning are infrastructure networks (Neuman and Hull 2011). What better asset to have under control? What better illustrates the importance of infrastructure than knowing that war planners seek to destroy it first? Why? Without it, the enemy cannot fight or survive. These same attributes make infrastructure the first to get rebuilt after a war or natural disaster. These extremes highlight how critical infrastructure really is.

In preindustrial societies – which we could call sustainable in terms of energy, materials, and environmental impacts – infrastructures were largely powered by the sun, wind, water, and gravity. Think of daylight, windmills, canals, aqueducts, rivers, watermills, and dams. Travel was on mediums also powered by water and wind, or animals and humans, without fossil fuels. They were built with sustainable and natural materials, using local knowledge gained from cultures intimately intertwined with nature. These factors made them sustainable, along with their small scale.

These principles underlying preindustrial, sustainable infrastructures will be explored in this book for their relevance today, even as we cannot go backwards in history nor should we idealize historical societies. New infrastructures that have their own principles and properties will also be surveyed. Novel advancements in infrastructure transform our lives, cities, and planet in ways beyond our control. Their scale, scope, magnitude, and centralized control can overwhelm individuals and ecosystems, and seem out of our control. In many instances, this causes dependence and despondence, leading to adverse effects to physical and mental health. Infrastructures can disconnect humans from nature, leading to emotional and spiritual maladies in addition to ecological and economic ones. Given the multifold effects of infrastructures, how can we plan, design, and build them so that good outweighs bad, beauty overtakes ugly?

The scale, scope, and ubiquity of infrastructure makes it an unsung hero and antihero in our world, for better and for worse. While the intent behind all infrastructure is to abet the greater good, at least in principle, the reality has become quite removed from that, as climate crises and economic inequities show. Infrastructures have become a double-edged sword, cogently analyzed in a landmark book: *Splintering Urbanism* (Graham and Marvin 2001). Another study, *The Promise of Infrastructure*, provides more recent scrutiny of the same dilemmas, across new terrains (Anand, Gupta, and Appel 2018).

Let's take a closer look at how these multilemmas play out by assaying a few megastructures designed to protect coastlines and low-lying interior cities and lands. On the one hand, they provide needed "insurance" against potentially catastrophic flooding, storm surges, and sea level rise. The value of what is being protected far exceeds the multibillion monetary costs of these gargantuan projects that were unthinkable not long ago. From a short- or even medium-term economic and social calculus, they make perfect sense. Their cost–benefit ratio in simple economic terms is almost unassailable.

On the other hand, credible and increasingly likely projections of greenhouse gas concentrations in the atmosphere and average global surface temperatures are that they will reach 500 ppm CO_2 and three to five degrees Celsius above today, respectively. Given that historic sea levels, when temperatures and CO_2 levels were that high, were 20 or more meters higher than today (Lambeck, Esat, and Potter 2002; Rohling et al. 1998), how well will these coastal infrastructures protect us in the future? This issue plagues grey infrastructures built for a single purpose according to limited criteria: cost and efficiency. These factors determined their rigidity and low resilience, and is a fundamental theme of this book.

The Late Eemian interglacial period, about 115,000 years ago, with the highest temperatures known in the *homo sapiens* era, of two degrees Celsius greater than today, had observed sea levels between six to nine meters higher than the present (Kopp et al. 2009; Dutton and Lambeck 2012). Will these and other contemporary flood barriers lull us complacently into inaction or inadequate action with their short-term promises of safety? Kulp and Strauss (2019) show how gross underestimates of coastal flooding reveal that low-lying coastal cities and regions will be flooded within our lifetimes, causing hundreds of millions of climate refugees from this source alone. Another study estimated 1.2 billion climate refugees by the year 2050, if present trajectories continue (Institute for Economics and Peace 2020).

Infrastructure Hubris

Ahkil Gupta eloquently marks this nature of infrastructure and how it affects thought and action in his phrase "the future in ruins", where he refers to the "temporality of infrastructure" (Anand, Gupta, and Appel 2018, 62). In other words, can we afford to be so short-sighted about the long-term impacts of infrastructures in the face of a radically different and perhaps unrecognizable world within the next generation?

Other examples of infrastructure hubris abound.

- The Thames Barrier, opened in 1982 at a cost of a half a billion pounds (£2 billion today), spans 520 meters across the River Thames in London. It is designed to protect approximately 125 square kilometers of central London from flooding caused by tidal surges.
- The Delta Works – the storm surge barrier that protects the Netherlands from flooding – was initiated after the catastrophic 1953 North Sea flood and completed in 1997 at a cost of 8 billion Dutch guilders, about $4 billion then (Aerts 2009).
- The deep sea barrier project for the North Sea called NEED – the Northern European Enclosure Dam – stretches from southern Norway to Scotland (300 miles) and southern England to France (100 miles). It could cost anywhere from $250 billion to $550 billion (Groeskamp and Kjellsson 2020).
- The Adriatic sea barrier megaproject MOSE (MOdulo Sperimentale Elettromeccanico – Experimental Electromechanical Module) protects Venice, Italy, it is estimated to cost upwards of $6 billion (Giovannini 2017).
- The 21-mile-long Saemangeum Seawall in Korea, completed in 2010 at a cost of over $2 billion, at an average height of 118 feet, may have a better chance to be effective over the long run (Wikipedia 2020).

These projects are but a tip of the iceberg when it comes to protection from storm flooding and sea level rise globally. Current projections suggest that they will not be adequate to hold back the sea in the face of catastrophic impacts from global warming. Yet these cautionary tales convey the audacity – of hope, technology, ambition, and hubris – that humans still maintain in attempts to control nature. This control is most often through infrastructure. Yet this "control" is mostly an illusion, with short-term and partial gains at best. Most likely is long-term damage at a larger scale with greater consequences (McPhee 1989).

If this was not enough, consider what happened in Australia in their summer of 2020. In the wake of a long, severe draught, bush fires devastated over twenty million acres, caused over $100 billion in property damage, and killed a billion animals along with at least 30 humans. As the country reeled in shock, one local aptly asked:

> How do you adapt when the changes coming are not simply new patterns but the very loss of a predictable pattern? How do you adapt to chaos? How do you affordably prepare a home simultaneously for drought, wind, rain, smoke, dust, fire, blackouts, rising sea levels, falling trees, floods, hail and record-breaking temperatures? (Pryor 2020).

These examples of sea control are merely one way to portray the dual nature and the multiple dilemmas that are part and parcel of all infrastructures. They all cut across, quite literally, places and peoples in different ways at different times. The same infrastructure might be a boon when it begins service, yet may become a burden over time. This can be seen with dams on rivers, cars on roads, and toxic electronic devices in landfills. An infrastructure might benefit some populations and harm others, depending on how they are managed. This is as true for "hard" infrastructure like transport, water, and power as it is for "soft" infrastructure like public health and safety, schools, and courts. Without universal access to water and learning and without fair adjudication of justice, some populations are disadvantaged.

The question is, can we design, build, and operate infrastructures so that they do not cut both ways, good and bad? I posit that the answer is yes, or can closely approach yes. This can be done by taking the long view and assessing the foreseeable consequences over the full life span of any infrastructure, including its repurposing and / or recycling. This way, planners, designers, and policymakers can make better decisions for truly sustainable and resilient infrastructure.

The Central Role of Cities for Infrastructure

To accomplish this, the central role of cities for infrastructure, and in particular its sustainability, must be considered. This is essential for its proper planning and design. Not understanding and acting on the mutual interaction of cities and infrastructures will only continue to hinder sustainability efforts. Exploring this mutual relationship is the subject of the book, in particular Chapters 3–6. Data and stories will be presented that articulate these factors. Key concepts such as networks, flows, life cycles, rate processes, and demand-capacity management will be introduced. It is argued that making infrastructure sustainable is the key to the sustainable city. This premise has been known to civilizations for millennia because it was vital to their growth and survival. It seems to have been forgotten, and this book seeks to reintroduce it for contemporary practice.

Cities are humankind's crowning achievements. Cities are the largest and most complex artefacts created by humans. Their size and complexity bear directly on the very possibility of their sustainability. More on this below and in Chapter 3. "Cities are the most visible signature of the Anthropocene: a new era in the co-evolution of life and the planet." This, from *Cities That Think Like Planets*, underscores a new condition of our age, and of the evolution of life on our planet (Alberti 2016, 11). If Sir David Attenborough has another series left in him to crown his quest to inform and inspire, he would do well to call it the *Grey Planet*, and address cities, the source of pressure on the species and planet he cares so much about.

Professor Alberti goes on to say that "Urban ecology faces a significant challenge: to position itself in the context of planetary change and to understand the role that cities play in the evolution of the earth" (Alberti 2016, 11). To understand the role of cities in the evolution of the earth and its ecosystems, knowing infrastructures is key. Cities themselves are ecosystems and infrastructures are their roots. Without infrastructure, cities simply could not exist. Infrastructures are the lifeblood and circulatory systems of urban ecosystems. Thus, we realize that urban metabolism and function extends far beyond the city limits and its hinterlands. Cities are connected globally and are the outposts and command posts of globalizations (Sassen 2001). City ecologies and their metabolisms are based on and can be estimated by proxy via infrastructure flows and processes.[4] Moreover, city-regions form new hybrid ecosystems with rural and natural areas as they increasingly intertwine. Further, infrastructures, especially telecommunications and transport, but also energy and education, are more than the roots of urban and hybrid ecosystems. They crisscross the globe and enable globalization. Indeed, infrastructure literally undergirds virtually all human endeavors.

Keeping Pace with Infrastructure

As cities explode in size and population, their infrastructures tend not to keep pace with urban needs and human desires. The result is illness, disease, pollution, poverty, traffic congestion, and more. While cities and economies have generated great wealth, why are infrastructures now often underfunded and deteriorated? The reasons are multifold, stemming from neoliberalism and its concomitant devaluing of the public sector and public services. This steady drawdown of governments' ability to raise funds to pay for infrastructure applies to its entire life cycle of planning, design, operation, repair, replacement, and recycling. While we are aware how important infrastructure is, the political will to fund investments is low and getting lower, considering infrastructure spending as a percentage of GDP (Kane and Tomer 2019; Congressional Budget Office of the United States 2019; Fay et al. 2019). This dangerous trend is ongoing, since before 1980 (Choate and Walter 1981).

We see report upon report extolling the virtues while simultaneously decrying the condition and inadequacies of our infrastructure. In the United Kingdom, the Eddington and Armitt Reports, the Institute of Civil Engineers, the Royal Town Planning Institute, the London Infrastructure Plan 2050, government agencies, foundations, think tanks, and others have chimed in. In this avalanche, London and the United Kingdom are far from alone. In the United States, the American Society of Civil Engineers (ASCE) produces a quadrennial "report card" of the national conditions: *State of America's Infrastructure Report Card*. The last was dire (ASCE 2020). It gave an overall grade for all infrastructures as mediocre: a C-. The prior report its most alarming: a near-failing D+ (ACSE 2016). The report's authors calculated that the cost to bring American infrastructure to current standards over the next eight years was $4.5 trillion. That amount does not account for new growth, new technologies, and raising standards, including sustainability and equitable access. Many nations have equivalent reports, as do international bodies, notably the World Bank, the International Monetary Fund, the United Nations and the Organization for Economic Cooperation and Development.

Given all this expertise and capacity, we have the knowledge to deal with these issues. To cite Sir John Armitt, Chair of the National Infrastructure Commission in the UK: "A second engineering adage comes to mind: 'give me a problem and I'll give you a solution'. We are good at engineering solutions, but we don't always fully examine the root cause of the problem" (Armitt 2015). There is an urban planning counterpart. Give planners a problem and they'll give you an analysis of the root causes, as well as the long-term impacts. This suggests that planners, designers, and engineers should work together more often, as they do in cities like Barcelona. This has implications for education as well as for policy and finance (Neuman 2020a; 2020b).

To know infrastructure, one first must know cities. To know cities, one must know infrastructure, as I develop in Chapters 2–4. Infrastructurists must be urbanists, and vice versa. Moreover, urban designers and planners see the long term and the big picture, design future scenarios, examine impacts, and develop assessment tools, while considering multiple interests in multiple contexts at multiple scales. Putting infrastructure, cities, and urbanization trends together in historical context illustrates how infrastructures begot the urban explosion (Chapter 4), as well as enabled massive consumption increases to go along with this explosion (Chapter 3). In our wasteful world, consumption yields waste, byproducts, and pollution. The trick is to use infrastructure to invert this equation and attain sustainability.

Can Cities Be Sustainable?

To appreciate this, ponder the scale and pace of urbanization today by comparing it to population, economy, and energy increases since the year 1500:

> In the year 1500, there were about 500 million Homo sapiens in the entire world. Today, there are [over] 7 billion, [14-fold increase]. The total value of goods and services produced by humankind in the year 1500 is estimated at $250 billion, in today's dollars. Nowadays the value of a year of human production is [over $80] trillion, [320-fold jump]. In 1500, humanity consumed about 13 trillion calories of energy per day. Today, we consume 1,500 trillion calories a day [115-fold rise] (Harari 2014).

According to my own calculations based on UN, IEA, CIA, and World Bank data since 1960, while human population has more than doubled, global economic output has octupled, and resource consumption gone up even more. (Estimates on resource depletion vary.) Thus, we are getting less efficient and *less sustainable* as we move to cities, not more, contrary to popular belief and professional dogma. Cities are voracious.

Prospects for the future are worse. A 2016 UN Environment Programme report projects world resource consumption will triple by 2050, even as world population will rise only by 28 percent (UNEP 2016, 17). Where will this end, if 50 years ago we already exceeded the planet's natural capacity to support our presence (Anderson et al. 2020; World Footprint Organization 2019; World Wildlife Fund 2018)?

In 1997, a number of preeminent ecologists and biologists published a linked series of studies in a special issue of *Science* titled Human Dominated Ecosystems. They provided evidence that every habitat, Antarctica included, is dominated by human activities. Ten years before that, ecologist Eugene Stoermer coined the term Anthropocene (Steffen et al. 2010). The Anthropocene is our present epoch that gives a name to human modifications to the biosphere. Per Benjamin Kunkel, it is the current situation "in which humanity, accidentally or deliberately, engineers the planet's condition" (Kunkel 2017). More and more scientists predict global collapse this century due to complete marine algae die-off at 500 parts per million of CO_2 in the atmosphere, which at current rates will occur by 2050, assuming an average 3 ppm annual increase over that period, and a base of 418 ppm in 2020.

Over and above these global projections, numerous studies suggest that causes and consequences are not distributed evenly among humanity. We know from numerous studies on equity that causes and consequences are not distributed evenly (Piketty 2014; Stiglitz, Sen, and Fitoussi 2009). Relating this to climate change and therefore infrastructure, Andreas Malm in *Fossil Capital* highlights that, "In the early 21st century, the poorest 45 per cent of humanity generated 7 per cent of CO2 emissions, while the richest 7 per cent produced 50 per cent" (Malm 2015). Capital is more implicated

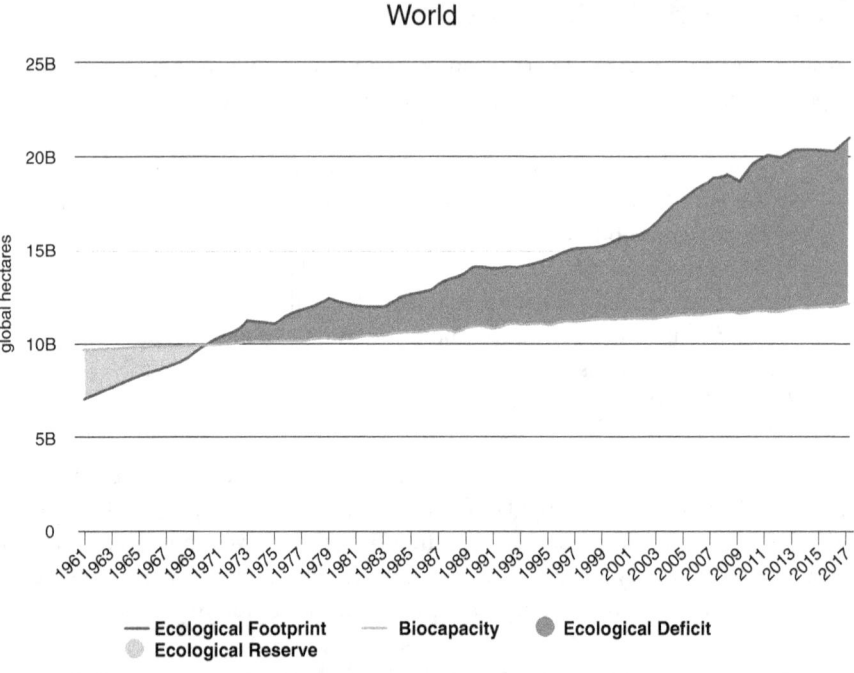

Figure 0.2 Global Ecological Footprint Chart since 1961

than carbon (Malm 2015). This, along with climate refugees, food shortages, and civil strife associated with the increasing number of, and increasingly severe, droughts, means that the climate crisis is a humanitarian crisis as well as an ecological one. Per Benjamin Kunkel, "The signal traits of contemporary capitalism are fantastic economic inequality and ecological devastation" (Kunkel 2017, 11).

The Power of Flows

Manuel Castells claimed over 30 years ago that the flows of power had been overtaken by the power of flows (Castells 1989), an endorsement of the power of infrastructure. The virtual world of digital flows has overtaken the tangible world of historic and longstanding institutions. Digital flows of capital and information, whether programmed ones in capital markets and commerce, or random ones across social media, overwhelm longstanding power structures and render them far less than effective than before. In part, this has fueled the ungovernability crisis, both in terms of political chaos and the private sector overwhelming the public. If infrastructure sowed, and accelerated, the seeds of our production, and later destruction, can we invert the equation to find in flows – and their conduits, infrastructure – a salvation that is cleaner, greener, and more equitable?

Let me employ my work with the State of California's infrastructure strategy and the *New Jersey State Plan*, whose principles for large-scale infrastructure planning are instructive.

The Public Policy Institute of California commissioned an examination of infrastructure in that state. It reported on all infrastructure for all state agencies and found some eye-openers (Neuman and Whittington 2000). One was an outcome of the "prison-industrial complex" (Schlosser 1998). Among other things, we found that California spent less in capital investment (facilities) per student at the University of California system that produced the most Nobel prizes than per prisoner in the prisons that produced the most vehicle license plates (*op. cit.,* 72). The prison lobby was the biggest lobby in California then (Page 2011).

Another finding was how backwards the process to finance infrastructure was, as revealed by Figure 0.3. The right-hand column describes the process for planning, budgeting, and financing infrastructure in California as of the year 2000. It was a budget- and finance-driven system. What got built was wholly conditioned by the money available to spend on it, rather than by actual current needs or projections of needs. Those funds were subject to / determined by political bargaining in the state legislature. In contrast, the left-hand column describes an evidence-based system that follows a life cycle method driven by actual and projected infrastructure needs. As one result of this research report, the State of California adopted a new law mandating a five-year strategic infrastructure plan at the state level. This first-time-ever requirement for a statewide plan changed planning and budgeting, with financing slower to follow. This is a case of research informing policy and law.

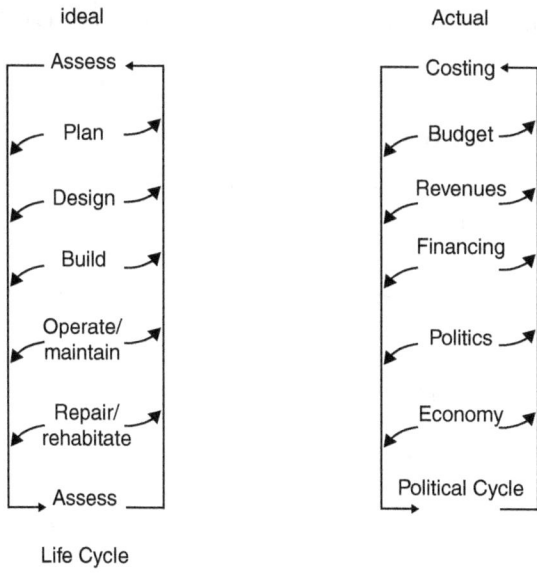

Figure 0.3 Life Cycle of Infrastructure – Ideal versus Actual

In New Jersey, a mandated component of their state plan (initially adopted in 1992) is an Infrastructure Needs Assessment for a population then of eight million, for all public infrastructure at all levels of government – municipal, county, and state. The assessment, which covered the 20-year period between 1990 and 2010, was required by the State Planning Act of 1986. This 300-page assessment of infrastructure needs was pioneering for being the first known use of life cycle analysis and life cycle costing for entire infrastructure systems (New Jersey State Planning Commission 1992).

The state plan itself was a strategic spatial plan to guide infrastructure. Significantly, like the UK's National Infrastructure Commission in the late 2010s, New Jersey's State Planning Commission was housed in the Department of Treasury. This was a political decision that took into account the inescapable link between capital funding and infrastructure facilities. Moreover, the Treasury is the management arm of government, coordinating policies and budgets both capital and operational for all agencies. Thus, the state plan links politics, policy, planning, management, and budget; all based on infrastructure investments supported by the Infrastructure Needs Assessment.

Two other examples illustrate the value of considering the regional scale in developing sustainable infrastructure solutions. One is the Texas Urban Triangle of Dallas–Fort Worth, Houston, San Antonio, and Austin; the heart of Texas and the motor of its economy. This case refers to built (grey, hard) infrastructures. The other is New Orleans and Southern Louisiana, and refers to natural (green) infrastructures. Both examples illustrate how infrastructure-led regional analyses and planning can address chronic problems effectively and affordably, as well as sustainably, conveyed by work conducted by teams of researchers and students, led by myself.

Grey and Green Infrastructures

The Texas Triangle houses over 20 million people, generating over 80 percent of the state's economy. It is a functioning urban megaregion whose name has entered the lexicon by conferring the region with a distinct identity. Work by an interdisciplinary team at Texas A&M University on a composite suitability analysis for future development mapped over 80 factors across 58,000 square miles, or 150,000 square kilometers. This work identified the most and least suitable places for both urban development and for land conservation (Neuman and Bright 2008). Among the more revealing findings was the superimposition of several development factors that showed the great degree of risk dozens of hazardous and toxic waste disposal sites in the Houston metropolitan area posed. This risk was compounded by several interrelated factors: Houston's sea level elevation, 15 feet of land subsidence at the heart of the city due to century-long water withdrawals from aquifers in the unconsolidated soils of the coastal plain, rising sea levels, increased flooding from tropical storms, and a greater risk of increasingly severe tropical storms (hurricanes). This analysis was enabled by the regional perspective on the interrelation of infrastructures such as waste disposal sites with the natural environment.

Follow-on research, funded by the Texas and US Departments of Transportation, developed a web-based Spatial Decision Support System to analyze the most suitable and sustainable route for high-speed rail in the Texas Triangle (Kim et al. 2014; Kim, Wunneburger, and Neuman 2013). This report included ecological and economic factors in the regional analysis in addition to the typical factors considered by engineers in high-speed rail route siting, mainly limited to turning curve radius and slope (gradient) of the train tracks. This method demonstrated the value of multidisciplinary and multiscalar analysis of spatial planning informed by GIS methods in the planning of sustainable infrastructure.

The second case refers to the regional spatial analysis for the sustainable redevelopment of New Orleans and the south coast of the State of Louisiana in the aftermath of Hurricanes Katrina and Rita in 2005 (Neuman 2007). These were two of the most powerful tropical storms in recorded history (Landsea et al. 2013). The analysis and plan for recovery after the hurricanes revealed that taking a regional and ecological perspective led to drastically divergent findings for the causes and solutions to storm damage and flood risk, compared to the reports prepared by individual professions such as architecture, planning, and engineering. This finding evolved from learning about two interrelated regional, ecological factors. First, that the erosion and disappearance of protective barrier islands and coastal marshlands (bayous in Louisiana) was due to the 150-year-long process of containing the Mississippi River's floods by earthen levees. These levees prevented coastal wetlands from being replenished by the river's sediments, a natural process that had been occurring for millions of years, and which created the state's coastal wetlands. Further, the construction of "Mr. GO" – the colloquial name of the Mississippi River Gulf Outlet, a wide ship canal carved into the wetlands to enable straight passage from New Orleans to the Gulf of Mexico – had devastating impacts. This passage, intended to enable ships to avoid the meandering river and the fearsome currents at its delta, had the effect of allowing hurricane storm surges to barrel at high speed straight from the Gulf to New Orleans. In the case of Hurricane Katrina, the storm surge was 29 feet (9 meters) high, swamping the city and causing over 2,000 deaths and over $125 billion in direct damage.

By contrast, post-Katrina reports by professional societies found other causes and responses. The civil engineers found that the earthen levees were too weak and needed to be strengthened. The architects found that the buildings were not strong enough and needed to be elevated and strengthened. The urban planners found that neighborhoods and towns were at risk, yet proposed "new urbanist" solutions of enhanced walkability and more compactness, meaning a higher density of buildings. While important, these solutions did not address the natural causes of devastation, and left structures, infrastructures, cities, and their inhabitants completely vulnerable to future storms. To how many other extant infrastructure systems designed to efficiency standards does this conclusion apply? The devastating fires in Australia and the American West in 2019–2020, a record tropical storm season in the Atlantic Ocean in 2020, and the coronavirus pandemic 2019–2021 drastically bring to the fore the need for new approaches, and new metrics for resilience and sustainability to be applied to the design, planning, and management of infrastructures and cities.

For example, we calculated that the distance between New Orleans and the Gulf Coast was the same distance over which the storm surge would have been attenuated had the wetlands and barrier islands remained intact. In other words, the ecological services provided by intact natural habitats (coastal wetlands) would have prevented flooding, sparing lives, and avoiding tens of billions of dollars in property damage. In this case, these natural coastal habitats served as "green infrastructure", although the terms are not directly interchangeable. Another multifactor and large-scale regional GIS-based spatial analysis demonstrated the vital importance of ecological infrastructure in protecting disadvantaged populations (low income, low education). The analysis found that these populations were more vulnerable, both in the city of New Orleans as well as in rural areas, than wealthier and more educated residents. Overall, we found that the root causes of flooding and related damage were regional and ecological, not local and technical, per the architects and engineers. This was due to our interdisciplinary and ecological approach.

Redefining Smart Infrastructure

This smart use of nature as green infrastructure is a less costly, less damaging, and more sustainable way to manage ecosystems and urban development simultaneously. It synthesizes environment and development. This enables a new approach to infrastructure development. In the past, we tended to think of infrastructure as the hard stuff, the grey matter, as if that was all that mattered. Yet is this mentality and the methods and systems that it spawned smart? How much urban infrastructure is concrete and asphalt, the dumbest materials around? Activity around so-called "smart infrastructure" has centered around sensing, software, apps, programming, and artificial intelligence as portrayed by the private sector consulting and technology firms. In my view, smart infrastructure is smart thinking about infrastructure. This means integrating the natural and built environments along the lines to be mentioned in this chapter, and the entire book. What provides the "smart" is the human brain, intelligently applied.

In contrast to hard urban infrastructure, take a quintessential terrestrial ecosystem – a forest. We know how alive, diverse, beautiful, productive, and complex forests are above ground. Let's go underground, to examine the complex root systems of forests – their infrastructure. Mycorrhizal, fungal, and root networks in forest soils comprise nature's infrastructure. They underpin and give life to the forest. Underground mycorrhizal networks channel the symbiotic relationships between undersoil fungal networks and the roots of all vascular plants, including trees. In fact, the two largest known organisms on the planet are largely underground. Both are clonal colonies with massive roots. A honey fungus, *Armillaria solidipes*, in Oregon covers 3.7 square miles (Sheldrake 2020). A quaking aspen colony, *Populus tremuloides*, in Utah has a unified root system for 47,000 trees. Estimates put it at 80,000 years of age, making it the oldest organism known. Tree species go back hundreds of millions of years. All thanks to roots, nature's infrastructure.

Trees communicate with each other and provide life support to each other through these networks, as if they were a close-knit family (Simard, Vyse, and Larson 2013). It turns out the film *Avatar* was not so far-fetched. Fungi do this too. These networks form the basis of forest ecosystems (Simard 2021; Gorzelak et al. 2015). They have been around for hundreds of millions of years.[5] What about urban ecosystems? Are urban infrastructures that smart? Can they talk to and support each other, self-regulate, self-regenerate, and create resilience? We need to move far beyond the criteria of function and efficiency that have dominated infrastructures and cities for centuries. To be fair, forests have had a several-hundred-million-year evolutionary head start on cities. Hopefully humans will have the time to catch up.

Trees are not the only ancient beings that communicate via roots. Fossils of the *Ediacaran* macrobiota (about 550 million years old) record diverse marine paleocommunities, including early animals, which predate the Cambrian Explosion. This group of aquatic species, called *Rangeomorpha*, were resilient and "dominated deep-marine ecosystems" of that era (Liu, *New York Times*, March 12, 2020). These fossils have been found worldwide. They had abundant filaments (root-like structures) that occurred in a dense network pattern that could extend up to several meters. The filaments constituted a prominent component of their ecosystems, and connected up to seven different species in what could have been colonies (Liu and Dunn 2020). The "extant [fossil record] suggests that Ediacaran [species] were likely clonal networks" (Liu and Dunn 2020, 1). The filaments served as channels for nutrients and chemical signals: "a means to communicate between the organisms," according to Liu in an interview in the *New York Times* on March 12, 2020.

The lesson is that nature has long used living "infrastructure networks" to support and nurture itself. These were more than mere circulatory systems. They had sentient, communicative, and intelligent (learning by evolutionary adaptation) properties involved in self-regulation as they formed living communities and ecosystems. They are principles that humans can learn and adapt into human infrastructure networks as we seek to become more sustainable.

To extend this analogy into the human realm, it is helpful to look at a circular economy. Its basis, unsurprisingly, is circular infrastructure, including circular logistics and production-distribution-consumption-reuse networks, abetted by circular thinking. Circular infrastructure networks are open, interconnected, and integrated, where the outputs of one form the inputs to others. (Which is why referring to "closing the loops" is scientifically incorrect. In nature, the loops remain open.) A key part of their openness is being open to new information and learning. This refers to the human element, embodied in a new type of governance and urban management. This is a tall order given the way infrastructures have been designed, built, and managed till now.

Scale and Modularity

We can go further to highlight the role of small-scale infrastructures that complement yet are overshadowed by "big ticket" megaprojects. Gargantuan megaprojects have equally gargantuan price tags and environmental and social impacts. Just to use some current projects (year 2020) in the United Kingdom as examples:

- £50 billion for a Railways Upgrade Plan
- £30 billion, for one London metro line, Crossrail 2
- £60–£100 billion, in 2020 values, for the high-speed rail line HS2 from London north to Manchester and surrounding cities
- £20 billion for a recently completed single metro line in London, Crossrail 1[6]
- £5 billion for the Thames Tideway Tunnel, a single "super sewer" of a few miles long

For cities nowadays, individual, large-scale, centralized infrastructures – such as transport, sewerage, solid waste, water supply, and energy systems – each typically have capital costs of upwards of billions of dollars / pounds / euros. Hundreds of millions can be added annually for operating and maintaining a single such system.

On the other hand, nature's infrastructures, also referred to as nature services, are virtually free, and mostly free of upkeep and maintenance, when humans do not disrupt them (Costanza et al. 1997). Nature is organized in ecosystems supported by numerous natural networks. Most individual units of nature, especially beings, aggregate in scale in modular and incremental ways to form habitats, communities, and ecosystems. It is these characteristics, and the operating principles behind them, that can be adapted to design infrastructure today. These characteristics are diametrically opposed to those of linear, rational infrastructure systems designed by engineers, as Figure 0.4 shows. These characteristics, and more importantly the principles behind them, are elaborated throughout the book. What does this mean for 21st century infrastructure that is truly smart?

We can use the example of a tree once again, at least by analogy. A tree has two major cycles, seasonal and life. Both involve countless other organisms in its cosm. A tree is a paragon of permanence and continuity, lasting centuries if not millennia, and providing stability to its surrounds.

One of humanity's great metaphors is the tree of life. Epics and legends extol the role of the tree, as symbol and as fact. Take a recent tree epic, the film *Avatar*: shelter, source of life and wisdom, storehouse and fount of knowledge – of how to live. The tree is the archetype of the web of life.

OLD / CURRENT	NEW / FUTURE
centralized	distributed / networked
fixed-in-place	mobile
inflexible	flexible
rigid	adaptable
large scale	small scale
unitary / indivisible	modular
expensive	inexpensive
risk prone	resilient
isolated	integrated

Figure 0.4 Infrastructure Characteristics – Old versus New
Source: author

Trees also exemplify the dialectic of continuity and change, standing erect for centuries, shedding leaves over seasons, rotting back to the soil over years. Trees are flexible as they sway in the wind. They are resilient as they absorb the rain. The provide shelter, shade, food, materials, playgrounds, store carbon, bind the soil; the list seems endless. Tree root system interactions with soil generate enormous biological complexity. Up to 15,000 different species live in a cubic foot of soil. (Don't treat your soil like dirt!) Trees are modular units that network to make forests, apex ecosystems that are central to life itself, including that of the planet's earth system. Trees filter out through their roots an incredible variety and quantity of toxic chemicals. Trees create microclimates and are indispensable to the global climate and Gaia herself. Trees produce their own energy and collect their own water using the intelligence of evolution. A tree in conjunction with its surroundings recycles its own litter and itself, fulfilling its life cycle while providing for countless others besides. Trees are open systems connected to other open systems through multiple natural networks, nature's infrastructures. These are the characteristics and operating principles that can be adapted to human infrastructures.

Asking the right question is more important than having the right answer. You can have what you think is the right answer, but if the question is wrong, the consequences can be disastrous. Just ask the residents of New Orleans after Hurricane Katrina in 2005, or Fukushima after the earthquake and tsunami in 2011.

In this spirit, we can ask: Why must a building consume energy? Why can't a building produce energy? Why must a building consume water? Why can't a building provide its own water? Why can't a building recycle its own outflows? Why can't a building be like a tree? Can we design buildings, infrastructures, and cities to be as smart as trees? That is, can we be as smart as a tree?

Using this thinking, for small-scale and modular infrastructures, also implies applying "last mile" thinking to all infrastructures, so that they interconnect with all points of a city, just as capillaries and venules are connected to arteries and veins to serve all cells in the body. Last mile, last drop, last bit (or byte), last joule, and so on.

When infrastructures are designed and built so that smaller scale networks are incrementally interwoven into larger ones, their modular components are incrementally embedded in larger scales. This endows flexibility, resilience, and adaptability. It allows for easier and cheaper network expansion, upgrades, and modifications, as well as adopting or retrofitting advances in technology. Thus, they are better able to serve changes in populations, their demographics, and their needs. These microsystems are less costly and can be deployed on each building or each space, unobtrusively and attractively. They include small rotary wind turbines, solar panels, rainwater tanks, green roofs, compost gardens, and so on. Our artists and designers are more than up to the task, given incentives to collaborate.

A fully green building with its own, self-contained infrastructure, while networked to other buildings and infrastructures, can approach 100 percent sustainability and even be carbon-positive. They also can feed into or obviate the need for expensive, large-scale systems. Small-scale, modular infrastructures can be, and are, funded by users, small-scale investors, and individuals via microfinancing and crowdsourcing precisely owing to their small scale and modularity. This "plug and play" approach contrasts sharply with large-scale and centralized systems that take years if not decades to plan and build, and then to burden the public purse, the citizenry, and nature. Moreover, centralized megaproject infrastructures make us dependent, rather than aware of and self-reliant regarding daily life. Home- and building-based microsystems, while not feasible in every instance, go a long way in educating about sustainability.

Developing modular, small-scale, and decentralized nodes of infrastructure that are interconnected to form integrated networks is less costly, more sustainable, more equitable, and more feasible because they can be retrofitted more easily into existing cities and regions. We already do this with the internet and smart devices. Why not translate that to other networks?

Circular Finance for Infrastructure

We can also apply the circular approach to funding. Life cycle funding may be the most important missing link in solving the infrastructure finance conundrum. Chapter 8 delves into financing, and Chapter 5 presents the life cycle, yet here we take a stroll in the past to remind us of the role of finance in infrastructure and city building, always foundational. We use an emblematic city – London – as a guide. In its evolution to world city, London shows the pivotal confluence of finance capital with infrastructure. Like Rome two millennia ago, all roads led to London, as well as rails and ships. Without discounting the roles of Liverpool, Manchester, Glasgow, and fellow cities at start the Industrial Revolution and the rise of the British Empire; it was London where the greatest merger of finance and transport made its mark in transforming London into the first global city, and not incidentally, knowledge capital. Financiers such as Frankfurt banker Nathan Mayer Rothschild arrived in London and set up a banking house in the city in 1798. He was aided by a large sum of money given to him by his father, Amschel Mayer Rothschild. This bank financed numerous large-scale projects, including railways and the Suez Canal (Ferguson 1998).

London was not alone. New York and Chicago followed as first in the New World to apply this "tale of two capitals" formula. The two capitals being finance and facilities, always married. Historian William Cronon's magisterial *Nature's Metropolis* (1999) described how the marriage of these two capitals made Chicago, and transformed much of the American continent besides.

Historically, most funding for infrastructure worldwide has historically been only to pay for the capital costs of construction. Taxes, tolls, and user fees were presumed to take care of operations and maintenance. Some funds were dedicated, many were not. Most did not keep pace with inflation, much less demand. Expenditures beyond operations and maintenance that are part of a cradle-to-cradle life cycle fell outside of standard funding mechanisms. As a result, most were not funded.

Yet capital costs represent only a portion of the life cycle of costs for infrastructure. Funding capital costs only is now in question. No matter the source, the amount needed and what it is needed for must be calculated in an entirely new way. Business as usual – funding capital costs only – digs the holes we have already dug in terms of chronic underfunding even deeper. Circular, life cycle funding avoids the "funding trap" caused by capital cost only approaches to infrastructure finance. The infrastructure funding trap has long short-changed infrastructure and led to unsafe systems, underfunded services, unsolvable backlogs, inequitable access, and more.

While the private sector has long been involved in infrastructure and its financing, around 1980 this activity accelerated. Several new factors came in to play at that time. First, neoliberalism took hold. One result was that governments at all levels in many countries suffered budget and therefore service cuts, including to infrastructure. Into this breach stepped the private sector, offering its presumed expertise and efficiency. This trend has continued to this writing, 40 years hence. Second, the deregulation of the financial industry. This further enabled firms and funds to enter the infrastructure and public sector space. Third, the World Bank, the International Monetary Fund, and related regional development banks supported both of these trends with research, publications, technical assistance, and mainly, loans to build massive infrastructure projects worldwide. Fourth, the complexity of infrastructure, and the focus on individual megaprojects rather than modular networks, has led to the twinning of extremely complex contracts governing their planning, construction, finance and operations with new institutional mechanisms to manage them, typically variations on public–private partnerships. Finally, continuing deregulation of and creativity in the financial sector has led to a wide range of funding / financing instruments. These new partnerships and their financing instruments simultaneously benefit the private sector by accruing the bulk of the returns on investment, and prejudice the public sector by transferring most of the risk to it.

Thus, it is easy to grasp why the private sector, particularly finance, now abetted by management consulting and high technology firms, has muscled its way onto infrastructure turf. The increasingly superior returns on finance capital compared to other types of capital, on top of multi-trillion-pound worldwide infrastructure spending, go a long way in explaining the ascendance of infrastructure in equity arenas. Savvy investors know that infrastructure investments return lucrative yields.

This book addresses how we can alter this equation so that infrastructures return double dividends, with both economic and ecological returns. Add increased social equity afforded by fairly managed accessibility that is provided by infrastructures, and we can see a triple return on investment. Three for the price of one. The old situation of government paying for it all is gone. What will replace it that will be both sustainable and equitable in serving the public good?

The Public Good

To make sure that the public interest remains served in this bold new world, value capture for infrastructure finance becomes paramount. That is a tall order in debilitated government regimes after 40 years of neoliberalism and austerity. Private equity prefers government to keep its hands off infrastructure, especially now that bond and cash yields are nearly nonexistent and equities are risky. This is paradoxical, as private equity and real estate developers at the same time seek certainty. This certainty in large part is guaranteed by strong and stable government, and the infrastructure it provides. Can society have it both ways? More to the point, can a short-sighted private sector have its cake and eat it too?

This debate is critical, and must go on. I believe it can best be informed and brokered by impartial institutions, such as universities and non-governmental organizations, and carried out dispassionately in independent fora and arenas. All sectors have their proper roles to play. Yet one sector cannot abdicate responsibility for infrastructure, and another sector cannot usurp it due to a single motive. Balanced partnerships in which multiple interests are served fairly are the aim. This used to be the job of government, providing *public* services that benefitted all.

Regardless of *how* financing is obtained, *what* it pays for and how those decisions are made are also of import. In this case, "what" does not mean which systems or projects, like which airport will get a third runway or which type of energy will be funded. Existing mechanisms have those decisions more or less sorted, though we can always do with more transparency, evidence, and civic input. Instead, we need to devise new decision criteria based on a cradle-to-cradle life cycle, equity, and sustainability.

We must be fully aware of the implications in this challenge. It could be a film called *Old Habits Die Hard, Sunk Capital Dies Harder*. The fixed costs of sunk capital and the fixed facilities it builds determine urban form and function, as they have for millennia. Those fixed forms, roads and rails, ports and parks, and so on, are priceless assets of the public trust, and civic works of art at their very best. Yet are these old, centralized systems truly sustainable and resilient long into the future? Can we transform equally fixed and discipline-bound methods and institutions? Where professions compete for and resolve conflicts regarding turf? Professional habits die hard too. Who would have thought Bruce Willis to be a philosopher of infrastructure?

The Public Trust

Long ago, infrastructure and public or common lands were known as the "public trust". Another historical term for the material public trust – lands and other common goods including public works – was "common wealth". Wealth that was held in common, by the people who were its owners, through the *trust* they placed in their *representatives* in government. How different it is today.

In recent decades there has been a steady, incremental, drip-by-drip erosion of the public trust, meaning public lands and public works (infrastructure) in today's terminology. This is but one consequence of neoliberalism. This was epitomized by prime minister of the United Kingdom Thatcher's claim that, "There is no such thing as society." Forty years on, this transformation is nearly complete, from public and common to private and individual.

It is revealing to note the terms in use today – public *capital*, *asset*, and *investment* – that have replaced what was called the public trust or common wealth. The terms have changed over time so that private sector language dominates now. Infrastructure projects are "deals". This change of discourse is important, because it is embedded in changes in policies and practices, and governs the way we think and act now. Less democratic and more particularized and polarized.

Another facet of public trust is that it serves as glue holding messy democratic processes together. This aspect of trust is embedded in social and political capital that keeps people engaged constructively over the long periods of time needed to accomplish infrastructure planning and financing. This glue consists of two interrelated ingredients: trust and transparency. Otherwise, no matter how carefully constructed the process, how cordial the proceedings, how fair the deliberations, and how carefully selected the stakeholders; any process could fall apart without public trust. Interpersonal trust is not sufficient. The erosion of this facet of the public trust has been most damaging to our collective responsibility to plan and finance infrastructure, and to ensure its services and impacts are equitable. For sustainable infrastructure to be planned and financed responsibly, civic trust needs to be rekindled.

Many cities around the world have poured vast sums into revitalizing their material public trusts to enhance their cities and their citizens' lives. European cities, for example, having been doing this by focusing on waterfronts and parks, public spaces such as plazas and squares, and civic places such as libraries and cultural centers. By so doing, they have been truly transforming their cities, and their citizens' relationships to them. They have been reinforcing the second aspect of public trust mentioned above – civic-mindedness – by creating higher quality material public trust: infrastructure, particularly public places where people can mingle and interact. This mutually reinforcing relationship is vital for civic life to flourish. The London Plan, for example, makes much of revitalizing the River Thames so it once again animates "a city that delights the senses" (Mayor of London 2016, 32). European cities are not alone. Infrastructure improvements have been bread and butter for city competitiveness for generations.

The Sharing Economy, Public Trust and Infrastructure

To conclude, we bring another aspect of the emergent circular economy into the realm of infrastructure: the sharing economy. Its distinction is trading on use value, not exchange value. Use value as an underlying principle places it properly in the realm of ecology instead of economy, notwithstanding their common root in Greek, *oikos*. This is because exchange is a relationship among partners. An exchange is an individual process that, when its flows are aggregated, yields an ecosystem of interacting individuals.[7] This model of a sharing economy is part of a greater sharing ecology, which is undergirded by mutual trust in our fellow citizens. In this way, individuals in a sharing economy perform formerly public services for a fee. We could simply call this sharing ecology *society*, or *community*.

We can craft multiple roles for new infrastructures in the sharing society. The new vision of smaller, modular, decentralized, and distributed networks suits the interpersonal nature of caring and sharing. This form of infrastructure, digitally enabled, helps bring out the best in us. Apps devised for distributing food waste and for enabling assistance during disasters or epidemics are but two demonstrations of the possibilities afforded by ingenuity. Reconceiving public services as small scale and personal rather than large scale and institutional is a giant step to long-term sustainability.

This approach is not limited to the private sector. A positive public sector example is the bicycle sharing services provided by cities worldwide. This type of infrastructure can go a long way in gaining greater social equity and distributive justice. Let us not overlook that sharing is caring. We can also grasp the benefits to democracy that stem from extending the sharing society. This is because cooperation is a key precept in society, heightened by caring and sharing.

As we know, infrastructure is paramount to all of us. New kinds of infrastructure for new ways of living can lead us into a bold new world that is not ominous like Huxley's. The aim is to shape thinking and institutions so that infrastructure is not seen merely as a physical substrate to buoy the economy. It is also the administrative substrate to serve society. Infrastructure has ramifications in every realm of human life, and can lift the human spirit.

Infrastructures enable cities to prosper and grow. They are key to their sustainability and our well-being. As infrastructure made cities possible, great infrastructure makes great cities possible, and sustainable infrastructure makes sustainable cities. This applies to towns and villages as well as cities; indeed to nations and economies. Think of Industrial Britain and you think railways. Preindustrial Britain and canals. Global Britain and networks. Great infrastructure makes great places. Continuing to do so into the future, we will be proud to be "citizens of somewhere". Somewhere special, in part made so by infrastructure that is planned, designed, and financed sustainably.

Notes

1 https://research.noaa.gov/article/ArtMID/587/ArticleID/2742/Despite-pandemic-shutdowns-carbon-dioxide-and-methane-surged-in-2020
2 https://www.esrl.noaa.gov/gmd/ccgg/carbontracker-ch4/
3 Due to the Great Influenza of 1918 to 1920, in "the United States, practically overnight, average life expectancy plunged to 47 from 54; in England and Wales, it fell more than a decade, from a historic height of 54 to an Elizabethan-era 41. India experienced average life expectancies below 30 years" (Johnson 2021a).
4 An early effort was led by a team from the Australian National University, which analyzed Hong Kong in the 1970s. They chose Hong Kong, a global city even then, as a city, state, and island; they believed it was easy to calculate what happened within its city limits. Today we know that it is difficult if not impossible to estimate precisely for an individual city, because of the interconnections manifest by globalization. See Boyden et al. 1981.
5 The oldest known tree species is *Wattieza*, 380 million years old. The oldest known living tree species is the *ginkgo biloba*, estimated at 270 million years. Trees are the oldest clonal and non-clonal living beings on the planet today, at 9,500 years for a Norway spruce in Sweden and 5,000 years for a bristlecone pine in California, respectively.
6 Crossrail 1 and 2 cost estimates obtained from their respective websites at the time of this writing, March 2020. https://www.crossrail.co.uk
7 Critiques have been published on large-scale, for profit corporate sharing corporations such as ride-sharing and home-sharing, and their effects on cities and citizens (Calo and Rosenblat 2020). My comments refer to the ideal, which would need to be planned, managed, and regulated to avoid or minimize negative effects.

Bibliography

Aerts, J. (2009). Adaptation cost in the Netherlands: Climate change and flood risk management. *Climate Research Netherlands*, 34–44.
Alberti, M. (2016). *Cities That Think Like Planets: Complexity, Resilience, and Innovation in Hybrid Ecosystems*. Seattle, WA: University of Washington Press.
ASCE (American Society of Civil Engineers). (2016). *America's Infrastructure Report Card*. Washington DC: ASCE.
ASCE (American Society of Civil Engineers). (2020). *America's Infrastructure Report Card*. Washington DC: ASCE.

Anand, N., Gupta, A., and Appel, H. (eds.). (2018). *The Promise of Infrastructure*. Durham, NC: Duke University Press.

Anderson, C., Weber, C., Fabricius, C., Glew, L., Opperman, J., Pacheco, P., Pendleton, L., Thau, D., Vermeulen, S., and Shaw, M. R. (2020). Planning for change: Conservation-related impacts of climate overshoot. *BioScience*, 70(2): 115–118.

Armitt, J. (2015). *ICE Presidential Address: Civil Engineers: Shaping Ourselves and Our World*. London: Institution of Civil Engineers.

Boyden, S., Millar, S., Newcombe, K., and O'Neill, B. (1981). *The Ecology of a City and its People: The Case of Hong Kong*. Canberra: Australian National University Press.

Calo, R. and Rosenblat, A. (2020). The taking economy: Uber, information and power. *Columbia Law Review*, 117(6) https://columbialawreview.org/content/the-taking-economy-uber-information-and-power/. Accessed August 25, 2020.

Castells, M. (1996). *The Rise of the Network Society*: Volume I of The Information Age: Economy, Society and Culture. Cambridge and Oxford: Blackwell.

Choate, P. and Walter, S. (1981). *America in Ruins: The Decaying Infrastructure*. Durham, NC: Duke University Press.

Congressional Budget Office of the United States. (2019). *Federal Investment 1962–2018*. Washington DC: Author.

Costanza, R., d'Arge, R., De Groot, R., Farber, S., Grasso, M., Hannon, B., Limburg, K., Naeem, S., O'Neill, R., Paruelo, J., Raskin, R., Sutton, P., and Van Den Belt, M. (1997). The value of the world's ecosystem services and natural capital. *Nature*, 387(6630): 253–260.

Cronon, W. (1991). *Nature's Metropolis: Chicago and the Great West*. New York: W. W. Norton.

Dutton, A. and Lambeck, K. (2012). Ice volume and sea level during the last interglacial. *Science*, 337(6091): 216–219.

Fay, M., Lee, H. I., Mastruzzi, M., Han, S., and Cho, M. (2019). *The Trillion Mark: How Much Countries are Spending on Infrastructure*. Washington DC: The World Bank.

Ferguson, N. (1998). *The House of Rothschild: Money's Prophets 1798–1848*. New York: Viking.

Giovannini, R. (2017). Venice and MOSE: Story of a failure. *La Stampa*, 10 December.

Gorzelak, M., Asay, A., Pickles, B., and Simard, S. (2015). Inter-plant communication through mycorrhizal networks mediates complex adaptive behaviour in plant communities. *Annals of Botany Plants*, 7: 1–15.

Graham, S. and Marvin, S. (2001). *Splintering Urbanism: Networked Infrastructures, Technological Mobilities, and the Urban Condition*. London: Routledge.

Groeskamp, S. and Kjellsson, J. (2020). NEED: The Northern European Enclosure Dam for if climate change mitigation fails. *Bulletin of the American Meteorological Society*, 101(7): 1174–1189.

Haq, B. and Schutter, S. (2008). A chronology of Paleozoic sea-level changes. *Science*, 322(5898): 64–68.

Harari, Y. (2014). *Sapiens: A Brief History of Humankind*. London: Harvill Secker.

Hetherington, K. (ed.). (2019). *Infrastructure, Environment, and Life in the Anthropocene*. Durham, NC: Duke University Press.

Institute for Economics and Peace. (2020). *Ecological Threat Register 2020: Understanding Ecological Threats, Resilience and Peace*. Sydney: Author.

Johnson, S. (2021a). How humanity gave itself extra life. *New York Times*, April 27.

Johnson, S. (2021b). *Extra Life: A Short History of Living Longer*. New York: Penguin.

Kane, J. and Tomer, A. (2019). *Shifting to an Era of Repair: US Infrastructure Spending Trends*. Washington DC: Brookings Institute.

Kim, H-Y., Wunneburger, D., Neuman, M., and Ahn, S.Y. (2014). Optimizing high-speed rail routes using a Spatial Decision Support System (SDSS): The Texas Urban Triangle (TUT) case. *Journal of Transport Geography*, 34: 194–201.

Kim, H-Y., Wunneburger, D., and Neuman, M., (2013). High-speed rail route and regional mobility with a raster-based decision support system: The Texas Urban Triangle case. *Journal of Geographic Information Systems*, 5(6): 559–566.

Kopp, R. E., Simons, F. J., Mitrovica, J. X., Maloof, A. C., and Oppenheimer, M. (2009). Probabilistic assessment of sea level during the last interglacial stage, *Nature*, 462(7275): 863–867.

Kulp, S. and Strauss, B. (2019). New elevation data triple estimates of global vulnerability to sea-level rise and coastal flooding. *Nature Communications*, 10(4844): 1–11.

Kunkel, B. (2017). The Capitalocene. *Times Review of Books*, 35(9): 1–13.

Lambeck, K., Esat, T. and Potter, E.-K. (2002). Links between climate and sea levels for the past three million years, *Nature*, 419: 199–206.

Landsea, C., Anderson, C., Bredemeyer W., Carrasco, C., Charles, N., Chenoweth, M., Clark, G., Delgado, S., Dunion, J., Ellis, R., Fernandez-Partagas, J., Feuer, S., Gamache, J., Glenn, D., Hagen, A., Hufstetler, L., Mock, C., Neumann, C., Perez Suarez, R., Prieto, P., Sanchez-Sesma, J., Santiago, A. Sims, J., Thomas, D., Woolcock, L. and Zimmer, M. (2013). *Documentation of Atlantic Tropical Cyclones Changes in HURDAT*. Miami: National Oceanographic and Atmospheric Agency, Atlantic Oceanographic and Meteorological Laboratory.

Liu, A. and Dunn, F. (2020). Filamentous connections between Ediacaran fronds. *Current Biology*, 30: 1–7.

Malm, A. (2015). *Fossil Capital: The Rise of Steam-Power and the Roots of Global Warming*. London: Verso.

Mayor of London. (2016). *The London Plan: The Spatial Development Strategy for London*. London: Author.

Mayor of London. (2014). *The London Infrastructure Plan 2050*. London: Author.

McPhee, J. (1989). *The Control of Nature*. New York: Farrar, Straus and Giroux.

Meier, R. (1968). The metropolis as a transaction-maximising system. *Daedalus*, 97(1):292–313.

Moore, J. (2015). *Capitalism in the Web of Life: Ecology and the Accumulation of Capital*. London: Verso.

Neuman, M. (2020a). Collaborative and interdisciplinary design education. In Coronado, J. M. and Solis, E. (eds.), *Ingeniería, Urbanismo y Universidad. Homenaje a José María de Ureña*. Ciudad Real: E.T.S.I. de Caminos, Canales y Puertos. Universidad de Castilla-La Mancha.

Neuman, M. (2020b). The power of infrastructure that shapes spatial strategy – Who is left behind? *Town Planning Review*, 91(5): 475–487.

Neuman, M. (2011). Infrastructure planning for sustainable cities. *Geographica Helvetica*, 15(2): 100–107.

Neuman, M. (ed.). (2007). *Rebuilding a Sustainable Gulf Coast: A Regional Plan for New Orleans and Environs*. College Station, TX: Texas A&M University.

Neuman, M. (2005). The compact city fallacy. *Journal of Planning Education and Research*, 25(1): 11–26.

Neuman, M. and Bright, E. (eds.). (2008). *Texas Urban Triangle: Framework for Future Growth*. College Station, TX: Southwest Universities Transportation Consortium.

Neuman, M. and Churchill, S. (2015). Measuring sustainability. *Town Planning Review*, 86(4): 457–482.

Neuman, M. and Churchill, S. (2011). A general process model of sustainability, *Industrial and Engineering Chemistry Research*, 50: 8901–8904.

Neuman, M. and Hull, A., (eds.). (2011). *The Futures of the City Region*. London: Routledge.

Neuman, M. and Whittington, J. (2000). *Building California's Future: Current Conditions in Infrastructure Planning, Budgeting, and Financing*. San Francisco: Public Policy Institute of California.

New Jersey State Planning Commission. (1992). *Assessment Of Infrastructure Needs To 2010 for the New Jersey State Development And Redevelopment Plan.* Trenton: Author.

Page, J. (2011). *The Toughest Beat: Politics, Punishment, and the Prison Officers Union in California.* Oxford: Oxford University Press.

Pryor, L. (2020). Has Australia reached a climate tipping point? *New York Times*, 24 February.

Rohling, E., Fenton, M., Jorissen, F., Bertrand, P., Ganssen, G., and Caulet, J. P. (1998). Magnitudes of sea-level lowstands of the past 500,000 years. *Nature*, 394: 162–165.

Sassen, S. (2001). *The Global City: New York, London, Tokyo.* Princeton: Princeton University Press, 2nd edition.

Schlosser, E. (1998). The prison-industrial complex. *The Atlantic*, December, 51–69.

Simard, S. (2021). *Finding the Mother Tree.* New York: Knopf.

Simard, S., Vyse, M., and Larson, A. (2013). Meta-networks of fungi, fauna and flora as agents of complex adaptive systems. In Puettmann, K., Messier, C., and Coates, K. (eds.), *Managing Forests as Complex Adaptive Systems: Building Resilience to the Challenge of Global Change.* New York: Routledge, 133–164.

Steffen, W., Grinevald, J., Crutzen, P., and McNeill, J. (2011). The Anthropocene: Cultural and historical perspectives. *Philosophical Transactions of the Royal Society A*, 369(1938): 842–867.

Stein, T. (2021). Despite pandemic shutdowns, carbon dioxide and methane surged in 2020. *NOAA Research News*, April 7.

United Nations. (1987). *Our Common Future.* Oxford: Oxford University Press.

UN Habitat (United Nations Human Settlements Programme). (2021). *Cities and Pandemics: Towards a More Just, Green and Healthy Future.* Nairobi: Author.

UNEP (United Nations Environment Programme). (2016). *Global Material Flows and Resource Productivity.* Paris: Author.

Wikipedia. (2020). https://en.wikipedia.org/wiki/Saemangeum_Seawall.

World Footprint Organization. (2019). *Humanity's Ecological Footprint Contracted between 2014–2016.* https://www.footprintnetwork.org/2019/04/24/humanitys-ecological-footprint-contracted-between-2014-and-2016/

World Wildlife Fund. (2018). *Living Planet Report 2018: Aiming Higher.* Gland, Switzerland: Author.

1

Infrastructure Investments, Public and Private Gains

This chapter provides an overview on infrastructure, cities, planning, economies, and sustainability; and their interrelationships in the context of economic, political, societal, and institutional frameworks and phenomena. It contends that for cities to be sustainable, infrastructure must be sustainable. It further means that investments in new infrastructure must also be sustainable. In so doing, it addresses the neoliberal context and the role of the various sectors and actors in planning, designing, financing, operating, and managing infrastructures. Finally, it argues that these facets, often separate, must be done together in an integrated way. Given current conditions, this implies serious reform if not transformation.

With nearly eight billion people, increasing at a rate of one billion every dozen or so years, the planet's current population is estimated to be approximately 84 percent urban, equaling 6.5 billion urban dwellers.[1] Urbanites consume at a far greater rate than rural dwellers (Neuman 2020a). Plus, the global aggregate rate of consumption is increasing. This leads to increasing quantities and rates of impacts, wastes, pollution, climate change, and so on. They paint a clear picture that if we want to survive as a species into the future, much less thrive, we must decrease both the overall amounts and rates of consumption. These increases – in urbanization, consumption, and impacts – implicate infrastructure at every turn.

The sustainability challenge for a consumer society is how to reduce consumption and harmful impacts while maintaining and improving life quality and at the same time redressing longstanding inequities among population groups. This is critical because most energy and materials are themselves consumed by or through infrastructures (Neuman 2020b, 479–480).

DOI: 10.4324/9780429323508-3

The approach taken in this book is to plan, design, and finance infrastructure in an integrative way. One that enhances with multiple positive gains, rather than zero-sum approaches replete with either-or tradeoffs. The types of integration that yield positive outcomes are many. One type integrates principles with practices. Another type of integration is between planning and design, also taught and practiced separately in many countries, especially Anglo-Saxon ones. By contrast, in the northern Mediterranean, planning and design are more integrated. A further type is to link budgeting, financing, and politics via modes of governance that take comprehensive, long-term, and life cycle views rather than short-term ones dictated by political cycles (and terms of office) and economic cycles (and quarterly income reports, monthly labor reports). Finally, better integrating infrastructures with structures in the city in order to arrive at a holistic understanding of the built environment. Throughout the book, examples of integration will be put forward. Integration is key to attaining sustainable infrastructures and thus sustainable cities. Integration is a new watchword for infrastructure planning and design.

Integrating in these ways, infrastructure networks can mimic biological and ecological networks. In nature, the outputs of any process become the inputs to other processes. These inputs and outputs are flows, continual and interconnected. They comprise a web of perpetual recycling in which waste does not exist. In nature, everything is used, whether material or energy. These flows are channeled in the conduits of nature, from rivers and root systems to glacial valleys and oceanic currents. Nature's conduits channel wind and water, rain and sun to support life via photosynthesis, metabolism, and decay. The networks formed by these conduits are interconnected and integrated, spanning geography and time. For example, a river's drainage basin can span the better part of a continent, nourishing many ecosystems and habitats along the way to its silt-laden delta; flowing for millennia if not millions of years, shaping its canyons, valleys, plains, and coasts. Nature's infrastructures are integrated into and form nature itself.

Built infrastructures are the equivalent human artifacts that perform similar functions in the ecosystems that we call cities. The difference is that our infrastructures are far from integrated. Thus, we have wastes and harmful impacts, inefficiencies and ineffectiveness. Our linear-rational and short-term methods of planning and design are far less evolved than those of nature. This makes sense when we consider that civilization and human settlements account for about 10,000 years of evolution, while nature accounts for billions.

This picture is sharpened by climate change and pandemics. Climate change has led to a climate crisis or emergency or catastrophe or apocalypse, depending on your perspective on the future. Of course, climate change is abetted by urbanization and globalization made possible by infrastructure. Pandemics have critical human and infrastructural causes and consequences as well. This is because of human development and other incursions into habitats where vector species live, via urbanization, tourism, resource extraction, and even research. This also happens in reverse via globalization, where vector species invade urban areas (Smith et al. 2014). Complicating matters, "pollution is the largest environmental cause of disease and premature death in the world today" (Lancet Commission on Pollution and Health 2018, 462).

Because of the global drivers of climate change, pandemics, and pollution, many cities and their infrastructures will not exist in a foreseeable future. This is because they will be under water or under siege, by floods, storm surge, and sea level rise or pandemics, pollution, wildfires, and droughts, respectively. Thus, it is ironic that cities, made possible by infrastructures, may see their decline because of human activities made possible by them. Adding to this, telecom infrastructures enable people to work remotely from cities during pandemics, and these workers have been questioning the importance of cities, at least for now. Many are reconsidering whether they want to return to cities after a crisis has passed, whether a pandemic or catastrophic storm or wildfire.

Regardless of the cause or source, cities and their infrastructures are eminently vulnerable because they are not resilient. It is impossible to move an entire city to another place that has less risk. The same can be said for most infrastructures. This is heightened from the financial perspective due to the sunk costs embedded in these large technical systems.

Sunk costs, in financial terms, means money that has been invested and cannot be recovered. Capital investments in infrastructure – capital costs for capital facilities – are sunk costs. Soon, in waterfront places, these costs will become sunk quite literally as rising seas swamp settlements along coasts. Some estimates suggest that upwards of 1.2 billion people will be displaced and become climate refugees as soon as 2050 (Institute for Economics and Peace 2020). Financially and literally, the sunk costs will not be able to be recovered. Abandoning whole cities and their infrastructure networks along low-lying coastal plains, which may be necessary within our lifetimes, could be the ultimate in non-sustainability. Clearly this should motivate all, including the financiers and politicians who fund and decide on infrastructure, to develop more sustainable models.

Adaptation and resilience are key, along with mitigation. Yet typical infrastructure is fixed, hardwired into the urban fabric. They historically have not been made resilient by design or by planning. See Figure 0.3 of the Introduction.

What does this mean for infrastructure and the cities that they enable and serve? They must change, rapidly and massively. No longer can they be your grandparents' infrastructure. No longer can they be fixed in place, centralized, massive, and "too big to fail". This latter term is an unfortunate euphemism for throwing unconscionable sums of money away on systems (and institutions) that are unsustainable. These same, old systems keep us set in our ways and trapped in our cities that may disappear forever, at least as we know them now.

While this may seem dire, this book lays out our current predicaments vis-a-vis cities and infrastructure in terms of what we can do to affect positive, sustainable transformation (Webb et al. 2018). Importantly, it addresses how we can redesign new ones and retrofit existing ones to adapt to rapidly changing climate and health futures.

The work infrastructure provides is not for free. Far from it. To keep infrastructure operating properly, it costs significant sums, much more than citizens typically realize. That is largely because current financing mechanisms for infrastructure pay for the capital (initial construction) costs only. Tax receipts plus tolls and user fees pay for operations and maintenance. The question is, what percentage of operations and maintenance costs are covered by reliable, dedicated revenue streams? Moreover, for most infrastructures, the rest of the life cycle typically remains unfunded. Infrastructures that do not have dedicated revenues suffer even more. Yet, if fully funded for the entire life cycle, and properly planned, built, and managed; infrastructure yields positive returns on investment, as any business or government can attest. Like any investment, it needs constant care to keep it reaping rewards over its lifetime.

Each infrastructure has a life span and a life cycle. Once built, infrastructure demands attention throughout the life cycle: cleaning, maintaining, repairing, updating, expanding, replacing, reinventing, and recycling; like any artifact. This requires intention, planning, and the application of will and resources. This book's premise is simple. To have productive, livable, healthy, and sustainable cities, we must have quality infrastructure that is cared for throughout its entire life cycle. As goes infrastructure, so go the cities, individuals, economies, environments, and societies that depend on it.

Infrastructure, Growth, Progress, and Sustainability

Today, society demands new types and arrangements of infrastructure to correspond to new needs like mobility, speed, agility, big data, the cloud, virtual reality, artificial intelligence, and so on. Is it finally time to employ our intellectual capital for innovative thinking for infrastructure capital investments? As one of the bigger, faster growing, and most lucrative sectors of the economy, particularly finance, infrastructure merits the best thinking. But this is not a call for unfettered capitalism, unregulated markets, indiscriminate techno-fixes, and a private sector takeover of public services. Instead, it is a caution about the necessary links between infrastructure and urban development, between public and private sectors. In the will to growth, which leads to the will to infrastructure, we find a logic not dissimilar to the will to power, with its inevitable consequences, especially conflict. These conflicts can be lessened through public–private partnerships that are focused squarely on the public good, of which infrastructure is a prime part.

Disciplined capitalism, in the form of intelligent investments, plays a critical role in making infrastructures sustainable. In 2011, a warning bell rang throughout the world that planned investments in fossil fuel infrastructures were leading to a "carbon bubble" of five times the carbon dioxide emissions that the planet could absorb and still remain within targets set by the IPCC (Carbon Tracker 2011). Ten years on, fossil fuel divestments inspired by that report have become mainstream, as pointed to by the world's largest investment firm, Blackrock, along with Marketa, which "separately concluded that investment funds have experienced no negative financial impacts from divesting from fossil fuels. In fact, they found evidence of modest improvement in fund return" (Sanzillo 2021). Money talks when it comes to sustainable infrastructure (McKibben 2021). This also applies to other infrastructures, such as transport and water, where financial markets are spearheading moves toward sustainability.

This seismic shifts may finally turn the tide, which has been flowing in a non-sustainable direction. While there has been progress in making the environment and development more compatible since the Brundtland Report's clarion call for sustainability (United Nations 1987), the aggregate data worldwide show that we have been going backwards on climate change and social equity. This reveals that development still takes a priority over the planet, even as this imbalance is changing. It also suggests a tremendous opportunity for infrastructure to help turn the tide, instead of merely serving to catalyze urban and economic growth, as booming markets for clean energy and green mobility show.

Sustained action to unlock the opportunities afforded by infrastructure hiding behind this conflict between environment and development awaits. Despite all the IPCC reports, climate accords, scientific research, climate protests, and so on; the main drivers of climate change – population growth, fossil fuels, and increases in per capita consumption – are far from abating, as all the data show. Any sober analysis – and there have been many – clearly shows that we cannot escape a fundamental rethink of growth and progress if we seek to remain on a habitable planet. Yet we can maintain quality of life *and* well-being even as population grows, if we do it right, and right away. One indispensable key is sustainable infrastructure.

Infrastructure is Indispensable

Wise investments can achieve the promise of infrastructure. To merely raise capital to build infrastructure is not enough. Infrastructure investments must simultaneously elevate both the public good and the private. To accomplish this in a complex, fragmented, and rapidly changing world that constantly faces multiple and interconnected crises requires new thinking and investing. Investing that is circular, like circular economies. Circular investing that is underpinned by life cycle methods and ecological thinking. How to accomplish this?

In a series of articles, I have demonstrated the scientific principles and theories along with mathematical proofs that underpin the mounting empirical evidence that shows that as cities become larger and more complex, they can *only* continue to consume more and become ever more unsustainable. This is due to the immutable laws of thermodynamics (Neuman 2011; 2005a; Neuman and Churchill 2015; 2011). Due to thermodynamics and other biophysical laws, unless we model cities and infrastructures on evolutionary and ecological principles, we can never attain sustainability. We cannot buy our way out of this predicament using new or more technology, mainly because spending and consuming according to existing ways that emphasize technological progress (business *still* as usual) have led us into it. We can think our way out, however. If we think and then act in a new way.

This new thinking entails sustainability. Strictly speaking, sustainability refers to the degree to which a process is sustainable, that is, can be maintained over the long run without depleting the resources and ecosystems that support it – carrying capacity – and without exceeding the capacities of natural systems and the planet as a whole to absorb the impacts of the process – resilience. When fully based on the synthesis of evolution, ecology, and thermodynamics; sustainability refers to *processes*, not things or places. This new conception is absolutely critical if we hope to attain sustainable cities, economies, and societies in practice. Yet this conception runs against prevalent notions of cities as places with form, not processes with flows. And of infrastructures as facilities, projects, or systems, not interconnected networks of processes and flows.

Today more than ever, rigid disciplinary thinking is called into question in the network society and the space of flows. What is the future of infrastructure when we recognize the primacy of processes in determining urban form? We live transactive lives on the go in transactive cities, presaged by urban theorist Richard Meier's article "The metropolis as a transaction-maximizing system" (Meier 1968). Transactions enabled by infrastructure. One beacon forward to greater sustainability is to recognize that these transactions are processes. These transactive processes form the basis to design – and redesign – sustainable infrastructure networks and the cities that they undergird.

The Reciprocal Relations of Infrastructures and Cities

How does this new understanding of cities as processes square with how cities and infrastructures have evolved side by side throughout history? Great cities are born of and give rise to great infrastructure. Seats of empire, such as Rome, Madrid, and London, owed their central standing to extensive infrastructure. These capitals could not govern the expanse of their dominions without superior transportation, communication, and administrative systems. They often pioneered new technologies to extend the reach and lucre of empire and the size of the capital city administering it. The Roman Empire, for example, could not have existed in its grandeur without roads emanating to its peripheral outposts and aqueducts supplying Rome with water. Other infrastructures critical to the rise of Rome include city walls, bridges, a seaport, reservoirs, public baths and fountains, and civic architecture that consisted of amphitheaters, the coliseum, circuses, and plazas (Benevolo 1980). The saying "all roads lead to Rome" clearly asserts the centrality of infrastructure for Rome and its empire.

Today, global cities owe their positions as command posts in the global economy to information, telecommunications, and transportation networks that concentrate knowledge, capital, goods, and people. Old notions of empire and hierarchy have been supplemented by a new order that shapes the symbiosis of corporate conglomerates with governments into networks, and posits world cities as nodes. The networking of society is in debt to the capital invested in networking infrastructures, which have recast relations among peoples, institutions, and places (McNeill and McNeill 2003; Sassen 2001; Castells 2001). The transformation of social space in general and urban space in particular is due to the transformation of infrastructure into globe-spanning networks, and the transformative power of infrastructure.

This relationship works both ways. Cities also give rise to infrastructure, as infrastructure is needed to sustain the city and its growth. The industrial era begat the modern era explosion of city growth, which infrastructure enabled and fueled. In addition to transport networks such as turnpikes, rails, and canals; waterworks and sewerage were technologies born out of the stresses of rapid and large-scale urban growth, including widespread epidemics such as cholera, smallpox, and malaria. At the same time, they fueled more growth. Witness how slowly New York City grew, for example, before it built its Croton water system in 1842 and the Erie Canal, which opened in 1825. How Paris grew before it developed its sewers in the 1830s. Compare this to how fast both grew after pivotal infrastructure installation. Today, Shanghai and Beijing provide testimony to the supercharging effect on growth by infrastructure. Infrastructure enabled each to grow at an average annual rate of a half million persons every year from 1990 to 2020.[2] Cities and infrastructure have always been mutually interdependent and coevolutionary.

Many identify with the notion of the "city as the maximum creation of civilization" as proclaimed by famed anthropologist Claude Levi Strauss. "The city is the most beautiful work of art of humanity", according to the philosopher Georg Wilhelm Hegel. City planner Edmund Bacon may be excused of professional bias when he stated that "the city is mankind's greatest achievement". In this era of globalization, the new nature of cities, especially big cities (world cities, global cities, metropolises, city regions, megacities, megalopolises), remains the same nature that cities have always exhibited: cities are transaction maximizing systems (Meier 1968) central places (Christaller 1966) and nodes of agglomeration economies (Jacobs 1984; Glaeser 2010). The issues today are what transactions are occurring, how are they being enabled, how (and why) they are being maximized, and what are the impacts of all these processes? Do they lead to sustainable cities and prosperity, public health and personal wellness, and fully realized lives and communities? Once again, infrastructure provides insights and answers to these questions.

One way to look at this is to see how infrastructure has changed over time, and led to greater amounts of growth and degrees of unsustainability. Telecommunications and transportation provide good examples. Technology advances in these two infrastructures have incurred and enabled the dislocation / separation / fragmentation of space and time. This is due to the multiple interpenetrations of infrastructure networks into daily life, and their nested embeddings in cities. As a consequence, we see a hyperization of all processes in the city, including acceleration in time, displacement in space, increased concentrations *and* dispersion, and increased frequency of interaction. Mega- and hypercities are becoming the norm.

Another effect of the proliferation of these particular networks is the mediating nature of telecommunications and transportation technologies. Increasingly knowledge and action are becoming mediated, and not a result of direct experience (McLuhan 1964). As we experience an increasing separation from reality by media, media can become the reality, leading to the disembedded nature of activity (Giddens 1990). Various media work between cognition and experience, placing a wedge between what we used to learn from apprenticeship, direct experience, and local knowledge. Now we learn from and through media. This dramatic and rapid change, compared to the entire human experience through evolution, has profound and multiple impacts, given the extent of life being lived online and through media. While these effects are beyond the scope of this book, I will distill some essences for cities and infrastructure.

Because of all these changes, some cities, called global or world cities, have global connections that are more important than local ones. They are distancing themselves from other cities and their own environs, forming a class unto themselves (Knox and Taylor 1995; Abrahamson 2004). Infrastructure enabled these critical changes in the dynamics of the city, so much so that its planning and governance must change to keep pace. As infrastructure is often a leading agent, or driver, of change, infrastructure planners must stay one step ahead in order to manage infrastructure and urban change responsibly. This distinguishes this book from others. Many texts deal with infrastructure as a static phenomenon, as a fixed facility or a project, with a focus on the physical network. Instead, we must deal with the fluxes it conveys, the nodes it connects, the activities it supports, and the multiple impacts it causes.

Consequently, I present a dynamic conception of infrastructure in the urban environment. This is done in several ways. First, by conveying the dynamic life cycles of infrastructure systems, in Chapters 5 and 6. Second, by stressing the flows that are carried by infrastructure and the processes used to operate and maintain them, in Chapters 2 and 3. Third, showing the historical relations among city planning, infrastructure, and urban development, in Chapter 4. Fourth, by aligning finance and governance with these precepts, in Chapters 7 and 8. Finally, by recognizing how infrastructure is embedded in the urban context and the society it serves.

The Reciprocal Relation of Infrastructure with City Planning

In history, the growth and construction of cities has been largely spontaneous, emergent, contingent, and evolutionary (Mumford 1961). Their development was dependent on local materials, local topography, local weather patterns and climate, shaped through local knowledge. By the same token, aspects of cities have been planned since the earliest civilizations of Mesopotamia, the Indus Valley, the Mediterranean, and China. These aspects include temples of worship and ritual, markets of commerce, and paths to connect them. The practice of modern, professionalized city planning as we now know it began during the Italian Renaissance and blossomed in the mid-19th century in reaction to the excesses of industrial European and American cities bursting at the seams (Benevolo 1980; Mumford 1961).

Throughout history, until the land use planning and zoning revolution of the late 19th and early 20th centuries, city planning was largely infrastructure planning. Infrastructure was the primary tool to shape the future of the city, and to determine the amount, location, and type of urban growth. Before land use zoning, the surveying and layout of a street network, squares, plazas, parks, prominent civic buildings, and waterworks were the primary occupations of city planners, regardless of whether they were trained as architects, engineers, landscape architects, surveyors, or colonial viceroys. A leading example of this approach was the Spanish Law of the Indies of the 16th century. It specified street patterns, squares, urban infrastructure, and their administration for Spanish settlements in the New World (Crouch, Garr, and Mundigo 1982; Neuman 2005b).

Of the two key sources of modern city planning – housing reform and sanitary reform – we can see that infrastructure has played a critical role in the founding of the profession and served as a mainstay of its early identity. This is illustrated clearly in the earliest and most influential comprehensive city planning schemes: Ildefons Cerdà and Barcelona, Georges Haussmann and Paris, Ebenezer Howard and the Garden City. For his part, Cerdà, the Catalan civil engineer who laid out the expansion of Barcelona in 1859, infrastructure was a primary object of his plan and means of its realization. The two signal and intertwined parts of the plan – roads and "islands" – were both conceived of as infrastructures. Islands were the individual city blocks containing housing that surrounded community open spaces within the courtyard between the four built sides of the block. The plan addressed economic, social, public health, and equity issues in addition to the built form (Neuman 2011).

Georges Haussmann, Prefect of the Seine (administrative district that included Paris) from 1853 to 1870, drafted a city plan that transformed Paris. He accomplished this chiefly by a modern assemblage of wide streets and boulevards connecting key points such as rail stations and markets (Haussmann called them "nodes of relation"), through demolishing buildings and neighborhoods to create boulevards and open spaces, sanitary infrastructure, omnibuses, and gas lamp lighting. He also created two large public parks east and west of the city and built numerous community facilities: schools, hospitals, barracks, and prisons (Choay 1969; Benevolo 1980). Based on planimetric and topographic surveys of the entire city, Haussmann's plan created complete circulatory and respiratory systems that would "give unity to and to transform into an operative whole" the City of Light (Choay 1969, 16).

Ebenezer Howard's Garden City was in fact a regional design that linked a regional town with smaller, neighboring towns in a productive economic and social unit. His infrastructures were transport, productive rural lands between the towns, and housing, largely what we would call today social housing. His scheme included finance and administration, and was widely adopted, though in truncated form (individual towns and suburbs) around the world (Howard 1902). We can see in all three, how infrastructure in the broad sense was instrumental. These three pioneers revealed how a holistically conceived city plan based on infrastructure could potentially solve many urban problems in unison. Again, early modern city planning was mostly infrastructure planning.

The Multiple Values of Infrastructure

Infrastructure inspires – the popular imagination, through books and films such as *A Bridge Too Far* and *A Bridge Over the River Kwai*. *Brookland* is Emily Barton's historical novel of family fortunes and the changes awaiting the emerging world city of early 18th century New York due to the flight of engineering fancy that was to become the Brooklyn Bridge. It conveys the destiny-determining nature of singular public works (Barton 2006). The story of Roman Polanski's film *Chinatown*, while dramatically distinct from Barton's, refers to the destiny-determining nature of another work, the Los Angeles aqueduct.

Infrastructure inhabits the public imagination and lifts the spirit – the Golden Gate Bridge, the Hoover and Three Gorges dams, the Pyramids, the Coliseum, the Appian Way; all testaments to civilizations present and past, monuments to the human spirit and progress. New York's Central Park and Berlin's Tiergarten are emblems of the myriad urban parks worldwide that afford recreation, entertainment, culture, and respite from chaotic urbanity; as well as provide settings for works of art like paintings, books, poems, and films.

Infrastructure is art – the Brooklyn Bridge, the Golden Gate Bridge, Prospect Park, Regents Park, the Eiffel Tower, the Coliseum, the Sydney Opera House, the Thames Barrier floodgates in London, bridges and communication towers by Spanish architect-engineer Santiago Calatrava. These names alone conjure images of the grandeur of infrastructure. On a more modest scale, city and town halls, schools and fire stations, squares and plazas, libraries and concert halls, and more represent civic infrastructure that embodies and projects the public spirit.

Infrastructure connects – bridges and tunnels, rails and trails, highways and byways, boats and planes, ports and airports, digital devices and networks; bringing people together. Travel, to the office or across the ocean, takes us to our daily routine as well as far away from it. From the Silk Roads and le Pont d'Avignon to the internet, infrastructure is the onramp to the extraordinary, the restorative, and the explorative; whether virtual or real.

Infrastructure unites – families with friends, water with crops, power to people. Utah's Golden Spike linked the American coasts via the transcontinental railway, opening the Western wilderness to settlement in the 19th century. Streets, sidewalks, and squares bind every community. The increasingly interconnected and expanding human web spreads across the globe, made possible by the networks of infrastructures. The human web is brought together by infrastructural webs that enable larger, more extensive, and richer social networks than ever before (McNeill and McNeill 2003). At the same time, we cannot discount the dark side of social media in dividing societies and communities, and a dark side of infrastructure that divides as well as connects (Graham and Marvin 2000).

Infrastructure serves – the common good by the community facilities and utilities that make possible, productive, and pleasant the day to day. Public works perform public services for all members of society. Freedom and opportunity are valued political rights enshrined in constitutions and the collective consciousness, made real by infrastructures that afford access to all, when they are planned and managed with the greater good in mind.

Infrastructure saves lives – whether levees or hospitals, sanitary sewers or waterworks, fire and police stations. Public health in cities is made possible by water supply and waste disposal systems. In fact, modern urban planning was a response to health epidemics in industrial cities, using sanitary infrastructures to eradicate disease vectors. Fire, police, and emergency medical services rely on and form part of community infrastructure. Heat and shelter provided by infrastructure enable survival and habitation in frigid climates.

Infrastructure endures – testaments to technical prowess and human ingenuity, and the collective will that musters resources to build and sustain them for centuries, even millennia. Wonders of the world, ancient and modern, are art and infrastructure combined into one, making men marvel. They capture the striving spirit of the human condition and ennoble ever more fantastic feats.

Infrastructure builds empires – Roman roads and aqueducts; Spanish Law of the Indies and its administrative, trade, and settlement building precepts; globalization based on the internet and other telecommunications and transportation networks. Schools, universities, and libraries are foundations for learning. They enable world trade and knowledge exchange. Infrastructure empowers political and corporate empires to span the globe. They mobilize, convergence and consolidate power as they undergird the ever-larger megacities and megainstitutions that they make possible. Again, these same infrastructures and the empires that they beget have a "flip side". They can divide and suppress, destroying cultures and habitats (Graham and Marvin 2000).

Infrastructures create wealth and add value – Central Park's influence on real estate values on Fifth Avenue, irrigation's on agriculture in the dry plains and desert, and ports' (sea, air, and land) on trade. "Location, location, location" should really be "access, access, access" or "value, value, value" afforded and created by infrastructure, infrastructure, infrastructure.

Infrastructures undergird human settlements – without infrastructure, cities themselves would be impossible. As societies and their infrastructures evolve, they made cities not just habitable, but prosperous, healthy, and creative. Society itself, urban or rural, could not exist today without infrastructure, so dependent on it have we become. The negative aspects of this dependence were introduced in the preceding introductory chapter.

As infrastructure is so prevalent, it is no surprise that it begat, or played a starring role in begetting, a number of professions: civil and environmental engineering, transportation engineering and planning, city and regional planning, public works and public administration. Other professions devote themselves to infrastructure as well – utility technicians, customer service representatives, accountants, public health practitioners, public administrators, financiers, engineers of most stripes; this list could go on. The term infrastructure is not found in the North American Industry Classification System (NAICS), which replaced the Standard Industrial Classification (SIC) codes. But by using utility, transportation, and other classifications of NAICS that correspond to our definitions of infrastructure in Chapter 2, according to the May 2020 US Census Bureau of Labor Statistics data, over 35 million people work in infrastructure fields.[3]

Another Side of Infrastructure

While infrastructure is a many splendored thing, it is far from everything. Moreover, infrastructure can be a double-edged sword, showing its dark side through malfunction, destruction, misuse, or poor planning, design and construction. It can divide and deny access as well as unite, connect, and provide access.

One cannot sing the praises of infrastructure without recounting its woes, otherwise the tale would be one-sided. The most obvious are the maladies, inconveniences, damages, and deaths caused when infrastructure fails. The breached levee, the blackout, the fallen bridge. Moreover, infrastructure can divide as well as connect. The "other side of the tracks" and the "digital divide" are old and new terms that speak to the schisms brought about by infrastructure. It can divide and fragment in other ways: ethnically, socially, and economically by keeping us "in" and them "out", and connecting "us" and not "them".

Gated communities and the meteoric rise of the security society, whether homeland security, cybersecurity, private security, public security (police, fire), and the military give the impression, sometimes false, of safety and protection, being out of harm's way, behind bastions of fences, gates, surveillance apparatuses, and armed, uniformed, and badged security personnel. The signals that security infrastructure sends, explicitly and subliminally, pervade our society and convey a way of life that disturbs the complacent post-World War II ideal of tranquil suburbs. Is this the direction we want our infrastructure to take us?

The human costs of failed or badly planned public works add up to a staggering toll across millennia and continents, most deeply felt by individuals and their loved ones. The faces of tragedy that haunt us as often as not owe their misfortune to infrastructure catastrophes, frequently brought about by extreme natural events that reveal the improper placement, planning, and design of the infrastructure that was destroyed by the calamity. The imperatives to get infrastructure right the first time are clear. With infrastructure as with anything else, you get what you pay for and what you plan for. And you pay dearly for what infrastructure you didn't pay for and didn't plan properly for.

The balance tallied on both sides of the ledger shows that infrastructure remains the lifeblood of communities and corporations, nations and militaries. Variously referred to as circulation systems and foundations, webs and networks, it is fundamental to supporting, enabling, and connecting people and activities. Infrastructure is the "fabric" of cities and the "tissue" of social and economic intercourse. These analogies connote solidity and stability that provide assurance and confidence to live a safe and productive life, able to enjoy well-being and pursue one's interests.

Notes

1 Compare to 55 percent as indicated in the most recent United Nations documentation. See https://www.reuters.com/article/us-global-cities/everything-weve-heard-about-global-urbanization-turns-out-to-be-wrong-researchers-idUSKBN1K21UU.
2 www.statista.com/statistics/1134787/china-natural-population-growth-rate-in-beijing/; and www.statista.com/statistics/466938/china-population-of-shanghai/
3 See Appendix 1 for year 2020 infrastructure employment data per NAICS codes.

References

Abrahamson, M. (2004). *Global Cities*. Oxford: Oxford University Press.
Barton, E. (2006). *Brookland*. New York: Farrar, Straus & Giroux.
Benevolo, L. (1980). *The History of the City*. Cambridge, MA: MIT Press.
Carbon Tracker. (2011). *Unburned Carbon: Are the World's Financial Markets Carrying a Carbon Bubble?* London: Author.
Castells, M. (2000). *The Rise of The Network Society: The Information Age: Economy, Society and Culture, Volume I*. Oxford: Blackwell, 2nd edition.
Choay, F. (1969). *The Modern City: Planning in the 19th Century*. New York: George Braziller.
Christaller, W. (1966). *Central Places in Southern Germany*. Engelwood Cliffs, NJ: Prentice Hall, translated by Carlisle W. Baskin. Originally published in 1933 as *Die zentralen Orte in Süddeutschland*. Jena: Gustav Fischer.
Crouch, D., Garr, D., and Mundigo, A. (1982). *Spanish City Planning in North America*. Cambridge, MA: MIT Press.
Giddens, A. (1990). *The Consequences of Modernity*. Stanford: Stanford University Press.
Glaeser, E. (2010). *Agglomeration Economics*. Chicago: University of Chicago Press.
Graham, S. and Marvin, S. (2000). *Splintering Urbanism*. London: Routledge.
Howard, E. (1902). *Garden Cities of To-Morrow*. London: Swan Sonnenschein.
Institute for Economics and Peace. (2020). *Ecological Threat Register 2020: Understanding Ecological Threats, Resilience and Peace*. Sydney: Author.
Jacobs, J. (1984). *Cities and the Wealth of Nations: Principles of Economic Life*. New York: Random House.

Knox, P. and Taylor, P. (eds.). (1995). *World Cities in a World System*. Cambridge: Cambridge University Press.
Lancet Commission on Pollution and Health. (2018). Lancet Commission on Pollution and Health. *Lancet*, 391: 462–512.
McLuhan, M. (1964). *Understanding Media: The Extensions of Man*. New York: McGraw Hill.
Meier, R. (1968). The metropolis as a transaction-maximizing system. *Daedalus*, 97, 1292–1313.
McKibben, B. (2021). The powerful new financial argument for fossil-fuel divestment, *The New Yorker*, April 3. https://www.newyorker.com/news/daily-comment/the-powerful-new-financial-argument-for-fossil-fuel-divestment
McNeill, J. R. and McNeill, W. H. (2003). *The Human Web: A Bird's Eye View of World History*. New York: W. W. Norton.
Mumford, L. (1961). *The City in History: Its Origins, its Transformations, and its Prospects*. New York: Harcourt, Brace & World.
Neuman, M. (2020a). Infrastructure is key to make cities sustainable. *Sustainability* 12, 8308: 1–17.
Neuman, M. (2020b). The power of infrastructure that shapes spatial strategy – Who is left behind? *Town Planning Review*, 95(1): 475–487.
Neuman, M. (2011). Ildefons Cerdà and the future of spatial planning: The network urbanism of a city planning pioneer. *Town Planning Review*, 82(2): 117–143.
Neuman, M. (2005a). The compact city fallacy. *Journal of Planning Education and Research*, 25(1): 11–26.
Neuman, M. (2005b). Infrastructure. In Roger W. Caves, (ed.), *Encyclopedia of the City*. London; New York: Routledge, 261–264.
Neuman, M. and Churchill, S. (2015). Measuring sustainability. *Town Planning Review*, 86(4): 457–482.
Neuman, M. and Churchill, S. (2011). A general process model of sustainability, *Industrial and Engineering Chemistry Research*, 50: 8901–8904.
Sanzillo, T. (2021). *Major Investment Advisors BlackRock and Meketa Provide a Fiduciary Path through the Energy Transition*. Lakewood, OH: Institute for Energy Economics and Financial Analysis (IEEFA) https://ieefa.org/major-investment-advisors-blackrock-and-meketa-provide-a-fiduciary-path-through-the-energy-transition/
Sassen, S. (2001). *The Global City: New York, London, Tokyo*. Princeton: Princeton University Press, 2nd edition.
Smith K., Goldberg M., Rosenthal S., Carlson L., Chen J., Chen C., and Ramachandran S. (2014). Global rise in human infectious disease outbreaks. *Journal of the Royal Society Interface*, 11(101): 1–6.
United Nations. (1987). *Our Common Future: Report of the World Commission on Environment and Development*. New York: Author.
Webb, R., Bai, X., Stafford Smith, M., Costanza, R., Griggs, D., Moglia, M., Neuman, M., Newman, P., Newton, P., Norman, B., Ryan, C., Schandl, H., Steffen, W., Tapper, N., and Thomson, G. (2018). Sustainable urban systems: Co-design and framing for transformation. *AMBIO*, 47(1): 57–77.

2
Infiltrating Infrastructure

Defining Infrastructure and its Role in Society

Infrastructure Network Theory

This chapter could have been titled Defining Infrastructure. However, the word "defining" limits the sense that can be imparted to infrastructure. To define means to circumscribe, to prescribe limits through language. *De*fining *de*limits the thing defined from other things. To use the word define with respect to infrastructure misconstrues the essence of infrastructure. Infrastructure permeates, through physical insertion and penetration, other structures. Synonyms that convey this image of infrastructure include implantation, interpenetration, embedding, perfusion, and intromission. Infrastructures are not simply substrates, as they are often misidentified in other texts. They do not merely lie underneath other structures, such as a building or a city. Similes for this older view of infrastructure include foundation, footing, base, pedestal, platform, and understructure. Infrastructures are not separate from cities or buildings, but rather connect to them directly in a vital way. They provide life to the structures that they infiltrate and perfuse. Infrastructures are life supports that channel water, energy, information, people, goods, and wastes to and from the structures that they support. This new reconception of the nature of infrastructure reveals how infrastructure infiltrates instead of underlies. In this chapter I aim to infiltrate infrastructures through this new ontological understanding.

Yet infrastructures do not merely infiltrate individual structures. Collectively, they also provide multichannel, multidirectional connections among the structures that they connect into networks. Infrastructures form the physical basis of networks. In addition to creating networks, infrastructures convey fluxes through them. A *flux*, technically, is the rate at which a fluid, particle, energy, information, or waveform flows through a surface. In infrastructure terms, I expand the term surface to include *conduit*. Flux in infrastructure is measured as a flow rate, as in gallons/liters of water per minute through a pipe or megabytes per second through a digital network. In common usage, flux also refers to a state of constant change. An extension of this latter meaning refers to the effect that the material or waveform in a flux brings about. A flux causes changes in the state of whatever it comes into contact with. For example, as water flows through a dam it can be harnessed to create energy by turning the blades of a turbine. These two meanings – flow and change – can be traced back to the origins of the word. Flux is derived from the Latin word *fluxus*, which meant both flow and change. This perfectly describes both the structural purpose of infrastructure (to convey flows) and the effects that the flow provokes (to cause change). In this way infrastructures serve triple roles as network creators, flux conveyors, and change inducers.

Infrastructures are often referred as infrastructure networks. The network consists, typically, of a generator of a flux, the channels or conduits through which the flux is conveyed, and multiple receivers, such as a reservoir and its water distribution network. Conversely, an infrastructure network may consist of many generators and a single receiver, such as a garbage disposal network. In between, many infrastructure networks consist of multiple generators and receivers, such as an electric power grid. Sources and receivers constitute the nodes of a network. Pipes, wires, rails, roads, channels, and the like make up the conduits of the network. Conduits can be more open and dispersed, such as air, water, or another medium through which the flux is transmitted, like microwaves through the atmosphere. Infrastructures add value to the nodes that they connect into networks by converting the potential of the fluxes that they carry into and through the receivers into more useful products and services.

To elaborate, consider the concrete cases of specific sources (generators) and receivers (users). A source could be a water reservoir, a power-generating station, or a university. These are examples of point sources. Sources can also be configured as networks. One example of a network source is an electric power grid. Another network source – for a knowledge network – is knowledge producers such as university and corporate research laboratories, and the organizations that fund them. Other nodes of a knowledge network include exchange sites and activities, such as conferences, journals, and universities; and repositories of knowledge, such as minds, books, libraries, websites, and databases. Receivers, like sources, can also be point receivers or network receivers. The point receiver of a sewage collection network, for example, is an individual treatment plant. An example of a network receiver is an institutional network, such as the repositories mentioned above in the case of the knowledge network, along with their users or clientele, broadly construed.

Sources and receivers can be one and the same, as in the case of a power co-generator which converts waste materials into energy, or the case of a university, which generates knowledge and uses it in the learning process. The mutual interdependence of sources and receivers, and their co-identities as both sources and receivers in some instances, emanates from the nature of the network itself. A network interlinks sources and receivers with various control and feedback loops which process and transform fluxes (material, data, energy) into more valuable and usable ones. This is the first way networks add value.

Networks add value a second way by conferring source and receiver status to the same entity, multiplying the usefulness of a source into both a source and receiver. A singular example of this type of value added by infrastructure networks is manifest in computer networks in which the processing power of the connected computers vastly exceeds the processing power of any of its individual computers. In urban areas, the collocation of a range of infrastructures, especially multimodal transportation networks, confers significant benefit to the real property located at that juncture, including increases in the monetary value of the property.

Thus, infrastructure network services perform a role in the economy and in society in ways analogous to "nature services". Nature services refers to the role that nature, via ecosystem functions, biological processes, and individual species' activities, performs for human benefit. For example, a forest and lake together perform water purification and reservoir services for free, saving the costs and impacts of constructing a water storage and purification system (Daily 1997).

Adding values in these and other ways specified throughout the text reveals the fundamental nature and purpose of infrastructure. These value-added investments are especially significant in cities and city-regions due to the density and intensity of interactions among infrastructure networks there. The net of the networks is more closely woven (the nodes are closer together) in a city, enabling more frequent mixing of fluxes and more benefits to users. Interactions can also entail negative costs to users. The composite portrait elaborated above comprises the basis of infrastructure network theory.

In contrast, standard definitions of infrastructure typically referred to built facilities and networks – either above or below ground – that support health, safety, and welfare. This take traditionally included publicly and privately owned providers of systems such as utilities (gas and electricity, water supply and sewerage, waste collection and disposal); public works (roads and bridges, dams and canals, ports and airports, railways); community facilities (prisons, schools, parks, recreation, hospitals, libraries); and telecommunications (telephone, internet, television, satellite, cable, broadband). Another overarching term that was common several generations ago was "collective consumption" (Castells 1978; Weisbrod 1964). While networks clearly are a part of this panoply, often the emphasis has been on a single project or public work. Within this project emphasis has been a focus on physical configuration and operations – the nuts and bolts, as it were.

Urbanist Josef Konvitz chronicled a professional etymology of the word "infrastructure". He found that the early English uses of the term were between the First and Second World Wars of the 20th century. The word was not included in either *Webster's Second International Dictionary* of 1934 or the first edition of the *Oxford English Dictionary* (OED). The word is found in the 1976 supplement to the OED, and in the *Webster's Third International Dictionary* of 1961. According to Konvitz, the word infrastructure "probably appeared for the first time in 1875, in French", and was associated with the military (Konvitz 1985, 131).[1]

Infrastructure is Empowering

Instead, we can characterize infrastructure as a mechanism or a means to empower another system – its receiver. The receiver is endowed with an added value that is proportioned by the flux that infrastructure carries into it. This added value is further increased by the interaction of the flux with processes of the receiver. For example, an electrical grid brings electricity – power – to a city or a building, and helps to convert the city or building from a mere assemblage of bricks and mortar into a productive urban economy or factory. Likewise, a telecommunications network brings information to an organization, which uses the information in its own developmental processes, thus converting the information to knowledge and the organization from a mere assemblage of individual persons into a productive unit. In these ways and others, infrastructure is transformational. Infrastructure transforms its receiver into something with greater capacity, with greater capabilities than it had without infrastructure. In this sense, infrastructure is empowering.

The capacity of infrastructure to transform is a double capacity. The first capacity is to transform the receiver into something greater, with more capacity than before. The second capacity is to transform the flux conveyed into something more valuable than its initial properties, by the interaction of the flux with the receiver through the medium of infrastructure. In this way, to continue with the first case of the preceding paragraph, a building and the human organization it contains are transformed into a productive enterprise, and the electricity itself is converted from energy to power (borrowing the literal meanings of those two terms from physics). Another way to conceive these positive transformations is from a potential status to an active condition. Infrastructure transforms natural resources into energy, waste into energy, digital bits into information, and so on. Infrastructure transforms a standing reserve into a dynamic state.

This repositioning of infrastructure marks it as an exemplar of technology that Heidegger envisioned in his revolutionary essay "The question concerning technology". For Heidegger, technology was not simply a machine or tool that enables humans to accomplish acts that they were unable to without it, or to make them easier to accomplish. Instead, he related technology's essence to its transformational power – to convert a thing upon which technology acts from a "standing reserve" into a function that serves a human purpose. Technology does the ordering, a process Heidegger calls "enframing". To him, enframing is the essence of technology (Heidegger 1977). Enframing is a concept that captures the effect technology has on human thinking and action. Enframing converts material objects into a standing reserve waiting to be acted upon by technology. Enframing has the effect of subordinating the natural essence of a thing to the processes and purposes of a technology that subsumes it. Enframing is a way of looking at the world that subjugates everything as subservient to human use. Technology, by enframing, reduces everything to its instrumental purpose of serving humankind. Infrastructure possesses the transformational power of technology.

However, there is a danger that Heidegger identifies with the transformation of a thing, especially nature, into a standing reserve awaiting human action upon it. Nature does not remain merely nature, adapting, evolving, and reproducing itself as it always has. Nature becomes artifice through its control by humans via technology, via infrastructure. Nature's processes become disrupted as they are placed into service for humans. Thus, we can begin to see the impacts infrastructure has on nature. In this way the essence of nature is concealed, and compromised, by technology. This is one of the dangers of technology about which Heidegger signals caution. Another danger he points out is that, to an extent, technology transforms humanity itself into a standing reserve, as in "human resources". Furthermore, humans adapt to the demands and rhythms of technology, and to a degree become its slaves instead of its masters.

The intent here is not to dissect Heidegger or to critique technology per se. This drastic truncation of a single part of one essay of Heidegger's vast output carries with it its own caution of misinterpretation. Rather, it is to reveal the nature of infrastructure through a range of interpretations. I aim to expose qualities of infrastructure that enable humans to rethink and redesign infrastructure into more benign, yet at the same time, useful technologies.

With this understanding, we see clearly how infrastructure empowers cities and transformed them from the *loci* of small city-states in classic Greece into the definitive centers of economic and cultural production and reproduction of the new millennium. If the 20th century was the American century, the 21st is the urban century. The planet's population possesses, for the first time, an urban majority. Cities now have global reach and have been transformed into metropolitan behemoths of 20 million persons or more, with geographic extensions exceeding 10,000 square miles (26,000 square kilometers) in extreme cases such as greater Los Angeles. New mega-agglomerations such as the Pearl River delta in Southern China and the Yangtze River delta in Eastern China approach 100 million human inhabitants. This urban explosion could not have occurred without infrastructure operating in its enabling and transformative modes. Infrastructures convert standing reserves into urban developments. Infrastructures are necessary for cities, but of course not sufficient.

Infrastructures and Their Roles in Society

Infrastructures refer to networks of built facilities – above and below ground – that support human development in settlements. Infrastructure plays a key intermediary part in lessening direct human contact with nature, and the necessity of having to extract sustenance directly from nature. Infrastructure enables settlements to grow into large and dense conurbations. Infrastructure types are listed in Table 2.1, where conventional classifications are used for convenience despite overlaps among them. The evolution of the term infrastructure and its synonyms is elaborated in order to portray the richness and historical legacy of a key primogenitor of urban society. Table 2.2 lists some terms that, while not synonyms, connote categories of infrastructure. Table 2.3 continues with a compendium of characteristics which are common to all types of infrastructure. The chapter closes with Table 2.4, which arrays the implications that these infrastructure characteristics pose. These issues are dealt with in the remainder of the book.

Even a casual scan of Table 2.1 reveals overlaps among categories that are artifacts of the history of each category and the term that denotes it. Moreover, one can see the connections within and among categories of infrastructure. Infrastructure does not exist and operate in isolation, but each type is connected in a variety of ways to other types. For example, solid waste collection and disposal is dependent on transportation networks to convey the materials that comprise waste. It further relies on telecommunications for operations and management, on utilities to provide power, knowledge networks to provide expertise. Infrastructure systems work synergistically to support all the functions of human settlements. They can also hinder the functioning of settlements if ill-planned, poorly operated and maintained, struck

Table 2.1 Types of Infrastructures

Utilities – gas and electricity, water supply and sewerage, stormwater management, waste collection and disposal
Public Works – highways and bridges, dams and reservoirs, ports and airports
Community Facilities – schools, parks, playgrounds, greenways, arenas, stadia and other sports and recreation areas and facilities, hospitals, libraries, civic buildings, auditoria, convention centers, fire and police stations, prisons, emergency management structures
Telecommunications – telephone, internet, television, radio, and multimedia; transmitted via satellite- and antenna-propagated waves and cable- and wire-channeled signals
Transportation – roads, sidewalks, trails, and bridges; railways, railway yards, and stations; seaports and airports; canals, rivers, lakes, and seas; mass transit (buses, subways, fixed-surface rail, cable-guided trolleys, and suspended trams); multimodal junctions and terminals; and their respective support facilities
Knowledge Networks – schools, universities, research institutes, libraries, museums, archives

Source: Expanded from Neuman and Whittington, 2000, 7–9

Table 2.2 Categorizations of Infrastructures

Utilities	Community Facilities
Public Works	Large Technological Systems
Civic Improvements	Urban Networks
Capital Facilities	Urban Infrastructures
Capital Investments	Critical Infrastructures

Table 2.3 Infrastructure Characteristics

1. A physical network or component thereof that channels a flux through conduits or a medium to its nodes (receivers) with the purpose of supporting a superordinate system connected to the network.
2. Delivers fluxes, goods, services, and people to a large number of locations, users, and consumers, a number which is anticipated to be steady or to increase over time.
3. Large investments of finance capital in order to build the physical network.
4. Relatively long life span (50 years or more) of the fixed components of the physical network, with the intention that the network serves indefinitely, or until obsolete.
5. Network capacity is designed to accommodate peak flows, perhaps with an additional margin to cushion external shocks or accommodate growth.
6. Economies of scale conferred by the performance of the entire network due to low per capita costs and long amortization periods, partially offset by design capacities that accommodate peak flows.
7. Interdependence among components within the infrastructure network, among entities it supports, and among other interlaced infrastructure networks which support it and which it supports.
8. Values added to and subtracted from the systems it supports and other interconnected infrastructure networks (externalities, when conceived in a non-holistic manner).
9. Values added to and subtracted from the real property and organizations connected, adjacent, or proximate to the network (externalities, when conceived in a non-holistic manner).
10. Immobility of the physical network, with exceptions like satellite-connected mobile (cell) phones.
11. Restricted substitutability of the physical network (not so of owners and / or operators), with exceptions like telecommunications and other decentralized, deregulated networks.
12. Low price elasticity based on the physical and operating characteristics of the network, and on its restricted substitutability.
13. Degrees of standardization within the physical network, in relation to technologies, pricing, controls, and measurement.
14. Degrees of standardization caused by the physical network, in relation to space (land prices, urbanization by a street grid, others), time (transportation schedules, telecommunications schedules, others), and homogenization of consumer acceptance.
15. Must be planned and managed.

Table 2.4 Infrastructure Characteristics and their Implications

Implications → / Characteristics ↓	Sustainability	Planning	Finance	Institutions
1. Physical network	* land consumption * material consumption * energy consumption * ecological impacts	* settlement patterns * development location * coordination with broader social goals	* determines capital investment budgets	* spatial (territorial) coordination across networks
2. Delivery of flux, goods, services, people to large number of users	* concentrated impacts * enables mass transit * more universal access	* develops standards of performance and accessibility	* enables accumulation of capital via large user base	* establishment of delivery systems * transaction costs in engaging users
3. Large investments of finance capital	* who pays? * who benefits?	* prioritize among networks	* ability to use debt financing * large sunk costs = risk	* capacity to raise and allocate funds * sector of ownership?
4. Long life span of the physical network	* durable materials * flexible re-use * risk of obsolescence	* locational impacts * life cycle planning and management	* long amortization for debt financing * repair and rehabilitation included in financing	* establishment of procedures to institutionalize long-term life cycle planning
5. Network capacity is designed for peak flows	* may exceed capacity of ecosystem to absorb peak flow impacts	* demand management * performance measures based on sliding scales	* differential user fees * design for < peak flow lowers system cost	* should network size be designed for peak flow capacity?
6. Economies of scale	* factor in externalities * network scale service delivery is sustainable?	* match scale of infrastructure network to scale of settlement	* easier to justify capital financing * decentralization?	* match scale of infrastructure network to scale of settlement
7. Interdependence among components	* potential savings from lower land consumption * concentration of impacts	* network collocation endows development synergies – MILU[4] * coordinated planning	* increases in indirect costs * co-financing potential	* high transaction costs for coordination among organizations and territories

8. Values added to and subtracted from systems supported	* work with, not against ecosystems	* cost–benefit calculus includes all ecological, socioeconomic, fiscal	* value capture financing with benefits going to public purse	* distributional (political) decisions benefits and impacts
9. Values added to and subtracted from real property and organizations	* impacts of high use & population densities * access inequalities	* land uses density, mix * transfer of development rights (TDR)	* Tax increment financing (TIF) * value capture finance	* TDR banks and markets across large areas
10. Immobility of the physical network	* persistent long-term impacts on land, water, air, communities, ecosystems	* predictability of development and its location	* risk of obsolescence if not able to convert or re-use	* place-based, scale-determined jurisdictional boundaries
11. Restricted substi- tutability of the physical network	* decrease in innovation * inequitable to users who can't access option	* vfewer alternatives to solve urban problems * off-grid or on-grid?	* monopoly price gauging risk * exclusion of users	* complacence, corruption, turf disputes * centralized vs. decentralized
12. Low price elasticity	* inequitable to users who can't afford option	* constrains alternatives in planning and implementation	* limited use of user fees for financing	* adoption of social equity remedies
13. Standardization of the physical network	* serves different social segments equally, and perhaps inequitably	* uniformity of services enables use of simple formulae to calculate capacities, densities, …	* more predictable cash flows for long-term budget estimates and capital requirements	* enables expansion across territory and time * facilitates coordination
14. Standardization caused by the physical network	* ecosystem ability to adapt to nonlocal impact * decrease in innovation	* creates homogenous places, detracts from local character	* restricted freedom to create new financing instruments	* people become statistics * standardization begets centralization
15. Must be planned and managed	* obliges consideration of local characteristics to attain local sustainability	* increases value of planning which is long term, impact evaluating	* life cycle financing	* institutions incorporate long-term, life cycle processes

by workers, locked down by owners, or damaged. The interaction of infrastructure networks with each other and with the physical and social fabrics of the city is of greater consequence than normally considered. This is but one reason that integration among infrastructures is essential for their sustainable design, planning, and operation.

The background in which infrastructure usually finds itself is immediately brought to the fore in cases of emergency. On close examination, infrastructure is revealed as a key factor in productivity, equity, development, learning, pleasure; in sum, any facet of daily life. As settlements and their panoply of infrastructure networks are so intertwined, it can justify amplifying and expanding the discourses of urban planning, public policy, and economic development so that the prime importance of infrastructure to urban growth and well-being is properly considered.

Evolution of the Term Infrastructure

Consider the origins of the term infrastructure. Synonymous with the word "base," it first referred to facilities built below the earth's surface: water, sewer, steam, and drainage systems installed under streets. It has lost clarity and precision as the complexity of our built world has increased over the past 100 years. Today, there are many meanings.

Large-scale capital-intensive monopolies, such as highways and other transportation facilities, water and sewer systems, and communications networks, are readily apparent examples of infrastructure. To this end, the World Bank considers utilities, public works, and other transport sectors (as denoted in Table 2.1) as infrastructure (World Bank 1994). These interpretations are clearly geared toward economic development and productivity. Another common interpretation limits infrastructure to public sector ownership (Gramlich 1994; World Bank 1999).[2] While public infrastructure may be easy to specify, it omits many facilities and networks that serve as infrastructures. Safety, health, and welfare facilities, military bases, prisons, schools, hospitals, parks and other recreational facilities, and police, fire, and disaster mitigation facilities add a social dimension to the economic. Broader interpretations include human capital investment, such as research and development facilities, and administrative infrastructure that supports organizational development and productivity. These latter two categories are not included in this book.

There are many different definitions of infrastructure. One type, definitions found in laws, often are so specific that they hamstring flexibility and innovation. For example, do initiatives, such as buying forests to protect watershed lands, and watershed management programs, which provide multibillion-dollar savings on hard facilities' construction costs, such as water supply reservoirs, wastewater treatment plants, and flood control structures, qualify as infrastructure or capital expenditure? Infrastructure is a moving target that seems to resist precise specification.

The tendency has been for the meaning of the term to expand over time to include more and different systems. This can be observed in operating definitions in state codes and manuals, in the language of specialists and managers, and in common usage by the general public. Infrastructure has become an encompassing term. It is true, nonetheless, that infrastructures have increased their presence on the human scene. As population and urbanization increase, infrastructure has enabled the pace of human activity to accelerate, aspirations to increase, distances to decrease, and time to shorten. Life has become increasingly mediated, and infrastructure is a key mediator. Infrastructure has permeated our lives and is now beginning to permeate our skin, and the skin of our pets, literally. Implanted chips portend a new, perhaps sinister, meaning of the adjective "infra" – within – that has until now been restricted to its embedding into other built structures.[3] The more rapidly infrastructure changes, the greater challenge it presents to anyone who seeks to define it, much less manage it.

On a practical plane, definitions of infrastructure are important and have significant consequences. Who pays for infrastructure and how it is financed is dependent on how infrastructure is defined. Financial accounting categories for construction and repair affect what gets done, or not, who does it, and what level of resources are afforded to different categories of infrastructure. In any national or state (regional) legislature one finds that the biggest budget battles routinely concern infrastructure. As definitions accumulate over time, each piece of legislation can have its own definition, and each is legally binding. Terms such as public works, capital facilities, capital improvements, public facilities, utilities, public utilities, community facilities, public development facilities, and infrastructure represent part of this statutory range. Given this atmosphere of confusion around the definition of infrastructure, it is no wonder that some documents have altogether avoided precise definition of the term.

Definitional and categorical problems have led to the creation of new terms like virtual infrastructure, wireless infrastructure, and portable infrastructure. These refer to the internet, mobile phones, and wireless laptops, among other devices enabled by Bluetooth and other wireless technologies. The convergence of formerly separate telecommunications platforms, including telephone, television, radio, and the internet, are expanding the penetration and pervasiveness of virtual infrastructures in society. Are terms such as wireless infrastructure oxymorons? In one sense wireless is the ultimate infrastructure, as its signals pervade (infra) other structures, including portable devices. In any event, wireless systems require plenty of fixed facilities, such as satellites, receiving and transmitting towers, switching systems, server farms, and more.

Over time, different professions (identified in parentheses) have proffered categorical denominations such as "urban infrastructure" (city planning), "public works" (civil engineering), "capital facilities" (business administration), "capital investments" (finance), "community facilities" (public administration), and "civic improvements" (architecture). Scholars and other commentators have called infrastructures "large technical systems", "networks", and "critical infrastructures". Examining these categories one at a time affords a deeper insight into infrastructure. It provides a good idea about how different entities (professions and governments) have managed infrastructure in different time and places.

Utilities refer to a subcategory of infrastructure known for its financing largely by user fees and by its subministration directly to the locale of the user – domicile or business. Electricity, water supply, wastewater treatment, natural gas, and waste collection are common types of utilities. Telephone service fits this listing of utilities, though it is rarely classed as one. Utilities have either private or public owners, and regardless of ownership, tend to have limited competition in their service areas. However, if a utility owner did once enjoy a monopoly, that is changing, especially in telecommunications and energy. If privately owned, they are subjected to regulatory supervision for consumer protection reasons.

Public works take as their starting point public sector ownership and benefit for the general public, as well as a tendency to consist of an individual, large-scale facility, or work. The first secular public works were aqueducts, baths, fountains, and roads. Dams and reservoirs, ports and canals, and highways and bridges were classic 18th and 19th century public works. Airports, a 20th century contribution, are almost exclusively the province of public sector construction. Ireland established the Office of Public Works in 1831 to supervise a wide range of government civil works, including roads, bridges, canals, railways, piers, harbors, and river and field drainage (Board of Public Works 1832). France also established a Ministry of Public Works in 1831, and other European nations soon followed suit (Benevolo 1967, 86–87).

What is becoming less pronounced throughout the world is the degree to which government finances, owns, or operates infrastructure systems. The strict validity of the modifier "public" is being eroded. All types of infrastructure nowadays have varying degrees of private sector involvement, and almost all are in a state of flux with respect to ownership. For example, for most of the 20th century, highways were entirely constructed and managed by the government departments of transportation. Recently, projects for private toll road development have been constructed across the globe, reverting to the turnpike model of the 18th and 19th centuries in England and the United States. Likewise, public ports and airports are afforded growth through significant contributions from ocean carriers and airlines in the private sector, even as they are managed by quasi-public agencies with reporting requirements to and oversight by higher levels of government.

Civic improvements is a term that was in vogue at the turn of the 19th to the 20th century that referred to the public improvements to the city for the benefit of its citizens. The term was in part associated with the City Beautiful movement on both sides of the Atlantic Ocean. Streets, sidewalks, street furniture, public lighting, parks, promenades, boulevards, and prominent public buildings such as city halls, museums, and libraries were typical civic improvements, as promulgated by the promoters of the City Beautiful in the Progressive Era. Civic improvements were designed by prominent architects and landscape architects and were meant to instill pride for the city, which had become filthy and crowded since the onset of the industrial era. Today the term civic improvements refers generally to the design and beautification of urban spaces through built projects. It includes public works or facilities that benefit the city in a visible way, meaning above ground projects.

The contemporary usage has expanded from its century-old City Beautiful roots, which were tied to bolstering appearance and attractiveness. It now encompasses more functional infrastructures such as marinas, ports, streets, sidewalks, street furniture, public transit, civic buildings, and so on.

Capital facilities take as their start the investment of financial capital into an individual facility. Thus, they share with the term public works the existence of individual projects or facilities. Yet unlike public works, the term capital facilities does not specify the nature of ownership. Capital facilities can be owned by public, private, non-profit, or mixed entities. Over time, the meanings attributed to capital facilities have evolved into one of the broadest classifications of infrastructure. It encompasses both individual facilities and networks of facilities, such as libraries and schools. It includes utilities, community facilities, and public works. It connotes any initial investment into a large physical structure or network that performs a service to its owners and users.

Capital investments is an expression that is more explicit about the role of finance capital in the infrastructure playing field, and the long-term return on investment anticipated by the investors. According to one specification of capital investments, Section 3.00 of the State of California's Budget Act defines "capital outlay" as "acquisitions of land or other real property, major construction, improvements, equipment, designs, working plans, specifications, and repairs necessary in connection with a construction or improvement project". This brings up an issue regarding capital financing, addressed in Chapter 8, by nominally relegating some costs of capital construction, namely repair and maintenance, to the operating budget instead of the capital budget. In practice, however, this is an accounting issue with local variations, and is not injurious to the overall concept of infrastructure as a capital investment.

Community facilities refers to the users and the location and scale of infrastructure. This category includes such facilities as schools and libraries, fire and police stations, emergency facilities, parks and community centers, city halls and public auditoria, and other buildings meant to serve individual communities at a neighborhood or municipal scale. These are usually owned and operated by the public sector. In the cases of small communities, some of these services are provided by citizen volunteers, such as fire fighting, and their facilities are financed in large part by fundraising. In the case of residential subdivisions planned by an individual developer, some of these facilities are provided privately, and managed by a community homeowners association.

Large technological systems is a term used by scholars to convey the scale, origin, and essential nature of infrastructure. This term represents an important advance in the study and understanding of infrastructure. This understanding was put forward by the historian of technology Thomas Hughes in his study of the development of large-scale electric power generation, transmission, and distribution in the United States and Europe in the latter 19th and early 20th centuries. His research looks at electric power as a *system*, a dominant intellectual current at the time (Hughes 1983). The principal advance contributed by Hughes was the incorporation of organizational, economic, political, professional, and academic factors into the overall infrastructure system. His view is of a technological system that is socially constructed, and consequently, society shaping.

According to Hughes,

> among the components in technological systems are physical artifacts, such as the turbogenerators, transformers, and transmission lines in electric light and power systems. Technological systems also include organizations, such as manufacturing firms, utility companies, and investment banks, and they incorporate components usually labeled scientific, such as books, articles, and university teaching and research programs. Legislative artifacts, such as regulatory laws, can also be part of technological systems. Because they are socially constructed and adapted in order to function as systems, natural resources such as coal mines, also qualify as system artifacts (Hughes 1987, 51).

Accordingly, the components of the system interact, and a change in any part of the system changes the whole

Hughes borrows standard theoretical constructs from systems thinking, such as system components deriving their characteristics from the system (Hughes 1987, 52). In so doing, he adapts a linear and sequential model of system performance that is constituted by several phases, one following the other: invention, development, technology transfer, system growth, and substantial momentum (Hughes 1983, 14). Hughes viewed systems as relatively closed constructs, in which all is subordinated to and organized around the system's goals. A system, when coupled with its control subsystem that monitors inputs and outputs using classical closed-loop feedback mechanisms, is dependent on rationalized processes and identifiable system boundaries. His approach to characterizing infrastructure regarding these points can be bolstered in fundamental respects.

In the first instance, the linear sequencing model provides an imperfect understanding of the actual development of a specific infrastructure. The evolution of a utility is anything but linear and sequential as it becomes subject to the perturbations of political economies dominated by belief and will, power and caprice, intransigence and negotiation, and other dislocations attendant to history and politics. Rather, the technological and institutional evolution of infrastructure is more satisfactorily explained by adapting more flexible concepts that allow for emergence and contingencies. In the second instance, stemming in part from the conditions which also inform the critiques of linear and sequential instrumental rationality, infrastructure is an open construct constituted by the whole of society, which in turn constitutes society, as Hughes acknowledged. The social construction stance engenders and necessitates an open paradigm in which boundaries are more fluid and permeable, control is more contingent, and institutional development is more coevolutionary. While Hughes is cognizant of these conditions and these critiques, an unbending adherence to the armature of systems theory has had the consequence of handcuffing the intellectual development and robustness needed for a fuller understanding of infrastructure in society. I address this situation in the discussion of governance institutions in Chapter 7.

Another important contribution to infrastructure theory was made by Gabriel Dupuy, who elaborated the idea of the **urban network**, particularly as it corresponds to urban development and the network theory of the city (Dupuy 1991; Tarr and Dupuy 1988). For Dupuy and his colleagues, network urbanism is a form of living in the city that is conditioned by the arrangement of infrastructures in networks. Corresponding to the European meaning of urbanism, which includes urban planning in addition to the study of urban conditions, network urbanism refers to interventions made to guide growth and development of the city. It explicitly recognizes the growth-inducing and growth-shaping nature of infrastructure.

This argument has been extended by sociologist Saskia Sassen to a phenomenon she calls the **global city**. Global cities are "command posts" in the global economy that are more connected to each other via infrastructure networks (and the financial, economic, social, and cultural networks enabled by them) than they are to their immediate hinterlands (Sassen 2001). This radical repositioning of cities as regards to their geographic environs eclipses the trade relation that industrial era cities had with their hinterlands. Industrial cities also used infrastructure networks to draw raw materials to them and distribute finished goods and services from them, as dramatically demonstrated by historian William Cronon for the case of Chicago (Cronon 1991). Geographers Jean Gottmann, Brian Berry, and Larry Bourne in their own research since 1960 each identified the role of infrastructures in connecting cities in geographic space and time (Gottmann 1961; Berry 1964; Bourne and Simmons 1978). More recently, urban theorists have addressed the reciprocal relations of the urban and its infrastructures within rapidly shifting regional and global contexts (Brenner 2019; Scott 2019).

The **network** argument has been transferred to the societal scale by sociologist Manuel Castells, who popularized the term network society (Castells 2000a). Sassen and Castells, in a series of incisive studies, have explored and explicated the interpenetration of the physical and social networks as mediated by telecommunications infrastructure and social institutions on a planetary scale (Sassen 1998; 2000; 2001; Castells 2000a; 2000b; 2001). The sociotechnical process involved in constructing networked infrastructures, and in turn, cities and societies, is routinely echoed. The influence of these scholars and their colleagues is beginning to clarify the occasionally confusing tendency found in the common usage of the term network, which refers to either the physical frameworks that comprise infrastructure (telephone network, power grid) or the social arrangement of the entities that use and are facilitated by infrastructure (personal network, organizational network).

Financial capital circulates more freely across the globe than people. Due to telecommunications networks, digital money flows 24/7 through global markets at the rate of billions of dollars per second. Yet due to similar networks, travelers and migrants are prohibited (or permitted) entry at airports, seaports, and land borders. Now public agencies responsible for immigration are using the same sophisticated surveillance and personal recognition technologies in public places on all persons which were previously exclusively the reserve of police agencies for use on criminals, or private companies to protect corporate secrets. Social media, artificial intelligence, cybersecurity, and remote sensing are now added to the surveillance mix.

The term **urban infrastructure** has been used to connote a specific location and type. Urban infrastructure exists in the city and supports urban. Yet urban is a restricting modifier of infrastructure in at least two ways. First, "urban" is a limiting adjective for the range of human settlements served by infrastructure. A highway just as readily serves a village or the countryside, as does an electrical power grid. This is equally valid in rapidly urbanizing southern continents and predominantly urbanized northern continents. The Covid-19 pandemic added a twist to this, as working from home, wherever workers chose their home base to be, including temporarily, stretched the definition of urban and put a premium on mobile connectivity. Furthermore, some infrastructures or significant parts of infrastructures that support the growth and development of human settlements are located outside of cities and urban regions. Examples include hydroelectric dams and their reservoirs, and interurban highways and rail lines. As a result, the term urban infrastructure is misleading.

Critical infrastructures build on the assumption that some infrastructures are more vital, more critical, than others. Behind this assumption lies the question: critical for what or whom? By one assessment, critical infrastructures include water, energy, transportation, and telecommunications (Thissen and Herder 2003). Yet what values underlie this assessment? Why are some infrastructures critical and others not? Could a city exist without disposing its wastes? In considering the interconnections among all infrastructures, it becomes apparent that they all are critical. The so-called critical infrastructures could not operate without the others. Consider also the long run. Could any contemporary economy, any society, exist if not for a category of infrastructure critical to all form of development: **knowledge infrastructure**? Universal and free public schools and libraries were essential to the democratization of knowledge and learning. Before the establishment of public libraries, books and other documents were closely guarded in private hands. Before the advent of public education, knowledge remained within the purview of the privileged elite. What about police, fire, and emergency management – aren't they critical? Who is to decide what is critical and what is not? Are not all infrastructures critical to contemporary cities and society?

The intent in defining a new category of infrastructure was spurred by the United States government, responding to concerns arising from security in an increasingly uncertain environment (President's Commission on Critical Infrastructures Protection 1997). It recognized the interconnection among infrastructure systems and sought to spotlight what it found to be the most critical among them. In their report, the Commission identified a need to integrate infrastructure systems that were in practice planned and managed separately. Infrastructures were deemed critical if they provided an essential and irreducible contribution to other infrastructures, such as energy, or if they were implicated in the management and control of other infrastructures, such as telecommunications. The concept of critical infrastructure accepts the interdependencies among infrastructures as fundamental, and seeks to safeguard the reliability of ones deemed critical. In this way it may entail actions outside of the soil of a sovereign nation into the affairs of others, such as protecting crude oil supplies necessitated by dependence on foreign sources. However, if a nation were not dependent on foreign oil, what implications would that have for "critical" infrastructures, including their definition?

The key issue identified by the President's Commission was reliability. In the face of the risks brought about by increasing security concerns, ensuring the reliability of the most critical systems was seen as a way to ensure the operability of all systems. This entailed vulnerability assessments, the implications of certain institutional arrangements, the implications of distributed generation, and the impact of wireless technologies, among other factors (President's Commission on Critical Infrastructures Protection 1997; Thissen and Herder 2003; see also *The International Journal of Critical Infrastructures*). The overall thrust of the critical infrastructures effort is to rethink infrastructure policymaking, and to reconsider the design of institutional arrangements for infrastructure management. Redesigning infrastructure management institutions led to a new conception of the interaction between a physical infrastructure itself and the various institutions engaged in its management. The overarching term "infrasystem" was coined to capture the physical, institutional, economic, and political elements related to infrastructure, and to distinguish this overall infrasystem from mere physical infrastructure (Thissen and Herder 2003, 283–284). Compare this approach to the one initiated by Hughes in his definition of large technological systems.

All of the above terms capture a part of the broad landscape of infrastructure. This befits the range of infrastructures extant today as they have developed historically over the centuries. They also reflect the expanding conceptions of what infrastructure is, and what roles it plays.

Common Characteristics of Infrastructures

This final section serves as a bridge between prior definitions and characterizations and our synthetic list of characteristics and a comprehensive definition. The list of characteristics and the definition capture the salient attributes in general terms. See Table 2.3 and Box 2.1 respectively. They are not exhaustive, and are not a closed catalogue. Technology changes too quickly, and society in response to it, for any listing or definition to be permanent. Instead, they are meant to indicate the scope and essential nature of infrastructure, and to inform and to guide infrastructure

> **Box 2.1 Definition of Infrastructure**
>
> Infrastructure is a physical or social–administrative network that channels a flux through conduits or a medium with the purpose of supporting a human population, whether located in a settlement or mobile, for the general or common good in addition to individual or private benefit. It consists of a long-lasting network connecting producers with a large number of users through standardized (while variable) technologies, pricing, and controls that are planned and managed by coordinating organizations.

planning and decision making. In this section I also array a listing of characteristics common to all infrastructures alongside a set of implications that each characteristic carries with it. See Table 2.4. These implications are organized into four categories, each corresponding to a following chapter in the book: sustainability, planning, finance, and institutions. This characteristic–implication matrix also serves as a bridge between the first two chapters of the book and the remaining ones.

Other scholars and organizations have put forward characteristics of infrastructure in attempts to identify commonalities with technical systems classified under the umbrella of the term. Notable among those include the early works of Hughes (1983; 1987), Firth, Boersma, and Melody (1999), the National Council on Public Works Improvements (1988), and the World Bank (1994).

Notes

1. Travaux de terrassement d'une voie ferrée, *Journal Officiel*, 18 août 1875, p. 6743, 3ᵉcol. ds *Littré Supplemente*.
2. The World Bank is an institution designed, by and large, for the effective delivery of infrastructure finance. The World Bank's definition of infrastructure draws on the work of development economists, who have used the term as an umbrella for social overhead capital. "Social" applies to services for the health, safety, and welfare of communal or societal, as opposed to individual, interests. "Overhead" refers to indirect costs that are not directly accounted for by the owning / operating incorporated entity in the production or sale of its goods or services. "Capital" is the money or property that is invested for long-term gain in the course of doing business.
3. In October of 2004 the United States Food and Drug Administration approved the intravenous implantation of microchips into humans for the purposes of medical identification. The Orwellian implications hardly need discussing. Implanted subcutaneous microchips are in use for identification purposes for security and convenience in a number of countries in Europe and Central America (Townsend 2004).
4. MILU refers to Multi-Functional Intensive Land Use. This planning and design approach was developed in the Netherlands in the late 1990s as an urban redevelopment strategy to build 24/7 activity zones integrated into the city on underused sites that had multiple infrastructure network intersections.

Bibliography

Benevolo, L. (1967). *The Origins of Modern Town Planning*. Cambridge, MA: MIT Press.
Berry, B. (1964). Cities as systems within systems of cities. *Papers of the Regional Science Association*, 13: 147–163.
Board of Public Works. (1832). *Public Works in Ireland, 1832–1833: First Report of the Commissioners upon the State of the Several Roads and Bridges Placed under Their Care by the Act 1 & 2 Will. 4, c. 33*. Dublin: HMSO.
Bourne, L. and Simmons, J. (eds.). (1978). *Systems of Cities: Readings on Structure, Growth, and Policy*. Oxford and New York: Oxford University Press.
Brenner, N. (2019). *New Urban Spaces: Urban Theory and the Scale Question*. New York: Oxford University Press.
Castells, M. (2001). *The Internet Galaxy: Reflections on the Internet, Business, and Society*. Oxford and New York: Oxford University Press.
Castells, M. (2000a). *The Information Age: Economy, Society, and Culture Vol. 1 The Rise of the Network Society*. Oxford, UK and Malden, MA: Blackwell Publishers, 2nd edition.
Castells, M. (2000b). *The Information Age: Economy, Society, and Culture Vol. 3 End of Millennium*. Oxford, UK and Malden, MA: Blackwell Publishers, 2nd edition.
Castells, M. (1978). *City, Class and Power*. New York: Springer.
Cronon, W. (1991). *Nature's Metropolis: Chicago and the Great West*. New York: W. W. Norton.
Daily, G. (ed.). (1997). *Nature's Services: Societal Dependence on Natural Ecosystems*. Washington DC: Island Press.
Dupuy, G. (1991). *L'Urbanisme des Réseaux: Théories et Méthodes*. Paris: Amand Colin.
Firth, L., Boersma, K., and Melody, B. (1999). Infrastructure concepts and classifications: A framework for scenario analysis of infrastructures in an economic perspective. In Weijnen, M. and ten Heuvelhof, E. (eds.), *The Infrastructure Playing Field in 2030*. Delft, the Netherlands: Delft University Press.
Gottman, J. (1961). *Megalopolis: The Urbanized Northeastern Seaboard of the United States*. New York: Twentieth Century Fund.
Gramlich, E. M. (1994). Infrastructure Investment: A Review Essay. *The Journal of Economic Literature*, 32 (3): 1176–1196.
Hanson, R. (ed.). (1984). *Perspectives on Urban Infrastructure*. Washington DC: National Academy Press.
Heidegger, M. (1977). *The Question Concerning Technology and Other Essays*, translated by William Lovitt. New York: Harper & Row.
Hughes, T. (1987). The Social Construction of Technological Systems. In Bijker, W. Hughes, and T. Pinch, eds., *The Social Construction of Technological Systems: New Directions in the Sociology and History of Technology*. Cambridge, MA: MIT Press.
Hughes, T. (1983). *Networks of Power: Electrification of Western Society 1880–1930*. Baltimore, MD and London: Johns Hopkins University Press.
Hughes, T., and Pinch, T. (eds.). (1987). *The Social Construction of Technological Systems: New Directions in the Sociology and History of Technology*. Cambridge, MA: MIT Press.
Kingdon, J. (1995). *Agendas, Alternatives, and Public Policies*. New York: Harper Collins, 2nd edition.
Konvitz, J. (1985). *The Urban Millennium: The City Building Process from the Early Middle Ages to the Present*. Baltimore, MD: Johns Hopkins University Press.
National Council on Public Works Improvements. (1988). *Fragile Foundations: A Report on America's Public Works*. Washington DC: Author.

Neuman, M. and Whittington, J. (2000). *Building California's Future: Current Conditions in Infrastructure Planning, Budgeting, and Financing.* San Francisco: Public Policy Institute of California.

Nossiter, A. (2006). A big government fix-it plan for New Orleans. *New York Times,* January 5, A2.

O'Brien, W. and Soibelman, L. (2004). Technology and engineering dimensions: Collecting and interpreting new information for civil and environmental infrastructure management. In Zimmerman, R. and Horan, T. (eds.), *Digital Infrastructures: Enabling Civil and Environmental Systems through Information Technology.* London: Routledge.

Parkin, J. and Sharma, D. (1999). *Infrastructure Planning.* London: Thomas Telford.

President's Commission on Critical Infrastructures Protection. (1997). *Critical Foundations: Protecting America's Infrastructure.* Washington DC: United States Government Printing Office.

Sassen, S. (2001). *The Global City: New York, London, Tokyo.* Princeton, NJ: Princeton University Press, 2nd edition.

Sassen, S. (ed.). (2000). *Cities in a World Economy.* Thousand Oaks, CA: Pine Forge Press, 2nd edition.

Sassen, S. (1998). *Globalization and its Discontents: Essays on the New Mobility of People and Money.* New York: New Press.

Scott, A. (2019). City-regions reconsidered. *Environment and Planning A,* 51(3): 554–580.

State of California. (1999). *Governor's Budget Summary 1999–2000.* Sacramento, CA: State of California.

Tarr, J. and Dupuy, G. (eds.). (1988). *Technology and the Rise of the Networked City in Europe and America.* Philadelphia, PA: Temple University Press.

Thissen, W. and Herder, P. (2003). *Critical Infrastructures: State of the Art in Research and Application.* Dordrecht, the Netherlands and Norwell, MA: Kluwer Academic Publishers.

Townsend, R. (2004). United States approves the implantation of microchips to identify patients. *El País,* October 15.

United Nations. (2004). *World Urbanization Prospects: The 2003 Revision.* New York: Author.

United Nations Center for Human Settlements. (2001). Decentralization and urban infrastructure management capacity. In *Cities in a Globalizing World: Global Report on Human Settlements.* London: Earthscan.

Weisbrod, B. (1964). Collective-consumption services of individual-consumption goods. *The Quarterly Journal of Economics,* 78(3): 471–477.

World Bank. (1999). *World Development Report: Knowledge for Development.* Oxford: Oxford University Press.

World Bank. (1994). *World Development Report: Infrastructure for Development.* Oxford: Oxford University Press.

Zimmerman, R. and Horan, T. (eds.). (2004). *Digital Infrastructures: Enabling Civil and Environmental Systems through Information Technology.* London: Routledge.

3

Sustainable Infrastructure Begets Sustainable Cities

Infrastructure is central to attaining sustainability in cities. The rationale for this follows a chain of reasoning. It is becoming ever more apparent that to have a sustainable economy and society, we must have sustainable cities. This is due to two factors. First, accelerating worldwide urbanization. Second, city regions have an outsized proportion of production, consumption, and impacts pertaining to sustainability, compared to rural places. According to the United Nations and the Intergovernmental Panel for Climate Change (IPCC), infrastructure and cities account for 1 percent and 2 percent of land on a global scale, respectively (IPCC 2020; UN Habitat 2020). Yet cities account for 55 percent of the world's population, 60 percent of energy consumption, 70 percent of global GDP, and 70 percent of greenhouse gas emissions (UN Habitat 2020).

To get more sustainable cities, we need sustainable infrastructure. This is because infrastructures collectively consume more energy and produce more carbon dioxide than any other element of the built environment. For example, transport alone consumes 25–30 percent of all energy, depending on the nation and its transport mix, and produces 25 percent of anthropogenic CO_2 globally.[1] Buildings, through the infrastructures that supply, operate, and maintain them, plus dispose of their wastes, consume approximately 40 percent of all energy (IEA 2020; 2021). To this we can add the enormous amounts of energy to build, operate, and maintain vast infrastructure networks, such as water supply, stormwater management, wastewater disposal, and power and telecom networks, among others. Note that these percentages refer to "advanced industrialized" nations, such as OECD countries. Other countries' percentages tend to be lower. Energy consumption is projected to continue to increase in the United States, tripling since 1950 in absolute terms, and easing in per capita terms. See Table 3.1.

Table 3.1 Energy Consumption

Year	United States Total*	United States Per capita**	World Total*	World Per capita**
1950	34.6	0.231		
1980	78.3	0.343	283	0.064
2000	99.0	0.396	446 #	0.070 #
2020	100.3 ##	0.302 ##	620	0.080
2050	110.5	0.283	910	0.094

* Unit = quadrillion BTUs (10^{15}) per year
** Unit = trillion BTUs (10^{12}) per person per year
\# World data from the year 2004
\#\# US data from the year 2019

Sources: US Department of Energy, Energy Information Agency. (2021). *International Energy Annual*. Washington DC: DOE; US Department of Energy, Energy Information Agency. (2021). *Annual Energy Review*. Washington DC: DOE; US Department of Energy, Energy Information Agency. (2021). *Annual Energy Outlook 2021*. Washington DC: DOE; US Department of Commerce, Census Bureau. (2021). *International Data Base*; author's calculation.

Infrastructure's immutable centrality to attaining sustainability goes far beyond energy and carbon. Water quality, air quality, food security, public health, jobs, education, and care – along with equitable access to them – are dependent on infrastructure. Social and economic equity and environmental justice are inseparable from sustainable development and infrastructure (Agyeman, Evans, and Bullard 2003). Infrastructure touches every aspect of sustainability just as it touches every aspect of our lives.

In order to provide a basis for sustainable infrastructure, this chapter introduces and explains key concepts, principles, and methods. After a brief historical exposition, it continues with the underlying science to inform how to measure sustainability, particularly vis-à-vis infrastructure. The science is underpinned by the marriage of thermodynamics and rate processes, without which a true understanding of sustainability is impossible. It follows with life cycle planning processes based on science tailored for infrastructure. The life cycle is "cradle-to-cradle", beyond the build-operate-maintain cycle routinely applied to infrastructure projects. The life cycle begins with resource extraction, transport, and manufacture at the outset and extends to reusing, retrofitting, recycling, upcycling, and disposal at the end. This expanded life cycle includes embodied energy and materials. It also is the principle underpinning a circular economy as embodied in interconnected infrastructure networks that mimic ecosystems where the outflow of one process is the inflow to another. The chapter concludes with a set of principles to guide the planning and development of sustainable infrastructure. This chapter, like the book, focuses on entire infrastructure networks and systems, even as when applied to individual projects and development sites.[2]

Infrastructure and the Global Condition

Across human history, wasteful economic activities accelerated the need to construct costly infrastructures. The very existence of many infrastructures has been occasioned by practices damaging to human health, to the natural and built environments, and to our livelihoods. An early instance was soil erosion due to careless agriculture that caused excessive silting of the Huang He (Yellow River) in China, where the silt sank to the bottom of the river as it snaked through the flat flood plain, leading to flooding over the dikes, or the river breaking through the dikes. This cycle was repeated as agriculture intensified and silt deposits increased (McNeill and McNeill 2003, 80). The accumulation of human wastes in cities and the need for sewage treatment to handle them has existed since the earliest urban settlements in Mesopotamia.

Today, with the exception of transport and telecom, many infrastructures are remedial in that they correct human activities that harm their environments. If human production, consumption, and living practices were environmentally benign, then infrastructure requirements would be markedly reduced. Infrastructure provision itself can assist societies work toward this goal by encouraging and incentivizing practices that are sustainable.

For many years, infrastructure has been positively correlated with increases in economic development, production, and consumption (World Bank 1994; United Nations Center for Human Settlements 1996). In addition to economic growth, infrastructure has long been correlated with urban growth (Mumford 1961; Tarr and Dupuy 1988). Reports have long noted the link between productivity and infrastructure, and managed infrastructure programs that invest large sums with high development expectations (National Council on Public Works Improvements 1988; World Bank 2004; UN Habitat 2020; McNichol 2019). Chambers of Commerce and other business associations worldwide routinely call for increased spending in infrastructure as a boost for economic growth. The United States government administered the public works programs during the great depression of the 1930s as a principal tool for recovery.

Some infrastructures are positively correlated with the increases in pollution, environmental degradation, and inequitable distribution of assets and impacts (UN Habitat 2020; United Nations Environment Programme 2019). These include but are not limited to highways, power generation, and solid waste disposal. Other green infrastructure networks, such as natural parks and corridors, and tertiary and biological sewage treatment, are positively correlated with environmental improvement (Melosi 2000). Infrastructure has also enabled improvements in public health and longevity, which is partly responsible for population increases, reflecting the reciprocal nature of infrastructure and development. It is astonishing that by the year 2050, 1 in 5 persons worldwide, of a projected population nearing 10 billion, will be 60 years of age or older (World Health Organization 2020).

Unequal Access to Infrastructure Generates Inequities

Infrastructures have impacts that reach beyond spurring economic growth, improving or harming the environment, and improving living standards. They both cause and solve vexing and persistent social and economic problems such as unequal income distribution and other inequalities and injustices. "Resources move from the poor to the rich, pollution moves from the rich to the poor." Vandana Shiva captures the essence of inequity of global capitalism in this phrase (Shiva 2000). These resources and pollution are generated and conveyed by infrastructures. Infrastructures are a leading factor in the accessibility to goods and services, and access is often inequitable. Environmental discrimination and injustice occur when the poor are located near toxic infrastructures such as incinerators and landfills. Conversely, environmental inequity occurs when the well-off have easier access via infrastructure to high quality locales. Access to better parks, schools, libraries, health care, and other public services typically favors wealthier communities and residents, detracting from social equity.

Common speech is replete with phrases that capture infrastructure-based inequities: "the other side of the tracks" and "digital divide" are merely two. Infrastructure is a long and sharp double-edged sword that cuts both ways: it provides for prosperity, access, and health as well as disparity, barriers, and illness. Intelligent planning can help ensure the former just as ignorance and poor planning ensure the latter.

A vivid illustration of social disparity was voiced by Kofi Annan, formerly Secretary General of the United Nations, at the URBAN 21 world congress in Berlin in July 2000. He referred to the Berlin Wall. After the Berlin Wall fell an economic wall rose in its stead between the northern and southern hemispheres. This invisible wall is just as much a barrier as the Berlin Wall before it. The average income per capita in the nation of Luxemburg is $40,000, whereas the average income per capita in Uganda is $40, a thousand-fold difference. Annan cited Abraham Lincoln's comment about the American civil war, "A house divided cannot stand".[3] While Annan was referring to the North–South divide in human and economic development on either side of the equator, others have long noted a parallel phenomenon within cities (Mollenkopf and Castells 1991; Goldsmith and Blakely 2010; Dickens 1859). A divided city cannot stand for long. The problems associated with the "dual city" are central problems, not marginal ones, often produced and / or worsened by infrastructure (Graham and Marvin 2000). Yet infrastructure is not the sole source of these dualities and harms. It is easy to recognize the cultural, religious, economic, and political causes of inequitable cities and societies.

Nature, Culture and Sustainability

The American architect Richard Neutra, known for his designs combining clean and pure Modernism inherited from Europe with an open and expansive sensibility that embraces nature and reflects New World frontier ideals, published *Survival Through Design*. His extended essay portrayed architecture and landscape design as forces to remediate an increasingly mechanized, impersonalized, and industrialized world. For Neutra, this world was becoming dangerously separated from the natural environment. His outlook was formed in the shadow of such influences as Fritz Lang's seminal film *Metropolis* and Charlie Chaplin's *Modern Times* (Neutra 1954; Lang 1926; Chaplin 1936). As apocalyptic warnings of the dangers inherent in technology and its effect on society, these two masterpieces captured many ills of industrial society.

Neutra's response was to reinsert nature into architecture, and architecture into nature, which was especially visible in his single-family homes. The title of Neutra's book suggests an important impetus for human design and planning: survival. Human ingenuity expressed in design was an evolutionary response that enabled our species to persist. As civilizations evolved, other values supplanted "mere" survival, including wealth accumulation, power projection, speed, size, and standardization. These new values threatened our survival, according to Neutra. He proposed that designers operate in a new mode to recover the balance with nature. Ian McHarg followed suit, at a larger regional scale in his masterpiece *Design With Nature* (McHarg 1969).

David Bourdon published *Designing the Earth*, a comprehensive worldwide survey of human design of landscapes. The book's subtitle captured another impetus for design: *The Human Impulse to Shape Nature*. Humans had progressed beyond survival. History was now shaped by will, not by instinct (Bourdon 1995). Reason, religion, myth, art, and other human activities accumulated and became known as culture, something distinct from nature. Over time cultural values began to guide design. Survival was assured, for the fortunate at least. Technology enabled humans to not just survive in nature, but to shape nature to our own likes and needs. We became its masters. We no longer compete with other species on a serious basis, except for some microbes and insects. We are our own most profound competitors. Our mastery has expanded to cover the entire planet, and we challenge only each other for supremacy. This complete control was signaled by a special issue of *Science* in 1997 titled simply *Human Dominated Ecosystems*. No subtitle was necessary.

We have begun to recognize the folly of unbridled control. McPhee and McKibben were not alone in signaling "the control of nature" (McPhee 1989) and "the end of nature" (McKibben 1989). Excess led to despoliation, destruction, profligate waste, and extinction of species and ecosystems, not to mention cultures and languages. Sustainability, as a response, is broadly understood as an attempt to inhabit the earth in a way that is more conducive for our long-term survival, as well as that of other species and ecosystems, and the planet itself. This new synthesis permits humans to inhabit the world according to culturally determined will and design, not just survival by chance and instinct. The difference lies in a new manifestation of human will that does not shape and subjugate nature and ourselves along with it. Instead, to live sustainably with nature, respecting it, adhering to its capacities and limitations while still realizing our own hopes and dreams.

Sustainable Processes Make Sustainable Places

"At present human society is one huge web of cooperation and competition, sustained by massive flows of information and energy. How long these flows, and this web, might last is an open question" (McNeill and McNeill, 2003, 322). Thus, the McNeills, in their world history, identified the link between sustainability and process at the global historical scale. They went on to recognize that at the urban scale, justice was at the heart of enduring human cohabitation since ancient times. "The Greeks invented a new master institution for themselves – the polis – by combining old ideas about justice with new was of defending themselves from outside attack. ... the pursuit of justice was always the foundation of the polis" (McNeill and McNeill, 2003, 73). The McNeills are not the only scholars who view cities and their infrastructure as intertwined with social justice.

Other urban observers have noted the same connection between cities, infrastructure, and sustainability in equity terms. "Study a city and neglect its sewers and power supplies (as many have), and you miss essential aspects of distributional justice and planning power" (Star 1999, 379). "All networks produce privileged places at their junctions and their access points" (Mitchell 1999, 31). While Mitchell was referring mostly to digital and knowledge networks, this principle can also be seen in water supply networks. In developing nations, potable water is many times more expensive for the poor living in shanty towns on the urban outskirts, who have to buy it by the bottle, than for the rich, who live in the city and have public water service provided through an infrastructure network. Even in advanced nations, basic services are not guaranteed, and social disparities are perpetuated by infrastructure.

The Process Basis for Sustainability

Sustainability is centered on processes. This is due to the definition of sustainability itself – to keep something going *over time*. A sustainable process is one whose rate is maintained over time without exceeding the innate ability of its surroundings to support the process, including the ability of the surroundings to absorb its impacts. This converts the general consensus of the term sustainability[4] – the general agreement about fundamental precepts of balancing development with the environment by addressing social, economic, and ecological concerns at the same time, with an eye toward future generations – into process terms (United Nations World Commission on Environment and Development 1987; United Nations Center for Human Settlements 2001; United Nations World Summit on Sustainable Development 2002). This is critical because the ways in which infrastructures are unsustainable and the need to convert them in order to be sustainable are described by the processes they perform and support. These are processes of production, consumption, pollution, accumulation, depletion, and assimilation. Moreover, they all produce impacts, inequities, and so on. The very flows conveyed by the conduits of infrastructure are processes themselves.

Sustainable processes have rates of production and regeneration that equal or exceed rates of consumption, depletion, extraction, and byproduct absorption. Sustainable processes are ones that replenish the flows of matter, energy, information, capital, and other evolutionary factors through a system (city, ecosystem) at levels in which the outputs are at least equal to the inputs, in terms of quality and quantity. Sustainable rates of waste and byproduct production are less than the rate in which the environs can absorb them and remain healthy and viable over the long term. Sustainable processes also lessen the differences among social groups. Sustainable processes give back in a circular way, with the outputs of one process continuously forming the inputs of others. Waste disappears in a sustainable process. This dynamic and multiscalar basis for sustainability overcomes limitations of static approaches such as footprints or carrying capacity analyses that measure values at one point in time and / or one place in space. In cities as in nature, processes are interconnected in open systems and networks. However, some current conceptions of sustainability assume a closed system which does not correspond to actual conditions.

Thus, sustainability refers to the degree to which an entity exists in a coevolutionary process with its environment whose inherent condition (essence) enables it to continue evolving and developing without jeopardizing its own life and livelihood, or the lives and livelihoods of those it affects, including the larger systems and networks in which the entity finds itself situated, over its lifetime. This amounts to a redefinition of sustainability as a state of being in which living processes self-perpetuate without harmful effects to their environment. Specifying this to cities and humans, sustainability refers to the ecology of human presence in place from a normative perspective. Can humans inhabit a city, region, ecosystem, etc. sustainably, without damage and ill effects to others?

This relation to surrounding environments can be expressed in theoretical, that is, mathematical terms. This theory links process with place under dynamic conditions. Mathematically, the processes can be specified as rate processes. Rate processes afford more precise theoretical characterizations by using mathematical formulae in which the rate of any given process to be sustained over time cannot exceed the innate ability of its surroundings to support that process. This rate includes the ability of the surroundings to absorb the impacts of the process. This confers a tremendous advantage to the rate process approach, as it can specify and quantify resilience. We adapt the rate process theory developed by chemical engineer Stuart Churchill (Churchill 1974).

The rate process theory of sustainability takes the simple mathematical form of differential equations. This formulation has several advantages. First, it treats sustainability in process terms, specifically as rate processes. Rate processes have a well-developed mathematics, and are well developed in engineering and other applied fields. Second, a mathematical treatment enables sustainability to be quantified, measurable, and replicable. We can assess whether we are improving over time and across comparable cases. Third, mathematics makes it near-universal, accessible across languages and cultures. Fourth, it enables a degree of rigor and precision that has until now been largely missing from the rhetoric and practices of sustainability.

Most importantly, it enables comprehensive and systematic assessments of continuous and dynamic processes.

As a general theory, it has the added advantage of being applicable to a wide range of factors that make a place or process sustainable. Moreover, it is a scale-independent theory that answers what until now has been the most intractable barrier in the search for a general theory of sustainability – what are we trying to sustain, and where are we trying to sustain it? The planet? An ecosystem? A city? A business? A way of life? Life itself? Yet another benefit is that the theory can be applied to dynamic, nonlinear, nonequilibrium systems as well as equilibrium systems because rate processes are derived from the second law of thermodynamics (Churchill 1974). Thus, it is applicable to complex urban, social, and ecological phenomena such as cities, organizations, and ecosystems.

One of the challenges for infrastructure planning and design is to integrate them fully not only into the city, but also into nature, sustainably. A guide for this is understanding nature's cycles and adapting them to cities and infrastructure. The cycles of nature – periodic, recurring, life cycles – all flow back into each other in networked, circular ways. Nature's cycles can be mimicked by infrastructure. Not just green infrastructures, but all of them. Doing this shapes a new view of sustainability via infrastructure. We can capture this new view in an elegant mathematical equation. See Equation 3.1.

$$\frac{1}{L}\frac{dx}{dt} = \sum_{k=0}^{n} r_i \qquad 3.1$$

Here dt is the change over time, referring to process, while dx is the change in the material x that is flowing in the process. L is a measure of the extent of the system, and r is the *rate* of accumulation or depletion of the process. The rate of accumulation or depletion is the mark of its degree of sustainability.

This new formula measures the sustainability of any process – natural, social, technical, economic – at any scale. This key unlocks the big black box in sustainability, and therefore sustainable infrastructure and urbanism – how do we measure it exactly? How do we know when an infrastructure network is sustainable, objectively? For example, in cities we occupy buildings that consume energy and produce heat. At what rates do we consume that energy and dissipate that heat? Thus, we see that designing buildings and cities takes into account rates of flows, of energy, water, information, etc. We can begin to see how thermodynamics and rates are fundamental.

Consider these examples – aquifer recharge and building heating and cooling – to illustrate. For aquifer recharge to be sustainable, the rate of water inflow into the aquifer must exceed the rate of water withdrawal, measured in volume per unit of time. For building heating and cooling, a rate measure for the degree of sustainability can be units of energy (say, kilowatt hours) per area or volume (say, square or cubic meter) per degree day. Lumens per square meter per day is a rate measure for daylight sustainability. See Appendix 2 for a more detailed presentation of this formula and several examples of application.

In both thermodynamics, the science of energy transformations, and ecology, the science of ecosystem dynamics, rate processes are key. Both are sciences of flows, processes, and transformations. How do we integrate them for a sustainable urbanism based on sustainable infrastructure? A good place to start, at least by analogy, is a tree.

A tree has two major cycles, seasonal and life. Both involve countless other organisms in its cosm. A tree is a paragon of permanence and continuity. The oldest tree species is *Wattieza*, 380 million years old. The oldest known living tree species is the *ginkgo biloba*, estimated at 270 million years. Trees are also the oldest clonal and nonclonal living beings on the planet today, at 9,500 years for a Norway spruce in Sweden and 5,000 years for a bristlecone pine in California, respectively.

One of humanity's great metaphors is the tree of life. Epics and legends extol the role of the tree, as symbol and as fact. Trees are shelter, source of life and wisdom, storehouse and fount of knowledge – of how to live. Throughout human history, the tree has been the archetype of the web of life.

Trees also exemplify the dialectic of continuity and change, standing erect for centuries, shedding leaves over seasons, rotting back to the soil over years. Trees are flexible as they sway in the wind. They are resilient as they absorb the rain. They provide shelter, shade, food, materials, playgrounds, store carbon, bind soil, regenerate ecosystems; the list seems endless. Tree root system interactions with mycorrhizae and fungi in the soil generate enormous biological complexity. Up to 15,000 different species live in a cubic foot of soil. Trees filter out through their roots an incredible variety and quantity of toxic chemicals. Trees create microclimates and are indispensable to the global climate and Gaia herself. Trees produce their own energy and collect their own water using the intelligence of evolution. A tree in conjunction with its surroundings recycles its own litter and itself, fulfilling its life cycle while providing for countless others besides. Trees are open systems connected to other open systems through multiple natural networks, nature's infrastructures. Can we design infrastructure networks that are as smart as trees?

Just as we connect tree to ecosystem, connecting cycles via networks, we can connect buildings, which need to be open to their surrounds, to the city, another open ecosystem, via infrastructure networks. Sustainable urbanism is network urbanism.

> If the city is to survive, process must have the final word.
> In the end the urban truth is in the flow.
> (Kostof 1992, 305)

Heading in New Directions

These conceptions of sustainability have obvious and direct implications for cities and their infrastructure. How we move about implicates processes dependent on energy, material, and information that produce pollution, noise, wastes, inequities, and damaging spatial and ecological impacts. Mobility processes enabled by transport networks consume fuel, time, space, and materials. Travel and access also produce positive economic and social benefits. Water and wastewater infrastructures also produce, consume, and convey materials and energy. For full life cycle calculations, we need to add the energy and materials embodied in these infrastructures, along with those consumed in the processes of building them. This applies to each type of infrastructure. Once we take this long-term and comprehensive view of sustainable infrastructures, we are better equipped to plan and design infrastructure networks that support substantially more sustainable cities.

Retrofitting the overall approach presented here into existing and future networks and cities will be a time-consuming, costly, and custom-designed task that will take our best thinking. It's not rocket science, a predictable and solvable physical science since the time of Newton. It is much more complex and challenging than that. Is there any human artifact larger and more complex than a city-region? Yet it is an essential task for our well-being and competitiveness, if not salvation.

While most infrastructures were invented in the industrial era to cope with the harmful impacts of rapidly growing industrial cities and to support their very growth, contemporary technologies such as telecommunications and knowledge infrastructures also consume materials and energy and produce pollution, environmental and economic impacts, and social and spatial inequities, named the digital divide. For example, people tend to assume that the telecom-propelled information society is more sustainable than industrial society because its data is digital and its presences are virtual, eliminating or reducing paper consumption and reducing the need for travel. Furthermore, it provides more opportunity and access due to the low cost and wide spread of telecom data, and purportedly pollutes less (as "light" or "clean" industry) than heavy industry.

Yet the opposite is true, because the more we connect virtually, the more we tend to connect in real life. Telecommunications infrastructure induces more travel demand and concomitant need for transportation infrastructure and energy to feed it, not less. Travel continues to increase worldwide, per the International Air Transport Association (IATA 2021, 11). See Figure 3.1. The same applies for material goods and their consumption. We consume more paper to print more documents precisely due to the explosion of digital data and easy access to them, thus producing more waste, per United Nations Food and Agriculture Organization data. While industrial smokestack emissions are lower, concentrated doses of high toxicity emanate from high-tech manufacturing facilities contaminate soils and groundwater (Chen et al. 2016).

Consider the delivery of goods and services globally. Amazon.com wouldn't work without global delivery networks. Smart phones, apps (most geared toward consumption, even if only of more data), and streaming all ramp up the demand for more digital devices, more internet connectivity, more data, and more servers. This leads inexorably to more energy and material consumption, of the kind that did not exist a generation or two ago. Five hundred megawatts or more power the

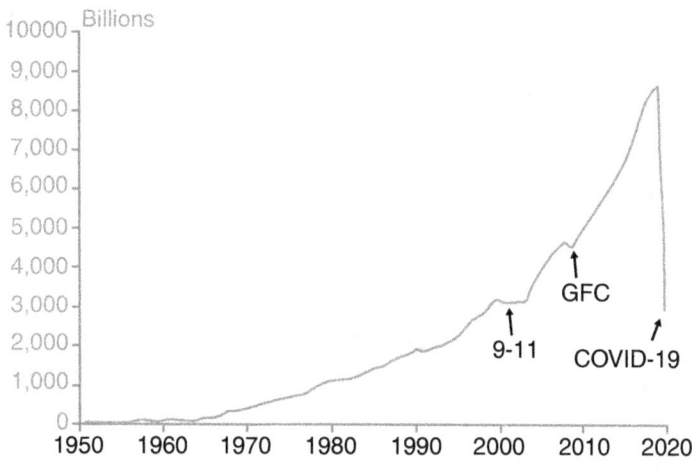

Figure 3.1 Worldwide Annual Air Travel Passenger Miles Flown since 1950

largest server farms or data centers that feed our insatiable appetite for the digital life. A typically sized server farm draws 200 megawatts, the equal of the annual energy consumption of 62,500 single-family homes, according to a 2011 report released by the US Department of Energy.[5] Web servers are a booming growth industry. In the US, Europe, and China alone, data centers in 2020 likely consumed over 500 terawatt hours of electricity (IEA 2020; Greenpeace 2019; European Union 2017; Lawrence Berkeley National Laboratory 2016). Overall, "Demand for data and digital services is expected to continue its exponential growth over the coming years, with global internet traffic expected to double by 2022 to 4.2 zettabytes per year (4.2 trillion gigabytes)" (IEA 2020).

Buying four books online? The searches caused by the clicks alone burn a kilo of coal. Packaging and delivery impacts not included. Searched for an image of your favorite singer or your latest travel destination online? You engaged 7,000 servers. According to an Uptime Institute report, "every time an image is posted on Instagram by the Portuguese soccer star Cristiano Ronaldo (who at the time of writing had the most followers on the platform), his more than 188 million followers consume over 24 megawatt-hours (MWh) of energy to view it" (Bashroush 2020). How much energy is used to synch hundreds of millions of iPhones, iPads, and iMacs daily?[6]

While many benefit, including the rural poor due to mobile phone service where internet is not available, the digital divide has added to social and economic exclusion, as those marginal to these networks become increasingly distant from mainstream activity. A significant example during the Covid-19 pandemic of 2020–2021 was school children in poorer school districts or poorer communities not having reliable – or any – access to online learning, leading to learning outcomes that were far below par.

Whether virtual or real, as a result of all this, the degree of sustainability of the use and multiple impacts of any infrastructure, is a complex matter that must be carefully calculated using this formula as an integral part of a life cycle planning process. While calculations can estimate existing or potential degrees of sustainability of an infrastructure network, what is important going forward is to plan and design / redesign / retrofit new and existing networks so that they are sustainable. To do so, we need guiding principles for design, provided below.

Principles to Plan and Design Sustainable Infrastructure

A conceptual guide for planning and design principles is found in the right-hand column of Figure 0.3 of the Introduction. It suggests that when infrastructure is designed and built so that smaller scale distributed nodes are incrementally interwoven (integrated) into larger scale networks, and are designed and built so that modular, cellular components are incrementally embedded in larger scales, these principles build in greater flexibility, resilience, and adaptability – that is, functionality, reliability, and sustainability – to infrastructure networks. And the cities they serve.

Nature has already provided a model, the tree and the forest, as indicated above and in the Introduction. Resource renewal, nature services, regeneration, and resilience are endemic to nature, and as such, nature offers a template to base the design and arrangement of infrastructure networks in territory.

1. Renewable resource priority

The use of renewable energy, materials, and resources has priority over the use of non-renewable energy, materials, and resources. To the greatest extent possible, use only renewable resources, whether they are directly from nature (primary), or recycled / upcycled / repurposed from existing human-made materials.

2. Nature services priority

Nature services refers to the functions that ecosystems and habitats perform that result in human benefit. The use of nature's services (also known as ecosystem services) as infrastructure has priority over the use of human-built infrastructures for the delivery of the same service. Nature and its natural processes and ecosystems as well as natural materials have the benefit of evolution, whose intelligence is imbedded into them. Nature's processes, ecosystems, and materials are sustainable by definition, with fewer disruptions of and impacts on natural habitats compared to human-built systems.

One example is wetlands, which perform a myriad of functions. Yet all ecosystems perform many functions that benefit humans, including oxygen and food production, water supply, carbon sequestration, toxic chemical remediation, storm absorption and attenuation, etc. These natural functions support both human health and ecosystem health. Green infrastructures such as parks, greenways, and waterways provide classic examples of natural, human-designed, or hybrid natural–human infrastructures employing nature services.

3. Biomimicry

When infrastructures are planned and designed to mimic or imitate natural ecosystems, they are more sustainable and have fewer negative impacts on both humans and nature. Biomimetic infrastructure emulates the form, function, and process found in nature. Biomimicry for infrastructure reflects and incorporates all the principles listed here, as they are drawn from nature, which is sustainable by definition. An example is wetlands that attenuate storms and manage stormwater for free, when the innate capacity of the wetlands to perform these services is not exceeded.

4. Resource regeneration rates

For a renewable natural resource, the rate of sustainable use can be no greater than the rate of its regeneration. For a renewable human-made resource, the rate of sustainable use can be no greater than the rate of the impacts of its production.

5. Resource substitution rates

For a nonrenewable resource, the rate of sustainable use can be no greater than the rate at which a natural resource can be substituted for it, or a synthetic resource can be substituted, as long as the synthetic resource has equal or lesser harmful impacts than a natural resource. The long-term goal is to convert all nonrenewable resources to renewable or less damaging nonrenewables.

6. Minimize embodied energy

Embodied energy consists of the sum of the energy manifest in a given infrastructure facility or network (or any structure or object). Embodied energy includes energy used to or embedded in extracting and transporting raw materials, converting raw materials into finished materials, transporting the finished materials to the construction site(s), preparing the construction site(s), building the structure(s) and network(s), transporting wastes and byproducts away from the construction site(s), and protecting from and remediating harmful environmental and social impacts of the infrastructure's construction and operation. (Conducting an embodied energy assessment using the rate process theory presented earlier in this chapter is incorporated into the life cycle infrastructure planning method in Chapter 5.)

7. Ecosystem resilience

Resilience applies to impacts *on* a system, whether building, infrastructure, city, or ecosystem; and impacts *of* a system on its surrounds. The first type – impacts on infrastructure – can refer to natural occurrences, such severe storms, weather events, wildfires, earthquakes, volcanic eruptions, tsunamis, etc. Impacts also include human-made instances such as war, genocide, terrorism, nuclear meltdowns, and oil spills. Finally, they can be combined human–natural disasters, such as a fire in the urban–nature interface, or a flood made more severe due to excessive impervious surfaces. For example, for pollution absorption capacity, the rate of sustainable pollution can be no greater than the rate at which that pollutant can be processed or absorbed by the environment, while maintaining the functional integrity and health of that environment.

8. Infrastructure resilience

To make infrastructure resilient generally, there are four design strategies:

1. Retreat to eliminate or minimize the risk: to locate away from the harm or risk by moving out of / elevating above the hazard zone, e.g. a flood plain or an area of projected sea level rise.
2. Distribute to spread the risk: to make more flexible and adaptable in order to absorb the impacts of a severe event by decentralizing a large metro-wide facility into small, modular, distributed micro-facilities.
3. Defend to deflect the risk: to harden the infrastructure to withstand physical impacts, such as a seawall or other barrier.
4. Reclaim to absorb the risk: to restore natural habitat to its functional / ecological integrity, so it can provide protection and other ecosystem service functions (green infrastructure).

9. Recycle and reuse: waste as a resource

Interconnect infrastructure networks, industries, and infrastructure service users so that the outputs, byproducts, and wastes of one process are recycled and reused as the resource inputs for other processes. This is a form of large-scale biomimicry in which interconnected infrastructure networks channel flows in linked processes in an urban ecosystem like nature's infrastructures do in natural ecosystems. Doing this creates seamless networks, like the interconnectedness of telecom networks in which wired and wireless digital signals from many nodes traverse numerous transmission modes to a wide range of user devices. A similar interconnectedness occurs with motor vehicles that go from garage and driveway to motorways and limited access highways via local streets, district arterials, urban boulevards, rural roads and highways, and so on.

10. Infrastructure renewal priority

Renewing existing infrastructures (if not obsolete, unsafe, or unhealthy) has priority over building new infrastructures. Using durable materials and flexible designs that are adaptable in the future extends the service life of infrastructure. Designing new and redesigning existing systems' operations, maintenance, and rehabilitation programs with long-term sustainability in mind keeps costs of renewal lower than costs of new construction.

11. Match the scale and type of infrastructure to the scale and type of its use

Renewable energy and water sources such as the sun, wind, and rain that are harnessed by individual, modular units that are on-site and off-grid. For example, site-specific or building-specific solar panels, wind turbines (helical and bladed), and rainwater catchment technologies have priority over metro-scale (or larger) grid-based networked infrastructures in certain circumstances. Embodied energies are lower in smaller, modular, on-site units, and there are few transmission losses. Inequitable service delivery is minimized, if everyone has these off-grid units.

12. Shared rights-of-way

Infrastructure rights of way have long been shared, as when electricity and telecom wires parallel railways and highways in the same right-of-way. Extending the networks in which this happens can serve to coordinate infrastructure planning, design, and investments; increase efficiency; and decrease costs, land consumption, habitat fragmentation, and environmental impacts. In dense urban settlements, this has been achieved by installing multiple infrastructure conduits in underground galleries or tunnels. Whether above or below ground, in rural or urban areas, shared rights-of-way also reduce maintenance costs and disruptions. In the late 19th century, Ebenezer Howard's pioneering treatise which later became the book titled *Garden City* stressed the co-location of infrastructures in the same right of way as a planning principle, as did Ildefons Cerdà in his *General Theory of Urbanization* (Howard 1898, 79; Cerdà 1867).

13. Integration among systems and settlements

Integration is a central tenet of the functions of infrastructure. It delivers flows and services to the places and peoples that it serves. Infrastructure is physically integrated into the structures which it services. Increasingly, infrastructures are integrated amongst each other, via shared rights-of-way at the simplest to integrated web-based mobile platforms and apps at the more complex. They are integrated across scales in a seamless way, so that movements across systems and scales flow smoothly. Think of driving from your home to your parents' home in another state or country: driveway to street to arterial to road to highway to motorway and back, across jurisdictions. Support infrastructures like bridges, petrol stations, signaling, and rest stops are integrated along the way. Seamlessness is a criterion to measure integration.

14. Equitable access to services

Sustainable infrastructure is designed, located, and operated so that all citizens have equal access to its services, and so that its services are provided and distributed equitably among all social groups. This holds for public as well as private infrastructures that serve entire populations, whether free for all users or fees are charged that are the same for all users, or apportioned fairly according to sociopolitical norms. Analytical models exist to measure and ensure the equitable distribution of infrastructure. For example, Pakzad and colleagues employed the Shannon Diversity Index to evaluate the distribution and diversity of infrastructure across neighborhoods (Pakzad and Osmond 2015).

Notes

1. Of the total 8 billion tons of CO_2 emitted by transportation in 2018, 45 percent came from passenger vehicles, 29 percent from road freight vehicles, 12 percent from aviation, 11 percent from shipping, 1 percent from rail, and the remaining 2 percent from other sources. International Energy Agency, https://www.iea.org/topics/transport. Accessed February 11, 2021.
2. For a superb introduction into infrastructure and site planning, see Hack, G. (2018). *Site Planning: International Practice*. Cambridge, MA: MIT Press. It focuses on how sustainability can be achieved through the development of sites from small to large. It illustrates emerging technologies that allow much of the energy, runoff, water, liquid and solid waste removal, and other functions to be handled on-site.
3. Transcribed by the author while attending Annan's speech in Berlin.
4. A common understanding of sustainability stems from the Brundtland Report: "Sustainable development seeks to meet the needs and aspirations of the present without compromising the ability to meet those of the future" (United Nations World Commission on Environment and Development 1987, 40). Its other main thesis was balancing environmental protection with economic development. Yet sustainability is not merely a matter of intergenerational equity, as the too-concise definition of the Brundtland Report implies. There are at least two limitations to equating sustainability with intergenerational equity. One is that it does not deal with the dimensions of space, and more specifically, local places. The second flaw is its use of the term "needs". The term need is complex and controversial, discredited because it can impose categorical thinking of one culture onto another, and because of the limitations of the concept of satisfying basic needs as a development strategy (Brundenius and Lundahl 1982). Dilip Dacuna offered a trenchant observation of the obsession to specify an exact definition: "defining sustainability is like playing god" (Dacuna, personal communication).
5. US EIA. (2011). *Residential Energy Consumption Survey*. Washington DC: US DOE.

6 There are standout examples of IT energy use. "Bitcoin mining, for example, is reliably estimated to have consumed over 73 terawatt-hour (TWh) of energy in 2019. This equates to the electricity use of 6.8 million average US households, or 20 million UK households. This is one cryptocurrency — of over 1,500 — and just one application area of blockchains. … Media streaming, which represents the biggest proportion of global traffic and which is rising steadily and globally, has become the energy guzzler of the internet. According to our analysis, streaming a 2.5 hour high definition (HD) movie consumes 1 kilowatt-hour (kWh) of energy. But for 4K (Ultra HD) streaming — expected to become more mainstream in 2020 — this will be closer to 3 kWh, a three-fold increase. … Data from the most developed countries shows what can be expected elsewhere. In the UK, which has more than 94% internet penetration, annual household broadband data consumption increased from 17 gigabyte (GB) in 2011 to 132 GB in 2016, according to official Ofcom data — a sustained 50% increase year-on-year for five years. (The growth figure is much higher in other parts of the world such as Asia and Africa.) Internet penetration, standing at 58% globally in 2019, is expected to increase by 10% in 2020. … While it will take a few years for 5G to further mature and become widespread, it is widely expected that the rollout of 5G from 2020 will substantially accelerate the data growth trends, with many new types of digital services in domains such as smart cities, IoT and transportation, among many others. The increased bandwidth compared with 4G will lead to increased demand for higher resolution content and richer media formats (e.g., virtual reality) as soon as late 2020 and rising more steeply, along with energy consumption, after that. The role of blockchain (of which Bitcoin is just an example) and its impact on energy consumption is still to be fully determined, but if the uptake is on a large scale, it can only be an upward force. Most analysts in this area have predicted a dramatic rise in blockchain adoption beyond cryptocurrency in 2020, helped by new offerings such as the AWS blockchain service. Not all blockchain models are the same, but it inherently means a decentralized architecture, which requires extensive infrastructure to accommodate the replication of data. This consumes more energy than traditional centralized architectures" (Bashroush 2020).

References

Agyeman, J., Evans, R., and Bullard, R. (2003). *Just Sustainabilities: Development in an Unequal World*. London: Earthscan.
Bashroush, R. (2020). *Data Center Energy Use Goes Up and Up and Up*. Seattle: The Uptime Institute. https://journal.uptimeinstitute.com/data-center-energy-use-goes-up-and-up/
Bourdon, D. (1995). *Designing the Earth: The Human Impulse to Shape Nature*. New York: H. N. Abrams.
Brundenius, C. and Lundahl, M. (eds.). (1982). *Development Strategies and Basic Needs in Latin America: Challenges for the 1980s*. Boulder, CO: Westview Press.
Cerdà, I. (1867). *Teoría General de Urbanización y Aplicación de sus Principios y Doctrinas a la Reforma y Ensanche de Barcelona*. Madrid: Imprenta Española.
Chaplin, C. (1936). *Modern Times*. Hollywood: United Artists.
Chen, M., Ogunseitan, O., Wang, J., Chen, H., Wang, B., and Chen, S. (2016). Evolution of electronic waste toxicity: Trends in innovation and regulation. *Environment International*, 89–90: 147–154.

Churchill, S. (1974). *The Interpretation and Use of Rate Data: The Rate Concept.* Washington DC: Hemisphere Publishing.
Dickens, C. (1859). *Tale of Two Cities.* London: Chapman and Hall.
European Union. (2017). *H2020 EU Resource Efficiency Coordination Action Project.* London: EU Resource Efficiency Coordination Action.
Goldsmith, W. and Blakely. E. (2010). *Separate Societies: Poverty and Inequality in U.S. Cities.* Philadelphia, PA: Temple University Press, 2nd edition.
Graham, S. and Marvin, S. (2000). *Splintering Urbanism.* London: Routledge.
Greenpeace. (2019). *Powering the Cloud: How China's Internet Industry can Shift to Clean Energy.* Beijing: Greenpeace China.
IEA (International Energy Agency). (2021). *Empowering Cities toward Net Zero Emissions Abstract Unlocking Resilient, Smart, Sustainable Urban Energy Systems.* Paris: Author.
IEA (International Energy Agency). (2020). *Tracking Clean Energy Progress: Data Centres and Data Transmission Networks.* Paris: Author.
IATA (International Air Transport Association). (2021). *Annual Review 2020.* Montreal: Author.
IPCC (Intergovernmental Panel on Climate Change). (2020). *Climate Change and Land: An IPCC special report on climate change, desertification, land degradation, sustainable land management, food security, and greenhouse gas fluxes in terrestrial ecosystems.*
Kostof, S. (1992). *The City Assembled: The Elements of Urban Form Through History.* Boston: MA: Little Brown.
Lang, F. (1927). *Metropolis.* Babelsberg: Universum Film AG.
Lawrence Berkeley National Laboratory. (2016). *United States Data Center Energy Usage Report.* Berkeley, CA: Author.
McHarg, I. (1969). *Design With Nature.* New York: Natural History Press.
McKibben, W. (1989). *The End of Nature.* New York: Random House.
McNeill, J. R. and McNeill, W. H. (2003). *The Human Web.* New York: W. W. Norton.
McNichol, E. (2019). *It's Time for States to Invest in Infrastructure.* Washington DC: Center for Budget and Policy Priorities.
McPhee, J. (1989). *The Control of Nature.* New York: Farrar, Straus and Giroux.
Melosi, M. (2000). *The Sanitary City: Urban Infrastructure in America from Colonial Times to the Present.* Baltimore, MD: Johns Hopkins University Press.
Mitchell, W. (1999). *E-topia: "Urban Life, Jim, but Not as We Know It".* Cambridge, MA: MIT Press.
Mollenkopf, J. and Castells, M. (1991). *Dual City: Restructuring New York.* New York: Sage.
Mumford, L. (1961). *The City in History: Its Origins, its Transformations, and its Prospects.* New York: Harcourt, Brace & World.
National Council on Public Works Improvements. (1988). *Fragile Foundations: A Report on America's Public Works.* Washington DC: Author.
Neutra, R. (1954). *Survival Through Design.* Oxford: Oxford University Press.
Pakzad, P. and Osmond, P. (2015). *A Conceptual Framework for Assessing Green Infrastructure Sustainability Performance in Australia.* Gold Coast, Australia: State of Australian Cities Conference.
Shiva, V. (2000). *Tomorrow's Biodiversity.* London: Thames and Hudson.
Star, S. (1999). The ethnography of infrastructure. *American Behavioral Scientist* 43(3): 377–391.
Tarr, J. and Dupuy, G. (eds.). (1988). *Technology and the Rise of the Networked City in Europe and America.* Philadelphia, PA: Temple University Press.

UN Habitat (United Nations Human Settlements Programme). (2020). *World Cities Report 2020: The Value of Sustainable Urbanization.* Nairobi: Author.
United Nations Center for Human Settlements. (2001). *Cities in a Globalizing World: Global Report on Human Settlements 2001.* Nairobi: Author.
United Nations Environment Programme. (2019). *Global Environmental Outlook 6.* Nairobi: Author.
United Nations World Commission on Environment and Development. (1987). *Our Common Future.* Oxford: Oxford University Press.
United Nations World Summit on Sustainable Development. (2002). *Report of the World Summit on Sustainable Development.* Johannesburg: Author.
World Bank. (2004). *World Development Report.* Washington DC: Author.
World Bank. (1994). *World Development Report: Infrastructure for Development.* Oxford: Oxford University Press.

PLANNING FOR SUSTAINABLE INFRASTRUCTURES II

4

City Planning and Infrastructure

This chapter sketches the history of the relations between infrastructure and city planning. Indeed infrastructure was a genesis of and long-time mainstay of urban planning. In some nations, North American ones in particular, their divorce came at great cost to society. A key aim of this book is to recover infrastructure into city and regional planning and design. Another is to provide a long-term perspective to all professions that deal with infrastructure. This chapter shows how infrastructure was integrated into planning practice historically, focusing on the industrial era to the present, especially in Europe and North America. In this chapter as in the book, the term city planning is not intended to specify a single discipline or profession. Instead, it encompasses all the practices, disciplines, and professions that together plan for a better future for the city-region: urban planning, urban design, urban policy, architecture, engineering (urban, civil, and environmental), landscape architecture, and public health, to name the most prominent.

> People follow plumbing.
>
> (J. B. Jackson)

A Deeply Rooted Relationship

Historically city planning has been deeply rooted in infrastructure. The first large-scale city planning operations in history were infrastructure interventions. From the first known water management systems that separated drinking water from waste water in the Indus Valley cities of Mohenjo Daro and Harappa five thousand years ago; the aqueducts, baths, fountains, streets, walls, and ports of ancient Rome and its one million inhabitants, along with its colonies across Europe, northern Africa, and the Middle East; through the street grids, squares, water systems, and walls of Spanish cities, both Iberian and New World; the demolition of European city walls, of which Paris and Barcelona in the 1850s gave rise to modern city planning with its straight wide boulevards and streets, public transit systems, sewage treatment systems, and so on; to the highways, high-speed rail, airports, internet, and mobile phones of the globalized urban society of contemporary times; all large-scale city planning was abetted by large scale infrastructure.

Transitions from one historical era to the next were marked by leaps in city building and infrastructure inventions. Infrastructures enabled urban populations on a scale and density not possible without them. Infrastructures also brought benefits to smaller cities and towns, endowing their inhabitants with a quality of life approaching larger cities.

Parallel to advances in construction and engineering introduced by urban infrastructures were innovations in administration and scientific methods that permitted the management of large infrastructure systems, as well as the cities and empires that went along with them. The Mesopotamian, Nile, Indus, and Huang He river valley civilizations introduced writing, numbers, money, accounting, taxes, rents, laws, bureaucracy, and other administrative novelties that enabled the raising and accumulation of wealth and the establishment of trade which in turn funded the construction of and fueled the need for large urban infrastructures, such as walls and dikes for protection, temples for collective ritual, roads and ports for trade, and canals for irrigation. The perfecting of bureaucratic hierarchies was epitomized by the Roman and Spanish empires, who coupled that with advances in infrastructure-led city building. The Spanish used the Law of the Indies and the Archive of the Indies in Seville, the seat of colonial administration, to settle the New World. Centuries later, the cartographic and statistical advances incorporated by Haussmann and Cerdà in the planning of Paris and Barcelona respectively each strengthened the union of infrastructure and urban planning.

The 20th century managerial revolution, with its early emphasis on standardization and mass production, late-century emphasis on mobility and flexibility, and entire century preference for speed, went hand in hand with the emergence of higher speed transportation and communications networks. High-speed transportation and communications infrastructure working 24/365 in real time created a new global economy replete with global cities, megacities, and megalopolises. These infrastructures fomented an information and knowledge revolution akin to the Industrial Revolution, and exerted a radical influence on city structure and function. They all serve as historical examples of administrative and methodological advances that gave rise to more complex, more interconnected, and larger scale infrastructures. Taken together, these innovations implanted the previously unimaginable possibility and implemented the reality of planning and designing entire cities in advance of their actual construction.

Whether in the service of capital cities, their empires, or not, early city planning was limited to infrastructure planning. It typically meant plumbing (flows of water, sewage, and stormwater), the layout of streets, squares, and open spaces, and the location of civic monuments and markets. This was true throughout the world. In Mesopotamia and the greater Middle East, notable were their ingenious innovations in sustainable and green infrastructures. Key among them are *qanats*. They are underground aqueducts that conveyed water in the desert from mountain streams to cities in the valleys throughout Persia, without evaporating. Compare to the volume of water that evaporates in American open-air aqueducts in California and the western states. *Bâdgirs* are wind catchers that cooled building interiors in hot urban summers, such as in Yazd. A *buj* is a combination stormwater drainage and irrigation channel which fed the verdant gardens and parks in large desert cities such as Shiraz (the "garden city") and Babylon. *Yakhchāls* are ice pits, literally translated from Farsi, which use evaporative cooling to store ice in the hot desert using natural materials and processes. All of these predate the time of Christ, some significantly.

In China, the Great Wall (770 BCE), the Grand Canal (468 BCE), the Forbidden City (1402 CE), and numerous canals, city walls, and markets spanning millennia are among the mainstays of urban and regional planning. In ancient Rome and its empire, aqueducts, roads, baths, temples, military outposts, markets, plazas, civic buildings, and a vast administrative apparatus were among the infrastructures that allowed this city to rule a vast empire and be the first to break the one million population barrier about two millennia ago. Its physical and administrative infrastructures operating in tandem formed a blueprint for empires to follow.

These examples are but three from around the world to which could be added cities and kingdoms in India, Central and South America, Asia, and Africa. Less known but not less spectacular or formative of urban and civilizations are the Xochimilco canal system in Mexico City and the massive prehistoric causeways, canals, and earthworks in the Amazonian rainforest (Erickson 2010). There is much to learn from how these disparate societies planned and governed a vast array of infrastructures in sustainable ways. Their principles for design and operation are models for sustainability today, even as their labor was exploited at best (slaves), and financing was not necessarily sustainable (pillage, tributes from colonization). Chief among ancient principles were local materials and knowledge, and working *within* the capacities of local ecological habitats and processes in adaptive ways. These advances enabled cities and their empires to prosper by linking finance, governance, climate, territory, and design in the service of infrastructure. While innovation occurred between antiquity and the industrial era, they were either incremental improvements on old designs, or incorporated new technologies of warfare and defense of cities, like walls, citadels, and moats.

Modern City Planning Origins

As populations grew in the industrial era, masses of people found their way to the manufacturing hubs – cities. Eighteenth and 19th century cities were exploding in size with limited and reactive planning, at best, hardly coping with the influx. Urban densities rocketed. For example, in the Lower East Side of Manhattan, 540,000 residents crammed into an area of two square miles in 1910 (> 100,000 per square kilometer) (Smith 1992, 64 and author's calculation). Daily life in these teeming districts comprised of congested streets, overcrowded housing, minimal open space, infectious disease, and poor public health due to the lack of proper sanitation, ventilation, and other factors. Urban conditions for most deteriorated in proportion to the scale, density, and speed of population growth.

Infrastructure abetted industrial scale urban growth in two ways. First, transport and energy infrastructures facilitated concentrated industrial activity. Rail, ports, canals, and turnpikes enabled the delivery of raw materials and growth-inducing trade. Second, the impacts of urban growth – pollution, illness, crowding – were alleviated somewhat by sanitary infrastructure: water, sewerage, and storm drains. Before the industrial age, cities that exceeded 50,000 inhabitants were rare exceptions (Benevolo 1980; Mumford 1961). Their small size let them fit into their environs more seamlessly. They did not tax the nature that supported them. Preindustrial town and country relations were idealized in Patrick Geddes's valley section (Geddes 1925, in Hall 2002b).

However, the scale and density of industrial metropolises changed the relations between city and country (Cronon 1983; 1991). As the metropolis exceeded the capacity of the natural ecosystems to support it, an ever-spreading web of infrastructure imported materials from further afield, with the effect of subjugating or supplanting natural systems with engineered ones.

Public Health and Planning

Modern planning began with sanitation reforms between 1840 and 1890 in European and North American cities to cope with their exploding size. The impacts on health and the environment were overwhelming. They led to famine, pandemics, misery, and poverty for many due to overcrowding. In order for industry to prosper and people to be fit to work, governments took action to improve conditions through sanitary reforms. The reforms operated on a miasma theory, whereby dirt and foul odors were disease bearing, and thus needed to be flushed away in order to secure adequate public health (Melosi 2000; LaPorte 2000). In 1842 the attorney Edwin Chadwick led the preparation of the "Report from the Poor Law Commissioners on an Inquiry into the Sanitary Condition of the Labouring Population of Great Britain", often referred to as the Sanitary Report, which chronicled unsanitary conditions in urban England. The report proposed correctives, including a comprehensive technological fix, consisting of an "arterial system of pressurized water which would place house drainage, main drainage, paving and street cleaning into a single sanitary process". This system was never implemented (Melosi 2000, 12; Peterson 1979).

Part of Chadwick's proposal, the water carriage sewage system, was adopted. It revolutionized sanitation. His self-cleaning sewer pipe successfully carried sewage away from the city by pressurized water flushing the wastes away, both from the home water closet and the city sewer pipes. In 1847, London established its Metropolitan Sanitary Commission to reform sewer system administration. In 1849, The Metropolitan Sewers Commission was formed in London to build a city-wide system. This organization was expanded in 1855 into a more comprehensive Metropolitan Board of Works. Many large European and American cities adopted this technology *and* institutional approach. Smaller cities followed suit. Mostly, sewage carried away by these systems was not treated, but rather pumped as raw effluent into surface waters. These lines were built in a piecemeal manner and did not constitute what would be considered now an integrated system (Melosi 2000). The first application of Chadwick's idea was by English engineer William Lindley, who designed Hamburg, Germany's sanitary sewers in 1842 (Peterson 1979, endnote 13).

In 1845, the first sanitary survey in the US was completed in New York, directed by physician John Griscom (1845) and titled "The Sanitary Condition of the Laboring Population of New York". It echoed the Chadwick report and demonstrated its transatlantic influence. This survey entailed a systematic data collection effort that mapped every property to document cases of contagious diseases (Levy 2009). New York built about 125 miles of sewer lines by 1865 (Peterson 1979; Melosi 2000). This was followed by Lemuel Shattuck's 1850 report on sanitary conditions in Massachusetts and surveys in numerous American cities. These surveys spurred evidence-based systematic government action. Shattuck's report concluded "since a large portion of the population was not abiding by proper sanitary principles, the state must assume the responsibility to ensure the public health" (Melosi 2000, 63). After Brooklyn, Chicago, and Jersey City built planned sewer systems, in comparison to the piecemeal efforts in New York and Boston; in 1866, New York adopted the first "comprehensive or systematic public health code" in the United States (Melosi 2000, 21). A building-by-building survey was conducted by collaborating physicians, engineers, and chemists that was documented in the 1866 "Report of the Council of Hygiene and Public Health of the Citizens Association of New York, Upon the Sanitary Conditions of the City" (Peterson 1979, endnote 40).

The beginnings of integrating public health into urban planning in America was propitiated by none other than Frederick Law Olmsted. Known in that era for his and Calvert Vaux's Central Park for New York City (1857), Olmsted had broader interests and activities. During the Civil War he was Director of the United States Sanitary Commission. Throughout his life and professional practice he strove to improve the health of cities and their inhabitants. A careful reading of his collected papers testifies that health was his driving concern (McLaughlin et al. 1977). Olmsted transformed the inherited American tradition of town planning through town layouts (streets and squares) to a more thorough practice that incorporated parks, parkways, landscaping, and sanitary infrastructure (Reps 1965). This can be seen in his seminal 1868 plan for Riverside, Illinois, which included stormwater drainage and sewerage. In this way, the nascent city planning movement began to link town layout, sanitary reforms, and housing provision; an achievement which would not be consummated until the turn of the 20th century.

Infrastructures like parks and open space, also part of the reforms of this period, sought to cleanse city air and to acquire land for public enjoyment. Following the creation of Brooklyn's Prospect Park and New York's Central Park were park and boulevard systems in Chicago, Boston, Philadelphia, Kansas City, and numerous North American cities and towns (Wilson 1964, 1989). In Boston, Frederick Law Olmsted Sr. designed the Fens, a linear park system or greenway that encompassed and enhanced a natural wetland. In so doing, he exploited its "nature services" such as flood control. Olmsted, with a skill for words as much as designs, named his fen way the Emerald Necklace. Boston's Metropolitan Parks Commission complemented its Sewerage Commission, which put forward the *Boston Metropolitan Sewerage Plan* in 1875 (Peterson 1979). American planning was beginning to expand its scale and scope to match its large European city counterparts, discussed next.

European Origins

The origins of comprehensive city improvements through physical planning in industrial Europe are usually attributed to the works of Baron Georges Haussmann, Prefect of the Seine (administrative district that included Paris) from 1853 to 1870, and Ildefons Cerdà, the Catalan civil engineer who conducted a comprehensive survey in 1855 and laid out the expansion of Barcelona in 1859 (Cerdà 1855). Here we note their use of infrastructure as their primary object of planning and as means of its realization.

Haussmann was a skillful and willful administrator whose plan transformed Paris, chiefly by a modern network of wide streets and boulevards connecting key points such as rail stations and markets (Haussmann called them "nodes of relation"). This was accomplished by demolishing buildings to create open spaces ("negative space", land not to be built upon), sanitary infrastructure (water supply, sewerage, and drainage), omnibuses, and gas lamp lighting. The goal of his circulation system was to unify the left and right banks of the Seine River. Not incidentally, it allowed passage for police and soldiers to quell civil unrest. He also created two large public parks east and west of the city, and built numerous community facilities: schools, hospitals, barracks, and prisons. To Haussmann, administrative infrastructure went hand in hand with physical infrastructure. Thus, he annexed outlying *communes*, partitioned Paris into 20 districts (*arondissements*), abolished old tax district boundaries, and coined the term "regularization" to denote the complex of actions he performed to bring order to the city (Choay 1969; Benevolo 1980; Saalman 1971).

The national housing reform and slum clearance law of 13 April 1850, adopted in response to a cholera epidemic, laid the legal groundwork for Haussmann to transform Paris (Benevolo 1967, 103). Significant to the future planning profession was his holistic view of the city, despite the ravages that wholesale demolition of buildings and entire neighborhoods wrought in order to accomplish his aims. Basing the plan on planimetric and topographic surveys of the entire city, he conceived of intervening to create whole circulatory and respiratory systems that, according to Choay, would "give unity to and to transform [Paris] into an operative whole" (Choay 1969, 16).

For his part, Cerdà was more daring than Haussmann. His surveys were far more comprehensive, covering social, economic, public health, housing, and physical environment conditions, in addition to the topographic work done by his Parisian contemporary. Furthermore, he coined the term "urbanization" and published an extensive multivolume *Teoría General de Urbanización*, whose first volume alone counted more than 800 pages (Cerdà 1867).[1] He too based his plan on circulatory and respiratory systems, and outdistanced Haussmann by providing for multilevel transportation interchanges that foresaw mechanized rail mass transit. Further, he conducted studies for the arrangements of housing and other buildings in blocks that integrated open public space into each block. His plan provided for other infrastructures: parks and plazas, sidewalks and gardens, roads and rails, water supply, sewerage, and storm drainage (Cerdà 1855). The tearing down of the city walls that began in 1854 in Barcelona was stimulus for the Barcelona plan.

For Cerdà, infrastructure was a primary object of his plan and means of its realization. The two signal and intertwined parts of the plan, roads and "islands", were both conceived of as infrastructures. Islands were the individual city blocks containing housing that surrounded community open spaces within the courtyard between the four built sides of a city block. This addressed economic, social, public health, and equity issues as integrated elements of built urban form, sealing the link between infrastructure and modern city planning (Neuman 2011).

With Haussmann's and Cerdà's plans, and the sanitary ideas of Chadwick and others, city planning began to take shape, with a decidedly infrastructural focus. Françoise Choay averred that the regularization Haussmann style endowed modern city planning with three prime attributes. The first was conceiving the city as an object for intervention and as a whole. The second was using analytic methods, of surveys and science. The third was that two objectives were given priority: traffic and hygiene (Choay 1969, 26–27). To this we can add three more 19th century contributions: the large-scale division of land into parcels for rapid urban real estate development and speculation, the creation of city parks systems, and museums in them, for popular enjoyment, and interurban infrastructure networks – rail, canals, telephones, and electricity.

Since Cerdà's and Haussmann's time, the urban planning profession has continued to consolidate around the physical elements of urban space, even as it expanded its scope beyond infrastructure. City planning's original ontological drive was to create urban place out of space through the intermediary of infrastructure.

Ongoing efforts to improve urban conditions, to make cities more livable and sustainable, comprise the history of city planning. Since the advent of the industrial era, historians have chronicled a series of reform movements that established the groundwork for contemporary planning practice (Hall 2002b; Fishman 2000; Tarr and Dupuy 1988; Krueckeberg 1983; Benevolo 1967). City planning before the industrial era was largely, though far from exclusively, a history of the partnership between infrastructure and city development. It is the essential argument of this book that the prospect of cities and life in them is largely conditioned by infrastructure, and that the way we plan infrastructure will ultimately determine whether cities and our urban way of life will be sustainable in the future.

Any history of infrastructure as a catalyst and ordering device for managing the city, like this brief and selective one, is part social history, part political history, and part economic, institutional, and technological histories (Hughes 1983; 1987; Tarr and Dupuy 1988; Dupuy 1991). The emphasis here is not on the technology itself. Nor is this a history of the inventors, the engineers, the entrepreneurs, the financiers, and others directly related to the invention and diffusion of any particular system. Rather, the emphasis is on the relation to the urban planning professions in the service of sustainable urban growth through adapting infrastructure to the urban environment.

A Strange Estrangement

By the close of the 20th century, however, the marriage between infrastructure and city planning was best described as estranged, principally in Anglo-Saxon nations. This was so even as the bond between infrastructure and cities was as tight as ever. The vital importance of infrastructure to cities had been repeatedly affirmed in case studies of cities (Lindstrom 2002; Erie 2002; Cronon 1991; Platt 1983) and general treatises and histories (Melosi 2000; Perry 1995; Benevolo 1980; Mumford 1961). Yet in practice and in the academy, the planning profession then abdicated much of its role in planning infrastructure to other professions. This was especially noticeable in the United States and Canada where infrastructure was called "the cinderella of urban studies" (Graham and Marvin 2001). The terms infrastructure and public works did not appear in the index of the most widely used history of planning (Hall 2002b). Why?

In the 1950s and the 1960s, the United States' interstate highway system began its assault on city centers. Originally, they were to stop at the metropolitan fringe and connect to local arterials, in order to spare the cities. Highway engineers mastered the drawing boards. It was left to activists, civic groups, and others to serve up a critique of the way in which infrastructure and urban planning were done, particularly in relation to low-income communities. Activists (reactive-ists) opposed the destruction of viable neighborhoods by ribbons of concrete and maze-like multilevel interchanges whose principal design criterion was free traffic flow.

Except for a few celebrated city planners and observers such as Paul Davidoff, Chester Hartman, and Jane Jacobs, who played vital roles in "freeway revolts" in Philadelphia, San Francisco, and New York respectively; at that time infrastructure went missing in American planning. In the main, the planning profession stood aside as traffic engineers, along with real estate developers, redrew metropolitan maps in favor of the suburbs (Rome 2001; Jackson 1985; Hartman 2002).

From about 1960 to 2000, North American planners' infrastructure roles outside of transportation planning tended to be limited to site plan, annexation, and development review functions. In these activities they typically coordinated meetings with developers, designers, and other interested parties to determine compliance with codes. Additional activities may have included assessing impact fees, ensuring the adequacy of easements, and applying design guidelines to projects. Depending on the capacity and expertise of the planning department, planners may also have been responsible for conducting infrastructure assessments, carrying out capacity analyses, or environmental assessments; although this was not common. Infrastructure, especially entire networks or systems, was not the primary concern, except perhaps at the metropolitan and state scales addressing transportation.

Further evidence of the separation is in the standard reference of local urban planning in the United States, the International City Management Association's (ICMA) "Green Book". The 2000 edition, titled *The Practice of Local Government Planning*, did not have a single chapter on infrastructure, utilities, capital facilities, or public works; while the current edition, *Local Planning: Contemporary Principles and Practice*, does dedicate one chapter to them (Hack, Sedway, and Birch 2009). Another leading text, *Urban Land Use Planning*, now in its fifth edition, allocates one chapter to infrastructure (Berke, Godschalk, and Kaiser 2005).

A review of contemporary comprehensive municipal plans in North America in the late 1990s and early 2000s revealed a similar level of disengagement. Plans typically reflected interest in demographics, land use, economic development, social concerns, urban design, and quality of life. This was shown in a content analysis by this author of the plans of cities where planning is prominent and influential: San Francisco, San Jose, Calgary, Philadelphia, Chicago, and Toronto. Infrastructure occupied a scant portion of their concerns. This was even more evident in the plans of smaller cities and towns. Specific infrastructure plans for transport, parks, community facilities, and utilities were once the main occupation of city planners. In the period 1960–2000 they were prepared by engineers, landscape architects, and fiscal specialists in public works and other agencies, not in the city planning department. In many cases, they still are.

Infrastructure concerns were left to utility providers, school districts, engineering or public works departments, parks departments, and so on. While planning agencies often coordinate with infrastructure organizations, and while infrastructure entities may have city planners or land use planners on their staffs, the degree and effectiveness of coordination among them varies widely, depending on a host of institutional, political, and historical factors.

Another part of the separation of infrastructure from public sector planning is that it is increasingly being done by the private sector, chiefly with new telecommunications infrastructures that are having a massive effect on urban form and development. Large telecommunications users are increasingly driving policy, and large telecom providers are planning de facto through construction. This shift to the private sector began over a generation ago, much of it fomented by the World Bank (World Bank 1994; Guy, Graham, and Marvin 1996; 2001). Its impetus was the dawn of neoliberalism in Western democracies, first evinced in national elections in the UK in 1979 and the US in 1980.

Where comprehensive planning did engage infrastructure is at larger scales, notably metropolitan, regional, and state. For example, the *New York Regional Plan* of 1996 and 2017, the *Portland Metropolitan Plan* of 1995, and the *New Jersey State Plans* of 1992 and 2001 are all based on governing growth-shaping infrastructure.

American planning was not alone in this estrangement. Commonwealth nations such as Canada, England, and Australia, as well as a few Northern European countries, did not stress infrastructure in their contemporary urban planning practices. Canadian planning mostly mirrors US practice, including provincial legislation that enables or encourages local master plans to deal with land use, growth patterns, infrastructure projects (not networks), and impact fees on private development. Exceptions include cities with a European heritage and form, like Montreal, Toronto, and Quebec City. Even there the differences were waning (Hodge and Robinson 2001). The centralized United Kingdom still relies on policy guidance from higher government levels, intergovernmental coordination, and functional specialization (housing, for example) to attain its planning aims (Cullingworth et al. 2015; Hall 2002a). Infrastructure is largely left to transport and other specialist engineers. In Australia, urban planning has largely benefited in its evolution from the English town and country planning code. Infrastructure is largely the province of the state departments of spatial planning, transport, and public works, and to an extent, federal agencies. Local planning follows through with development details (Gurran 2011; McLaughlin 1992; Sandercock 1990). The most recent Australian bible of planning only dedicates 2 of 20 chapters to infrastructure (Sipe and Vella 2017).

In general, when urban planners, especially Anglo-Saxon ones, have been left aside in contemporary infrastructure planning practices; engineers, utility specialists, and fiscal managers have leaned in to exercise leading roles. Planners are bypassed for several reasons: disciplinary specialization due to technical sophistication, privatization and public–private partnerships vitiating public responsibilities, and the changing relations among levels of government. On the one hand, devolution of governmental responsibilities from higher to lower levels yields decreased planning involvement where lower level institutional capacities are not as fully funded and realized. On the other hand, where a powerful central government acts in concert with intermediate levels (regions, provinces, and states) to exercise regulatory oversight and provide capital, it gets the job done, yet usurps local power.

Where Infrastructure Still Leads City Planning

Infrastructure as a basis of planning at the city scale and larger was and still is prominent in European spatial planning. In Italy, Spain, and Latin America, city planning is allied to and often a specialty within architecture, and infrastructure does occupy a prominent position in professional activity. Likewise in Southeast Asia (Korea, Taiwan, China) and India, where engineer-planners and architect-planners center their efforts on the shaping of urban form via infrastructure. In Europe, the mode of planning has transformed from "blueprint to strategy", especially at regional and European scales. Infrastructure is used as the strategic kingpin to intraconnect and interconnect metropolitan regions (Albrechts, Balducci, and Hillier 2016; Reimer, Getimis, and Blotevogel 2014; Faludi and Waterhout 2002). As Klaus Kunzmann has noted, the various networks connecting Europe's metropolises, including production, information, memories, power, and culture, are all predicated by physical infrastructure. Without it, these and other networks could not exist (Kunzmann 1997).

This was most apparent in the planning of the great capital metropolises since World War II. In Europe we observe that spatial planning for metropolitan regions and larger scales *is* infrastructure planning. This is not surprising, as the genesis of contemporary metropolitan planning in Europe was post-World War II reconstruction, which repaired damaged infrastructure, especially transportation and power, and rebuilt bombed and shelled cities. The Greater London Plan of 1944 by Abercrombie and Forshaw is prototypical in this regard.

The rebirth of Barcelona in the post-franquist period is a showpiece of the profound impact that infrastructure-led urban design and planning can have on the fortunes of a city. Fueled since the mid-1980s by preparations for the 1992 summer Olympics, continued at a less feverish pace with the preparations for the global event Forum 2004, and a phase of "large projects" in between; planning efforts in Barcelona were led by architect- and engineer-planners. Their unprecedented 20-year run to 2005 of intensive and inventive planning is widely recognized for the improvement of public spaces, the redevelopment and conversion of the historic center into a cultural city, the reconnection of the city to the sea, the redevelopment of former industrial districts into new high-tech zones, and the conversion of its old industrial port to a contemporary leisure port and entertainment zone. These advancements to city planning became known as the Barcelona model, and have been exported to cities throughout Spain, South America, and beyond. These enhancements fused urban design with infrastructure projects.

Major construction projects in the Catalan capital included seaport, airport, and freight rail updates and expansions, and their linking to form an advanced logistics activity zone that is propelling Barcelona to the top of Mediterranean ports. This is due to the added volume and added value that advanced logistics processing is afforded by the co-location synergies of transportation infrastructure. Building high-speed rail also transformed the city. Water quality and supply were foci of massive infrastructure projects aimed at improving environmental quality. The cleaning up and rerouting of the two rivers that form the northern and southern flanks of the city, the Besós and the Llobregat, are visible indicators of infrastructure planning. Invisible examples include the reconstruction of the stormwater sewer drainage system, plus placing various utility, telecom, and water supply cables and lines in a single underground gallery or tunnel which eases repair access, minimizes surface street disruption during maintenance, and facilitates system upgrades and expansions. These innovative contributions to infrastructure planning through multidisciplinary design are reverberating throughout the planning world (Neuman 2011; Montaner 1999).

On the other side of the world, infrastructure has also been a major factor in China's urban and regional development. For most of the post-1949 period, in particular since 2000, infrastructure occupied a high priority in China's national development. Before 1978, the main emphasis was on transportation, power, and water infrastructure that supported regional development. This was an economic policy aimed at bringing growth to impoverished rural areas, to reduce the disparities between urban and rural areas, and to support strategic aims. Few public works were built in cities. Since opening to the world in 1978, it became apparent that inadequate infrastructure systems hindered China's urban development. As a result, the central government changed its policy and began to build urban infrastructure. Updating transportation systems was given top priority, and was guided by city planning. Changes in infrastructure financing, coupled with more local freedom to attract private development including foreign direct investment and funds from the World Bank, all enhanced urban infrastructure building capacity.

The period since the 1990s is marked by massive urban infrastructure investments, accelerating in each decade since. At the outset of the 21st century, China's cities stepped onto the global stage. Policy stressed infrastructure that enhances environmental quality and supports growth in leading centers, such as Beijing's hosting of the 2008 summer Olympics and Shanghai's emergence as a global financial capital and hosting of the 2010 World's Fair. Telecom and high-speed rail investments place both networks at the global forefront.

This selective scan of infrastructure and city planning highlights as much diversity as it does identify trends. In order to better understand how we arrived at this position today, the following sections of this chapter will illustrate in greater detail the intersecting historical tendencies of urban development, infrastructure, and city planning as a succession of urban reform movements. We begin at the conclusion of the mid-19th century sanitary reforms in England and the United States that were highlighted above, and continue through to the present day.

Infrastructure, Planning, and Reform Movements – The United States

Towards the end of the reform period, around the year 1900, in the United States the municipal art movement began. Sometimes referred to as the civic art movement, it reinforced the tendency of the nascent planning profession to center its efforts on the physical form of the city. Cities were beautified by architects and landscape architects through the embellishment of streets and the creation of parks, museums, promenades, and accessible waterfronts. A pinnacle of this movement was an urban design achievement – the design of a civic center. Civic centers clustered important public buildings such as city halls, courts, auditoria, and libraries around a monumental open space, usually a hard-surfaced plaza. The groupings of these buildings around a square meant to suggest civic splendor and foster civic pride (Wilson 1989).

This approach to improving the city's appearance through redesigning its physical form, led as it was by architects and landscape architects, was termed the City Beautiful movement. This movement owed a large debt to Frederick Law Olmsted. Olmsted "advanced many of the arguments associated with the City Beautiful conviction of the inseparability of beauty and utility" (Wilson 1989, 29). His theory of urbanism advocated the dispersion of high concentrations of growth by the comprehensive planning of parks and boulevards in relation to urban growth. He believed in the restorative powers of parks and natural landscapes, and demonstrated the economic value of his theory by showing that property values were higher near them (Olmsted 1870, cited in Wilson 1989).

In the United States, Municipal Arts Societies in support of this movement sprang up in hundreds of localities. Founded by Richard M. Hunt in New York City in 1892, the Municipal Art Society was a forerunner of civic groups engaged in urban improvements.[2] By 1906 there were 2,215 member groups of the American Civic Association (ACA). The ACA identified three aims of their work: beauty of an entire municipality; an inclusive idea of improvement, both functional and aesthetic; and the inseparability of beauty and utility. The ACA, together with the National Municipal League (founded in 1894), were the organizational engines that underpinned the City Beautiful movement and led the public call for the establishment of city planning as a government function. In New York, the Municipal Art Society pressed for an official city art commission and city planning authority (Wilson 1989).

These civic groups benefited from the inspiration provided by the 1893 Columbian Exposition in Chicago. This exhibition was housed in the Great White City, a temporary urban district built for the fair and designed by Frederick Law Olmsted Sr. and John Root. Daniel Burnham is often credited with planning the fair, and his title was chief of construction. Yet Burnham himself credited Olmsted with the plan: "In the highest sense he [Olmsted] is the planner of the Exposition" (Wilson 1989, 34). While these three designer-planners were greatly influenced by the 1889 Paris World's Fair, which sported the Eiffel Tower, transatlantic planner Thomas Adams observed that "the Fair represented the culmination of a period of over twenty years' activity in the sanitary and aesthetic improvement of cities" (Adams 1935, 173).

Infrastructure and its planning played an important and visible part in the success of the Chicago exposition. The Great White City took its name from the uniform whiteness of all the façades and the millions of electric lights that showered a brilliant light on the whitewashed plaster buildings. Canals, streetcars, and water and sewerage systems not only supported the fair's operations, but also were prominent exhibits. The fair showcased the integration of functional and aesthetic values in engineering, architecture, and civic design that went on to inspire a generation. Architect-planner Arnold Brunner coined the term "beautility" to convey the inextricable connection between beauty and utility that was intrinsic to City Beautiful (Wilson 1989, 83). In this, Brunner was indebted to corresponding theories of architecture and planning during the Renaissance, in which artist-architects such as Brunelleschi, Alberti, and Michelangelo struck a balance between beauty (*voluptas*) and usefulness (*commoditas*) (Konvitz 1985, 38). San Francisco, Cleveland, and Chicago became leading large city exemplars in the United States of the municipal arts movement.

Infrastructure, Planning, and Reform Movements – Europe

Parallel to the American City Beautiful movement was an equivalent in Europe. One manifestation was found in the international expositions, which were held in leading capital and other cities throughout the continent, starting with the 1851 Crystal Palace Exhibition in London. Expositions were also held in Paris in 1871, 1889, and 1900, and Barcelona in 1888; and many others took advantage of the world fair not only to showcase their city and provide a setting to display the latest wonders from around the globe. A principal motive behind hosting and staging these cumbersome logistical enterprises was to revitalize portions of their hosts' cities, or to convert an entire district from an obsolete use to a new one. Such was the case in Barcelona in 1888 where a demolished citadel site was transformed into the fairgrounds of its Universal Exposition. The thick defensive stone walls surrounding the citadel were torn down, and the area was annexed into the city. It currently serves as a city park named La Ciutadella (The Citadel in Catalan). This pattern of reusing temporary districts as functional parts of the city was to be repeated in the aftermath of world's fairs and Olympic games ever since.

Another manifestation of the City Beautiful idea in Europe was spurred by Camillo Sitte's book *City Planning According to Artistic Principles* (Sitte 1965 [1889 original]). This slim volume was especially influential in German-speaking lands and Northern Europe. It rekindled interest in the qualities of public spaces, notably squares and streets and their disposition in relation to the built urban fabric. Even though the text did not concern itself with infrastructure besides streets and squares, it sought to bring back the "art" to city building, which he saw to be disappearing in the shadows of functional-technical infrastructure construction. He valued "the ideal of the ancients", Rome and Athens, over the "rigid" and artless "modern systems" (Sitte 1965, 84, 58).

Changes to the Mode of Planning

The distinction between the early modern era of the late 19th century and the contemporary period is fundamental. The modern ideal, highly prized, was a unitary city; a single coherent morphological entity unified by comprehensively planned and coordinated infrastructure systems. The street grid was the primary glue that bound the city together. Less visible systems such as water distribution, sewerage, and power grids performed comparable functions below and above ground. The urban core of the industrial city was the economic and cultural hub, with radial infrastructure connecting less dense residential suburbs to the center. The modern city, as it swelled in size and importance, could not grow "organically" anymore. Gradual growth according to long-accepted practices gave way to explosive expansion according to the industrial logic that seized and subordinated terrain to capitalist logic (Lefebvre 1991). Prior to the modern city planning project, industrial urban growth proceeded chaotically, without comprehensively planned interventions. This led, of course, to the industrial city's ills and evils documented earlier in this chapter, and the nascent planning profession's rise in response. The production of space thus acceded to a new set of equations that gave planned infrastructure a superordinate position that dictated the terms of urban development.

Among these new equations was the integrating comprehensiveness of a plan for the whole city. According to Daniel Burnham, prior to his time, cities "had built great public works in piecemeal, unrelated and without the unity of a comprehensive general plan" (Wilson 1989, 69–70). Such was the shift that it led Burnham to confidently proclaim the "great truth" of the 1893 Columbian Exposition in the February 1902 issue of *Century Magazine*. This truth became even more apparent to him after he completed his 1901 plan for the national capital, known as the McMillan Plan: "the supreme one of the need of design and plan for whole cities" (Wilson 1989, 69).[3]

This new comprehensive planning placed function alongside beauty for coequal consideration. Burnham and his associate Edward Bennett's brand of civic design was a plan map and artistic renderings showing the location and form of future infrastructure networks: parks, transportation, streets, and the civic center. In 1909, the Commercial Club of Chicago released Burnham and Bennett's *Plan of Chicago*. It was a culmination of their large-scale civic design projects, having completed plans for Cleveland, San Francisco, and other American cities in the feverish first decade of the century. The Chicago plan and the McMillan Plan before it were landmarks in North American planning.[4]

Burnham was not alone. Other leading exponents of North American city planning of that era, Frederick Law Olmsted Jr. and John Nolen, voiced identical views in the classic text *City Planning*. Olmsted's introduction to that edited volume declared in the first sentence "City planning is the attempt to exert a well-considered influence on behalf of the people of a city over the development of their physical environment as a whole." He continued that this new term city planning stands for a "growing appreciation of a city's organic unity" (Nolen 1916, 1).[5] To Nolen and his contributors, all leading planners of the era, the principal elements of a city plan were comprised of infrastructure: streets, public buildings, recreation facilities, parks, water supply, waterways, railroads, and transportation and railways. Only five chapters of eighteen were allocated to administrative issues such as legislation and financing. Nolen's book became the benchmark for the rapidly developing planning profession.

In stark contrast, the current era of urban development is witnessing the persistent fragmentation, inequities, and diversification of cities that are the compound product of many forces. They include massive migrations, changes in modes and locales of production, the spread of capitalism and democracy, and the individuation of living and movement. Critically, these are all enabled and abetted by networked communications and transportation infrastructures.

Over the generations, various terms have been coined to capture aspects of these changes: urbanization, suburbanization, globalization, and glocalization. Now, metro areas are increasingly spatially and functionally divided by networked infrastructures and by the legal tool of zoning into zones that possess greater accessibility and concomitant wealth and zones that have less accessibility and wealth. Graham and Marvin have identified this segregation by infrastructure as "splintering urbanism" (Graham and Marvin 2001). This is a new urban truth, "a mode of truth, not centered and coherent, but angular and splintered" (attributed to Jorge Luis Borges). This new truth is tearing the city apart, instead of pulling it together. It is a contradictory truth that represents the double-edged sword of infrastructure.

Infrastructure has always been the medium that separated the haves from the have-nots. The exceptions, which stand out as shining beacons of an ideal which does serve people equitably, are where infrastructure and related services are truly universal and accessible to all. Public libraries, schools, and public water systems serve as exemplars in this regard. The urban predicament of segregation by lack of access to infrastructure has motivated reforms in the ways cities were built and managed and continues to do so.

What happened between 1900 and 2020 was the gradual leaning away from infrastructure through a series of social movements that became ingrained in planning practice. The first was the City Functional, whereby city plans were becoming less occupied with aesthetics and infrastructure and more concerned with administration and the control of private property by zoning. New York City's 1916 Zoning Code was popularized by Hugh Ferris's powerful renderings of building setbacks, and by a written legal code in support of the renderings.

The diffusion of the New York code to towns and cities nationwide led to the rapid adoption of zoning as the principle municipal tool to accomplish planning, supplanting comprehensive plans drawn by civic designers. According to a section of attorney Alfred Bettman's pivotal *amici curiae* brief to the United States Supreme Court in the 1926 case *Village of Euclid et al. v. Ambler Realty Company*, titled "The Remarkable Spread of Zoning in the United States", by 1926 a total of 420 American municipalities had enacted zoning ordinances, and "hundreds of other municipalities are engaged in [their] preparation" (Bettman 1946, 159). As a result of the zoning revolution, land use zones prescribed by ordinance supplanted urban form and infrastructure as the objects of planning.

Increasing professional specialization and the encroachment of municipal engineers onto the turf of landscape architects and urban planners, that begun in the City Beautiful period, increased to the extent that one scholar was able to remark that from the bastions of appointed municipal office, engineers

> made a daily impress on the city's physical form that the landscape architects would never match. Though they made some contributions to comprehensive planning, engineers more often won civic admiration for solving specific, immediate problems of drainage, water supply, and traffic. Engineers and public administrators were proponents of cost-conscious, efficient, technologically proficient conduct of urban government (Wilson 1989, 37).

At the same time, as institutional considerations came to the fore, infrastructure-based physical planning receded, especially at the municipal level. New techniques such as zoning and a legally binding master plan, administered by newly formed planning commissions, altered the tone of how planning was done and who did it. Before it was architects, landscape architects, and engineers. Now, more lawyers and new professionals called city planners took on these tasks. The diffusion of the US Commerce Department's Standard Zoning Enabling Act in 1922 provided a model state law which many states adopted. These laws permitted or prescribed municipal zoning, administered by zoning commissions. In 1926 the Department followed suit with the Standard Planning Enabling Act, also adopted by many states. Tellingly, zoning preceded planning in this sequence, as it has done since in many American localities, despite the theory that zoning is a tool that implements the urban plan, and thus is subsequent to it. This had the effect of placing more importance on legal procedures, and less on physical planning and infrastructure. Control of private development via zoning replaced guiding it by infrastructure planning.

The radical mark that zoning left on the metropolis was to haunt cities, especially North American ones, for the remainder of the 20th century, and into the 21st. Zoning – segregating different land uses from each other into single use zones – split the city apart. Separating functions from each other – residences from employment, industry and other nuisance-generating activities from suppliers and distributors – was one way zoning divided the city. Zoning also split the city socially by establishing gradients among use classifications. The wealthy were located into certain residential zones, the middle class in others, and the poor in yet others. Economic activities were similarly classified, with laborers and professionals often in different zones. This persistent separation by zoning flew counter to the logic that had guided city growth throughout recorded history. The logic that guided city development – bring people and activities together – was the crowning achievement of cities and their contribution to human civilization. Zoning dealt a near catastrophic blow to cities, which they are beginning to recover from by using compact city planning.

The New Realities of the City-Region

The preparation of metropolitan and regional plans recognized that urban growth occurred in suburban sprawl as well as in downtown concentration, and the interrelations of the two required coordinated planning for more than just the central city. Inspired by the Scottish biologist and regionalist Patrick Geddes, planners on both sides of the Atlantic produced regional plans. Paragons were the *Greater London Plan* in 1944 and the Regional Plan Association of New York's (RPA) 1929–1930 *Plan for New York and Environs*, led by the English planner Thomas Adams. Geddes also exerted a strong influence on the Regional Plan Association of America, a nemesis to the RPA, by proposing an alternate plan led by a group spearheaded by Geddes's acolyte, Lewis Mumford (Hall 2002b).

The *Plan for New York and its Environs* was essentially a regional design, using regional infrastructure systems as the framework for most recommendations. (The neighborhood unit proposed by Clarence Perry was a notable exception.) The two-volume plan, when combined with the eight volumes of surveys and studies, amounted to an encyclopaedia of planning. It captured the state of the art on both sides of the Atlantic. Robert Moses, a vehement antagonist of the RPA and the New York City Planning Commission, who was the city's Park Commissioner and Chair of the Triborough Bridge Authority, made an international reputation for himself as the "master builder" by building highways, bridges, tunnels, parks, parkways, and public housing (Caro 1974). What is often overlooked is the ironic fact that the locations for these infrastructure facilities were prescribed in the RPA's 1929–1930 regional plan. The RPA has published four plans, about every 30 years, the last in 2017.

Another example is the Tennessee Valley Authority (TVA), a federal agency created in the 1930s to build dams, reservoirs, hydroelectric plants, munitions factories, and ancillary facilities in a multistate Tennessee River region in the southeastern United States. Intended as a regional development strategy for one of the chronically poorest regions in the nation, the TVA was an icon of New Deal planning (Selznick 1949). Widely influential, both the RPA and TVA plans stand as convincing evidence of the link between planning and infrastructure at the metropolitan and regional scales.

In the United Kingdom, Thomas Adams, still a partner in his planning firm while leading the RPA, prepared eight advisory city-region plans between 1924 and 1932. He also introduced the American idea of a parkway into metropolitan design in his work around the city of London. Patrick Abercrombie, prior to leading the development of the *Greater London Plan* of 1944 and the *Clyde Valley Plan* of 1946 for the Glasgow urban region of Scotland, produced a series of advisory regional plans in the 1920s (Hall 2002b). These plans used the same tools to shape growth as the 1929 New York regional plan. They were regional designs that guided the physical form of the region, and the location and size of new or expanded settlements. Infrastructure did the shaping.

Back in the United States, the National Planning Board, created under President Roosevelt in 1933, operated through 1943 under other names such as the National Resources Committee and the National Resources Planning Board (NRPB). It coordinated federal planning for public works and national resources. It conducted long-range research studies in the support of its planning, and stimulated local, regional, and especially state planning. In the 1930s most states set up state planning boards, modeled on the NRPB, which itself was influenced by the New York State Commission of Housing and Regional Planning, which was established in the 1920s and produced the *New York State Plan* in 1926. (Roosevelt was governor of New York from 1929–1932.) After 1939, at the dawn of World War II, the NRPB withdrew from public works planning and supporting state planning boards, most of which were dissolved or left idle, in favor of special duties related to national defense (Clawson 1981). Its prime legacy is the thousands of public works projects that still grace communities throughout the United States.

The shift away from infrastructure toward zoning and administration was nearly complete by the 1950s. Stuart Chapin's landmark text *Land Use Planning* (1957) signaled the shift:

> It changed the way planning was practiced in the United States, by shifting the core of planning from design [and infrastructure] to land use. This meant a move away from Olmsted's "complex unity" of the city to land units segmented into [zones]… Even as the book acknowledged that land use planning was is one part of comprehensive planning, it nevertheless stressed quantitative analysis over design synthesis. … In part its success derived from the fact that a land use basis (as opposed to a whole-city basis) fit more neatly into the way North American institutions dealt with real property (deeds, laws, zoning). … Dividing land into uses and other categories of analysis lent itself handily to various control technologies being used in the governance of land … With the land use control model, planning employed a divide and conquer mentality decidedly distinct from the order and build mindset of previous physical plans (Neuman 1998, 214).

Infrastructure, which shaped prior physical plans, was not a significant part of Chapin's planning. His book signaled changes on the horizon.

This was never so evident as with the 1956 Interstate Highways and Defense Act and its massive impacts on all of America, including metropolitan land use patterns. Interstate highway impacts, along with other stimulants of postwar suburban sprawl – inexpensive home loans, urban flight, and baby boom demographics – have been extensively chronicled (Jackson 1985). The interstate highway act helped continue the separation of infrastructure, especially transportation and stormwater management, from city planning's purview into the hands of specialists. Absent plans other than for zoning, suburban planners were left to react to subdivision and other development proposals without the infrastructure planning tools that guided earlier city growth.

In the city itself, the housers and other urban renewal advocates and professionals held sway, priming the city for the "federal bulldozer" of North American-style urban renewal (Anderson 1964). Apart from interstate highway assaults into the city, which were in some cities fiercely and effectively resisted, infrastructure was not a part of the urban renewal vocabulary. In general, infrastructure planning, except at the metropolitan and larger scales, was largely replaced by housing and community planning. An exception to this came as a result of the Metropolitan Planning Organizations, created by federal law in the 1960s. They were principally engaged in transportation planning. Institutionally they were weak initially, and subject to numerous federal criteria and constraints.

City Grassrooted

The turbulent decade of the 1960s ushered in a profound reconsideration of urban planning's scope and mission. Emboldened by Jane Jacobs's call to pay greater attention to the fine-grained details of city living, especially in the neighborhoods, planners began to fight the increasing hold that transportation engineers and urban renewal experts exerted on urban development (Jacobs 1961). The freeway revolts in Philadelphia, San Francisco, and other places were led and informed by planners. The American planning profession was impelled by Paul Davidoff's inspiring article "Advocacy and Pluralism in Planning" to give voice to the underrepresented, to advocate on their behalf in the planning arena (Davidoff 1965). Cities neared the top of the US domestic policy agenda, placed in the limelight by civil rights, riots, decay, depopulation, and pollution. The Department of Housing and Urban Development, established by law in 1965, applied federal muscle to the urban agenda.

Infrastructure was not included as a main part of the new department's mission. Instead, federal responsibility for infrastructure was and continues to be scattered among numerous departments and agencies. Additionally, routing highways through residential neighborhoods and the placement of large utility, waste disposal, airport, seaport, and sanitary facilities in poor neighborhoods comprised the new currents of planning that led to grassroots opposition rather than infrastructure's reincorporation into planning.

These movements accelerated the estrangement of planning from infrastructure, and moved it towards urban redevelopment, community planning, and housing. Social planning, advocacy planning, equity planning, policy planning, and other monikers denoted two related shifts in planning. One was to critique infrastructure planning and physical planning from a social, local, place-based perspective. The second was to continue the gradual shift away from physical form that had dominated planning since the mid-19th century.

Another seismic shift of the 1960s, the environmental movement, was to have a similar effect on the planning profession. While many were called to planning, particularly environmental planning, by such seminal texts as Ian McHarg's *Design With Nature*, efforts to improve the environment relied on natural methods (McHarg 1969). Environmental infrastructure became the near-exclusive province of civil engineers, and a new specialty, environmental engineers (Melosi 2000).

The separation between infrastructure and urban planning in the United States was mirrored in American-led international initiatives. During the reconstruction of Europe and Japan after World War II, the Marshall Plan channeled vast sums of money into infrastructure. These sums were managed by politicians and professional bureaucrats rather than planners or engineers. As the United Nations and the World Bank evolved, significant portions of their aid efforts were directed towards infrastructure. Through them, economists and other social scientists and financial managers directed activities. As nations in Asia, Africa, and Latin America developed industrial economies under the influence of international aid and globalization, their own national and local institutions absorbed the economic calculus of infrastructure decision-making. We cannot discount the influence of Robert McNamara as the head of the World Bank in this era, applying his "whiz-kid" policy analysis grounded in operations research and his tenure as president of Ford Motor Company.

Nonetheless, some regions, including Europe, Latin America, and Southeast Asia, maintained infrastructure as the strategic focus of urban and regional planning and economic development. Regional dichotomies such as these reflect disparities that come into conflict as Western theories and practices have been propagated throughout the world.

In Europe, local grassroots efforts to improve urban living arose in many cities across the continent. Among the early efforts, reform in Bologna, Italy was spearheaded by architect-planner-activists under the protective umbrella of a supportive city administration. Like urban and environmental activism in the United States, their efforts focused on the quality of the urban environment and housing in the neighborhoods. In Madrid and Barcelona, Spanish urban social movements, locally called citizens movements, led major urban renovations in a style completely distinct from the federal bulldozer. They were led by planner-activists in response to two overarching conditions, the flood of rural migrants into the cities after World War II and the Franco regime's lack of response to the influx (not building adequate housing, infrastructure, and community facilities). Citizens protested to improve their shanty-town communities with such vigor that they nearly toppled the dictatorship, and shook up the planning profession and local government from top to bottom. The Spanish citizens movements signaled an exception to the generalized (but far from total) Euro-American departure from infrastructure as a planning concern (Castells 1983). In contrast, European large-scale infrastructure network planning was largely left to regional and national governments.

What Caused the Estrangement of Infrastructure from Planning?

This overview of the history of the development of city planning in the modern era, after 1850, reveals that it was based initially on the twin pillars of sanitary reform via infrastructure provision and poverty alleviation through housing reform. Planning evolved to assume more functions, such as civic beautification, land use and development control via zoning and other legal provisions, regional and state planning, economic and community development, and environmental protection.[6]

We should take care to note the distinction between physical form as a basis of planning and infrastructure as a basis of planning. While there are obvious links between the two, they had different origins and differing impacts on the planning profession. The limits of the physical planning approach, especially its tendency to leave out some infrastructure, were in part what gave way to the expansion of planning into social, economic, legal, institutional, and other arenas. City planning has never been exclusively about physical planning or infrastructure, not even in Europe or Asia. It has always been a means to achieve broader social and economic and political goals, and sometimes those means included infrastructure and physical planning.

Along the way, city planning's involvement with infrastructure has waned. Others, notably engineers, usurped its advocacy and management. William Wilson and Martin Melosi's meticulous analyses of the United States indicate that, "Beginning in the nineteenth century, municipal engineers deliberately preempted several planning areas, especially those involving sanitation, street grading and surfacing, drainage, and the oversight of [capital] improvement construction" (Wilson 1989, 285; Melosi 2000).

This preemption of the planning profession's scope amounts to an estrangement in the uneasy relationship between planners and engineers, due in large part to the differences in training that they receive. Engineers, with a mathematically oriented systems approach to problem solving that omits knowledge of cities and of governance, speak a language distant from the combination of legalese, social survey, process orientation, and a bit of urban design that planners have evolved. Yet they are both design professions.

A drift back to urban form was the new urbanism movement in the US and the compact city movement in the rest of the world. Led by architects and urban designers, they criticized suburban sprawl and the loss of community life engendered by it, in their view (Duany, Plater-Zyberk and Speck 2001). A critique of suburban sprawl and a solution to the perceived loss of community that accompanied it, new urbanism submitted its proposals along three connected lines. One was the compact city, replete with higher densities, finer grain of mixed land uses, and pedestrian orientation. Second was an emphasis on public spaces – streets, squares, and parks – with the environmental determinist premise that enhancing public space would foster public interaction. Third is the public health connection with active living and active transport. Together, along with a revaluing of cities, especially their centers, as places to live, work, and recreate, these trends have helped to start to bring infrastructure back into planning.

The compact city sparked a debate about some aspects of infrastructure (streets, public spaces, public transport) and the relationship between planners and engineers. The same can be said about sustainability for environmental and energy infrastructures. New urbanists and compact city advocates agree that planning has for too long abdicated its former role of guiding street layout and the urban design relationship between structures and streets. A renewed debate about community life, sustainability, public health, and the physical manifestation of communities captured broad civic and political attention. As this book contends, infrastructure is at the center of all these debates, and can effectively integrate concerns and solutions for the city to become more sustainable.

Notes

1 When coupled with his numerous statistical surveys of the 1850s and his Barcelona Extension Plan of 1960, the *Teoría* could be said to be an equivalent of the multivolume Regional Plan Association of New York's (RPA) *Plan for New York and Environs* of 1929–1931, in that it comprised an equally voluminous compendium of city planning of his time. The difference between Cerdà and the RPA document is that the Catalan produced it himself, and that his work is nearly entirely original.
2 The American League for Civic Improvement (ALCI), founded in 1902, was originally the American Society of Municipal Improvements, which was founded in 1894, and morphed through National League of Improvement Associations, founded in 1900. In 1904 the ALCI merged with the American Park and Outdoor Art Association (founded in 1897) to become the American Civic Association.
3 The 1901 McMillan Plan for Washington, DC. Senator James McMillan was Chairman of the Senate Committee on the District of Columbia and was involved in the city's centennial celebration in 1900. McMillan's Committee and the American Institute of Architects selected an interdisciplinary team to replan the Mall, which included Burnham, Frederick Law Olmsted Jr., Boston architect Charles McKim, and sculptor Augustus Saint-Gaudens. According to Wilson, the McMillan Plan's contribution to the City Beautiful movement was "palpable and immediate, in both the architectural and popular press" (Wilson 1989, 69).
4 Around this time, a six volume *Pittsburgh Survey* (1907–1908) conducted by Paul U. Kellogg under the auspices of the Sage Foundation focused on the conditions of city dwellers rather than civic improvements. Its contributors were sociologists, political scientists, and economists. Endorsed by Mayor Guthrie, it resulted in a bond issue for $6,775,000 passed by popular vote. Curiously, the bond-funded infrastructure, even though the survey highlighted human conditions. The technological fixes the bond funded were a new hospital, playgrounds, a water treatment plant, garbage incinerators, sewers, a boulevard, and street widening (Griffith 1983, 122–123).
5 *City Planning* (Nolan 1916) explained the principles of and justifications for preparing a general plan. A second edition appeared in 1929, which became a precursor to the

International City Management Association's *Local Planning Administration* series, now the standard reference for urban planning in the United States. Nolen's book was an impetus for the establishment of the American City Planning Institute (ACPI) in 1917, America's first professional planning association. Its first elected president was Frederick Law Olmsted Jr.
6 Housing, while a strong planning root in Europe, is not as much a root in the United States. A debated puzzle in American planning history is why housing played a lesser role.

Bibliography

Adams, T. (1935). Outline of town and city planning: A review of past efforts and modern aims. *Town Planning Review*.
Albrechts, L., Balducci, A., and Hillier, J. (2016). *Situated Practices of Strategic Planning: An International Perspective*. London: Routledge.
Anderson, M. (1964). *The Federal Bulldozer: A Critical Analysis of Urban Renewal 1949–1962*. Cambridge, MA: MIT Press.
Benevolo, L. (1980). *The History of the City*. Cambridge, MA: MIT Press.
Benevolo, L. (1967). *The Origins of Modern Town Planning*. Cambridge, MA: MIT Press.
Berke, P. Godschalk, D., and Kaiser, E. (2005). *Urban Land Use Planning*. Urbana, IL: University of Illinois Press, 5th edition.
Bettman, A. (1946). *City and Regional Planning Papers*. Cambridge, MA: Harvard University Press.
Caro, R. (1974). *The Power Broker: Robert Moses and the Fall of New York*. New York: Alfred A. Knopf.
Cerdà, I. (1867). *Teoría General de Urbanización y Aplicación de sus Principios y Doctrinas a la Reforma y Ensanche de Barcelona*. Madrid: Imprenta Española.
Cerdà, I. (1855). Ensanche de la ciudad de Barcelona. Memória descriptiva de los trabajos facultativos y estudios estadísticos hechos del orden del gobierno y consideraciones que se han tenido presentes en la formación del ante-proyecto para el emplazamiento y distribución del nuevo caserío. In *Cerdà y Barcelona vol. 1*. (1991). Madrid: Ministerio de administraciones públicas and Barcelona: Ajuntament de Barcelona.
Chadwick, E. (1842). *Report from the Poor Law Commissioners on an Inquiry into the Sanitary Condition of the Laboring Population of Great Britain*. Reprint, Edinburgh: University of Edinburgh Press, 1965.
Chapin Jr., S. (1957). *Urban Land Use Planning*. Urbana, IL: University of Illinois Press.
Choay, F. (1969). *The Modern City: Planning in the 19th Century*. New York: George Braziller.
Clawson, M. (1981). *New Deal Planning: The National Resources Planning Board*. Baltimore, MD: Johns Hopkins University Press.
Cronon, W. (1991). *Nature's Metropolis: Chicago and the Great West*. New York: W. W. Norton.
Cronon, W. (1983). *Changes in the Land: Indians, Colonists, and the Ecology of New England*. New York: Hill and Wang.
Cullingworth, B., Pendlebury, J., Davoudi, S., Nadin, V., Hart, T., Vigar, G., Webb, D., and Townshend, T. (2015). *Town and Country Planning in the UK*. London: Routledge, 15th edition.
Davidoff, P. (1965). Advocacy and pluralism in planning. *Journal of the American Institute of Planners*, 31: 103–115.
Duany, A., Plater-Zyberk, E. and Speck, J. (2001). *Suburban Nation*. New York: North Point Press.

Dupuy, G. (1991). *L'Urbanisme des Reseaux: Theories et Methods*. Paris: A. Colon.
Erickson, C. (2010). The transformation of environment into landscape: The historical ecology of monumental earthwork construction in the Bolivian Amazon. *Diversity*, 2(4): 618–652.
Erie, S. (2002). Los Angeles as a developmental state. In Dear, M. (ed.), *From Chicago to L.A.; Making Sense of Urban Theory*. Thousand Oaks, CA: Sage, 133–159.
Faludi, A. and Waterhout, B. (2002). *The Making of the European Spatial Development Perspective: No Masterplan*. London, New York: Routledge.
Fishman, R. (ed.). (2000). *The American Planning Tradition: Culture and Policy*. Washington DC: Woodrow Wilson Center Press.
Graham, S. and Marvin, S. (2001). *Splintering Urbanism: Networked Infrastructures, Technological Mobilities and the Urban Condition*. London: Routledge.
Griffith, Ernest. (1983 [1974]). *A History of American City Government: The Progressive Years and Their Aftermath, 1900–1920*. Washington DC: University Press of America.
Griscom, J. (1845). *The Sanitary Condition of the Laboring Population of New York*. New York: City of New York.
Gurran, N. (2011). *Australian Urban Land Use Planning: Principles, Systems, and Practice*. Sydney: University of Sydney Press.
Guy, S., Graham, S., and Marvin, S. (1996). Privatized utilities and regional governance: The new regional managers? *Regional Studies*, 30(8): 733–739.
Hack, G., Sedway, P. H., Birch, E. L. (eds.). (2009). *Local Planning: Contemporary Principles and Practice*. Washington DC: ICMA Press.
Hall, P. (2002a). *Urban and Regional Planning*. London and New York: Routledge.
Hall, P. (2002b). *Cities of Tomorrow: An Intellectual History of Urban Planning and Design in the Twentieth Century*. New York: Blackwell, 3rd edition.
Hartman, C. (2002 [1984]). *City for Sale: The Transformation of San Francisco*. Berkeley, CA: University of California Press.
Hasselberger, B. (ed.) (2017). *Encounters in Planning Thought*. London: Routledge.
Hodge, G. and Robinson, I. (2001). *Planning Canadian Regions*. Vancouver: University of British Columbia Press.
Hughes, T. (1987). The social construction of technological systems. In Bijker, W., Hughes, T., and Pinch, T. (eds.), *The Social Construction of Technological Systems: New Directions in the Sociology and History of Technology*. Cambridge, MA: MIT Press.
Hughes, T. (1983). *Networks of Power: Electrification of Western Society 1880–1930*. Baltimore, MD and London: Johns Hopkins University Press.
Jacobs, J. (1961). *The Death and Life of Great American Cities*. New York: Random House.
Jackson, K. (1985). *The Crabgrass Frontier: The Suburbanization of the United States*. New York: Oxford University Press.
Konvitz, J. (1985). *The Urban Millennium: The City Building Process from the Early Middle Ages to the Present*. Baltimore, MD: Johns Hopkins University Press.
Krueckeberg, D. (1983). *Introduction to Planning History in the United States*. New Brunswick, MJ: Center for Urban Policy Research.
Kunzmann, K. (1997). The future of the city region in Europe. In Bosma, K. and Hellinga, H., *Mastering the City: North-European City Planning 1900–2000*. Rotterdam: NAI Publishers and The Hague: EFL Publications, Volume I, 16–29.
LaPorte, D. (2000). *The History of Shit*. Cambridge, MA: MIT Press.
Lefebvre, H. (1991 [1974]). *The Production of Space*. Oxford: Basil Blackwell.
Levy, J. (2009). *Contemporary Urban Planning*. Upper Saddle River, NJ: Prentice Hall.

Lindstrom, B. (2002). Public works and land use: The importance of infrastructure in Chicago's metropolitan development, 1830–1970. In Weiwel, W. and Persky, J. (eds.). *Suburban Sprawl: Private Decisions and Public Policy.* Armonk, NY: M. E. Sharpe.

McHarg, I. (1969). *Design with Nature.* New York: American Museum of Natural History.

McLaughlin, J. B. (1992). *Shaping Melbourne's Future? Town Planning, the State and Civil Society.* New York: Cambridge University Press.

McLaughlin, C. et al. (eds). (1977). *The Collected Papers of Frederick Law Olmsted.* Baltimore, MD: Johns Hopkins University Press, 6 volumes.

Melosi, M. (2000). *The Sanitary City: Urban Infrastructure in America from Colonial Times to the Present.* Baltimore, MD: Johns Hopkins University Press.

Montaner, J. (Ed.) (1999). *Barcelona 1979–2004: Del Desenvolupment a la Ciutat de Qualitat.* Barcelona: City of Barcelona.

Mumford, L. (1961). *The City in History: Its Origins, its Transformations, and its Prospects.* New York: Harcourt, Brace & World.

Neuman, M. (2011). Ildefons Cerdà and the future of spatial planning: The network urbanism of a city planning pioneer. *Town Planning Review,* 82(2): 117–143.

Neuman, M. (1998). Does planning need the plan? *Journal of the American Planning Association,* 64(2): 208–220.

Nolen, J. (1916). *City Planning: A Series of Papers Presenting the Essential Elements of a City Plan.* New York: D. Appleton.

Perry, D. (ed.). (1995). *Building the Public City.* Beverly Hills, CA: Sage.

Peterson, J. (2003). *The Birth of City Planning in the United States, 1840–1917.* Baltimore, MD: Johns Hopkins University Press.

Platt, H. (1983). *City Building in the New South: The Growth of Public Services in Houston.* Philadelphia, PA: Temple University Press.

Reimer, M., Getimis, P., and Blotevogel, H. (eds.). (2014). *Spatial Planning Systems and Practices in Europe: A Comparative Perspective on Continuity and Changes.* London: Routledge.

Reps, J. (1965). *The Making of Urban America: A History of City Planning in the United States.* Princeton, NJ: Princeton University Press.

Rome, A. (2001). *The Bulldozer in the Countryside: Suburban Sprawl and the Rise of American Environmentalism.* Cambridge: Cambridge University Press.

Saalman, H. (1971). *Haussmann: Paris Transformed.* New York: George Braziller.

Sandercock, L. (1990). *Property, Politics, and Urban Planning: A History of Australian City Planning, 1890–1990.* Piscataway, NJ: Transaction Publishers.

Selznick, P. (1949). *TVA and the Grassroots: A Study in the Sociology of Formal Organization.* Berkeley, CA: University of California Press.

Sipe, N. and Vella, K. (eds.). (2017). *The Routledge Handbook of Australian Urban and Regional Planning.* London: Taylor & Francis.

Sitte, C. (1965 [1889]). *City Planning According to Artistic Principles,* edited by Collins, G. and Crasemann Collins, C. New York: Random House.

Smith, N. (1992). New city, new frontier: Lower East Side as Wild Wild West. In Sorkin, M. (ed.), *Variations on a Theme Park.* New York: Hill and Wang, 61–93.

Tarr, J. and Dupuy, G. (eds.). (1988). *Technology and the Rise of the Networked City in Europe and America.* Philadelphia, PA: Temple University Press.

Wilson, W. (1989). *The City Beautiful Movement.* Baltimore, MD: Johns Hopkins University Press.

Wilson, W. (1964). *The City Beautiful Movement in Kansas City.* Columbia, MO: University of Missouri Press.

World Bank. (1994). *World Development Report: Infrastructure for Development.* Oxford: Oxford University Press.

Big Dig Project

Facts

Who: United States Department of Transportation, Federal Highway Administration & The Massachusetts Turnpike Authority

What: The largest civil works project in US history

Where: Boston: eight miles of Interstate highway construction, approximately four miles of I-93 between Roxbury and Somerville, and approximately four miles of I-90 between Chinatown and East Boston

When: Federal legislation passed 1987, ground broken in Boston 1991, completion 2007

Why: To reconnect the city and to alleviate traffic bottlenecks

How much: $24,300,000,000

Planning and Sustainability

Boston, Massachusetts's Central Artery is one of the most congested highways in the United States. Traffic has crawled for more than ten hours each day and the annual cost to motorists from this congestion was estimated to be $500 million. The elevated highway also cut off Boston's North End and Waterfront neighborhoods from the downtown, limiting these areas' ability to participate in the city's life. The solution, called the Central Artery/Tunnel Project (CA/T), is operated by the Massachusetts Turnpike Authority.

The project includes two main elements – the extension of Interstate 90 from its current terminus south of downtown Boston under Boston Harbor to Logan Airport, and the replacement of Interstate 93 through downtown Boston, including a tunnel through the heart of the city. This is one of the largest, most technically difficult and environmentally challenging infrastructure projects ever undertaken in the United States.

Planning for the Central Artery/Tunnel Project began in 1982, with work on environmental impact reviews. Preliminary design began in the 1980s. Final design began in the late 1980s, after Congress approved funding and the project's basic scope in April 1987. Construction began in September 1991 on the Ted Williams Tunnel and a special bypass road through South Boston to take truck traffic off of neighborhood streets. The total cost was estimated at $24.3 billion, making it the most expensive highway project in US history.

Along with improving mobility in notoriously congested downtown Boston, the Central Artery project was conceived to reconnect neighborhoods severed by the old elevated highway, and improve the quality of life in the city beyond the limited confines of the new expressway. Apart from a 12 percent reduction in city-wide carbon monoxide levels, major project benefits include creation of more than 260 acres of open land, including 27 acres where the existing Central Artery now stands, more than 100 acres at Spectacle Island in Boston Harbor, and 40 more acres of new parks in and around downtown Boston. Clay and dirt from the project were being used to fill and cap landfills throughout the Boston area.

The entire project was finished in 2007, including demolition of the elevated highway and restoration of the surface.

Finance and Cost

The project was funded from a variety of sources including federal transportation funding, cash, and many kinds of bonds. See Tables 1 and 2.

Table 1 Overall Revenues by Source (US $ millions)

Source	Revenues
Federal	7,049
Transportation Infrastructure Fund	2,343
Grant Anticipation Notes	1,500
Mass Port Authority	302
State Bonds / Notes	1,588
State interest on MTA found	45
Turnpike Authority	1,658
Insurance Trust Revenues	140
Total	14,625

Table 2 Cost Estimate by Major Project Element as of 2003 (US $ millions)

Element	Cost Estimate
Design	1,049
ROW	607
Construction	9,417
Project Management	2,139
Insurance	615
Force Accounts	602
Contingency	196
Total	14,625

5
Infrastructure Planning

What, Who, When, Where, Why, and How

Infrastructure systems and networks are always planned. Infrastructure planning is a process that is always situated in spatial territory. As a process, infrastructure planning also is situated in time in an institutional setting. While infrastructure is most often thought of as a fixed facility or system, it also changes over its life span. That is why this book bases infrastructure planning on the life cycle process. This chapter presents the principles, tools, and practices of infrastructure planning in a pragmatic way that incorporate time and place. The 5 W's and one H – What, Who, When, Where, Why, and How – comprise a rubric to guide the development of a life cycle process for infrastructure planning.

What infrastructures get planned may appear obvious – all of them. Yet each system typically gets planned and designed independently of others. A common though not unique exception is stormwater drainage that is planned in conjunction with surface transport – roads and rails. Cooperative planning among infrastructures should be the norm, so that all networks and the settlements that they occupy and traverse are considered at the outset of, and throughout, the planning process. This is evident for linear infrastructures that share rights-of-way, yet applies to all types. Benefits of coordinated planning with other infrastructures include efficiencies, cost savings, lower land acquisition costs, lower maintenance costs, less habitat fragmentation, and less environmental impact, among others. Farsighted planning also accounts for growth, expansion, updates, and space for future infrastructures. Flexibility in planning is thus key, a challenge given the specificity and fixity of infrastructure.

Who plans infrastructure is a question of vital importance with significant consequences. Who determines whether for better or worse, as the cases of the $24 billion project called the Big Dig in Boston (described earlier) and the tragic devastation wrought by Hurricane Katrina (described in the Introduction) both illustrate. These are but two egregious examples from the United States among any number worldwide. In contrast, better infrastructure decisions come from collaborative planning among city leaders, planners, landscape architects, urban designers, architects, engineers, financiers, citizens, and users. When it is under the purview of one discipline, as it has been for a long while in many jurisdictions, shortsighted mistakes are costly. Another example of this type of uni-disciplinary approach is from the 1960s, when Interstate Highways destroyed parts of many American cities.

Who is not merely which individual or profession. Which organization(s), institution(s), and / or grouping(s) is more apt for the scale, cost, and complexity of infrastructure. Who is involved and at which stage(s) of the planning process is a matter of its design. Those involved get selected, yet the designers and coordinators of the planning process benefit from being open to new partners and collaborators as the process unfolds.

When infrastructure gets planned may be less obvious. It has several answers, depending on the time horizon. Given that infrastructure can have a several-hundred-year life span, or longer, the long-term view is essential. To an extent, different steps of the infrastructure planning process occur at different times, depending on its stage in the life cycle. The most significant planning, including design, engineering, costing, budgeting, financing, and prospective impact assessment, occurs at the outset, before it is built. Yet the initial planning is not the endpoint. Not everything can be foreseen, and no planning process is ideal in that political and fiscal constraints, among others, impinge.

The steps mentioned above recur throughout the life cycle, as needs of the system change, as service areas expand or contract, technology is innovated, policy (law, regulations) changes, economic and budget contexts evolve, ownership of private systems change hands, and so on. For example, effects of climate change and natural disasters reveal the low level of resilience of many old, fixed-in-place systems that need to be redesigned and retrofitted. Or consider the programming of scheduled maintenance and repair that can occur during initial planning and become integrated into the life cycle. This contrasts with maintenance that is ad hoc, reactive, and prone to budget cuts – which is why many systems are in poor repair.

Another time factor to consider when planning an individual facility, system or network is its intersections with the life spans and life cycles of other infrastructures, and the territory itself. For example, stormwater management along highways can be redesigned to be more porous and less impervious. Using green rather than grey infrastructure allows more aquifer and surface water recharge, less runoff and flooding, and more pollution filtering. A continuous consideration of other infrastructures is vital throughout all stages of an individual network's life cycle.

Where is of vital importance, given the spatial dimension. Allowing for the many impacts that an infrastructure network has, and how they are interconnected with other networks and the built and natural environments, many factors need to be taken into account. This stresses the need for spatial planners (urban designers and planners, city and regional planners, environmental and ecological planners, and landscape architects, for example) to be involved throughout.

Why is because without proper planning and design, infrastructure can itself become or cause a disaster, with significant consequences. Peter Hall's book *Great Planning Disasters* (Hall 1982) is about infrastructure whose planning is lacking or misguided. Hall's book is more than a cautionary tale. Suboptimal service, operations, and maintenance are all consequences of limited or inadequate planning, as are the wide range of social, economic, equity, and environmental impacts. Capital facilities are of capital importance.

How is the topic of the rest of the chapter. Currently, infrastructure systems tend to be planned individually, in isolation from each other and from urban planning. This short-sighted approach entails great costs to society and the environment that can be avoided. Uncoordinated planning also involves higher risk (Altshuler and Luberoff 2003; Flyvberg, Bruzelius, Rosengatter 2003). In contrast, the life cycle planning methods outlined here, which apply primarily to networks and systems (though it can be adapted to individual projects), afford outcomes with less risk, more resilience, greater sustainability, fewer negative impacts, and more positive outcomes in terms of service and being woven more harmoniously into cities and landscapes.

Introducing the Life Cycle

Cities, infrastructure, and infrastructure planning all have life cycles. Understanding the complex relationships among them is vital to the success and effectiveness of each. Here I lay out the key elements of their relations as they support life cycle planning. The life cycle of cities, though examined by Kevin Lynch in his last two books, *Good City Form* and *Wasting Away*, is rarely incorporated into infrastructure planning (Lynch 1981; 1990). His thesis, which we adopt, is that cities are alive with periods of boom, bust, renewal, and decay.

The same is true for infrastructure. Different infrastructure planning strategies can be tailored for these periods. However, this integrated approach tends not to be elucidated in mainstream planning. The planning approach herein integrates urban life cycles with infrastructure cycles, via life cycle infrastructure planning. The term life cycle in this book refers to the "cradle-to-cradle" life span, which includes how to recycle, upcycle, repurpose, and dispose of an infrastructure once it reaches the end of its service life. We adapt cradle to cradle from a book of the same name (McDonough and Braungart 2010).

The "bones" of a city – its infrastructure – are instrumental to literally support it and keep it vibrant over time. Rejuvenating those bones, even full replacements, are critical. There has been much research as to why cities thrive, fail, or any shade in between these two endpoints. In the case of capital cities, the fortunes of its nation or empire typically go lockstep with the capital. A demise may be political or related to the succession of the ruler. In other instances it can be related to climate change, draught, and / or famine. While one factor may be decisive, others come into play. Growth of a city is likewise attributed to many factors, acting in concert. Infrastructure is critical to all stages of a city's life cycle, whether developing or declining. Understanding the roles of infrastructure in both promoting development (the usual scenario), or stemming or reversing decline, is to recognize the interplay of cities and infrastructures across both of their life cycles. The long-term perspective is crucial to effectively navigate their interplay. The disposition of life cycle planning is thus fundamental to the relations among cities and infrastructure.

The Infrastructure Life Cycle

Numerous texts – particularly engineering – put forth different means to handle the infrastructure life cycle. However, they are not explicated in spatial terms regarding their relation to urban or natural environments. Moreover, life cycle methods tend to exist in isolation, without considering two other essential parameters in comprehensive sustainability approaches. The first of these is preparing a demand-capacity analysis, which determines the overall demand for an infrastructure at a future date (the planning period or planning horizon) in a specific territory (spatial unit, geographic area), consistent with the economic, social, and political capacities of the area to support population and economic growth that the infrastructure(s) will serve. This method, which takes in to account the spatial territory, differs from a typical infrastructure needs assessment. This will be fully developed in the next chapter.

The second is conducting an assessment in terms of rate process calculations that measure the rate of energy and material consumption and byproduct production of an infrastructure in relation to its surrounding environment. The result of a rate process calculation is used to facilitate the choice of an infrastructure by conducting a comparative assessment among technology options, to determine which among them are more sustainable. The demand-capacity and rate process analyses, when coupled with a life cycle analysis of an infrastructure network, permit sustainable stewardship over the entire working life of an infrastructure. All three steps are integral to a full-blown sustainability assessment. Combining these three steps links life cycle infrastructure planning with sustainable urban planning. See Box 5.1.

Linking infrastructure to urban planning in this way offers a three-part responsive planning methodology that is contextually considerate and institutionally savvy. It provides a more complete context for decision-making so that technical considerations do not dominate decision-making processes. It provides an optimization framework that lays out a fuller range of sustainability criteria, rather than just cost and function. See Box 5.2.

> **Box 5.1 The Infrastructure Planning Process**
>
> **INFRASTRUCTURE PLANNING PROCESS**
>
> 1. DEMAND CAPACITY MANAGEMENT
> 2. RATE PROCESS ANALYSIS
> 3. LIFE CYCLE ANALYSIS

> **Box 5.2 Three Steps That Integrate Infrastructure and Urban Planning**
>
> 1. *Demand-capacity analysis* – determination of the overall demand for all infrastructure systems at a specific future time in a determinate geographic area, consistent with ecological, social, and economic capacities of that area.
> 2. *Rate process calculations* – facilitate the choice of an infrastructure network or facility by conducting a comparative assessment among various technology options. The comparative assessment determines the absolute and relative degrees of sustainability of each option.
> 3. *Life cycle planning* – permits the sustainable stewardship of infrastructure networks and facilities over their entire working lives.

Fifteen Stages of Life Cycle Infrastructure Planning

The life cycle approach to infrastructure planning and management starts with a needs assessment, here called a *demand-capacity assessment*. It goes on to encompass planning, technology selection, programming, design, costing, impact analysis, budgeting, financing, construction, operations, maintenance and repair, rehabilitation and replacement, evaluation of service provision / satisfaction, and finally,

> A. Demand assessment (from demand-capacity analysis)
> B. Planning
> C. Technology selection (from rate process analysis)
> D. Programming
> E. Design
> F. Costing
> G. Impact analysis
> H. Budgeting
> I. Financing
> J. Construction
> K. Operations
> L. Maintenance and repair
> M. Rehabilitation and replacement
> N. Evaluation of service and physical network
> O. Reassessment of needs – return to the beginning

Figure 5.1 Fifteen Stages in Life Cycle Infrastructure Planning

reassessment of needs. Life cycle planning is distinguished from service life costing, a method used in engineering and accounting that is more restricted and does not, consequently, lead to comprehensive sustainability. The 15 stages are outlined below. See Figure 5.1 for the stages of life cycle infrastructure planning.

Demand Assessment

This is a long-term infrastructure *demand assessment* – 20 years or more. Typical needs assessments are linear calculations based on projected population and economic growth (that tend to be straight-line projections) and existing systems' capacities. Thus, a straightforward equation can express this relationship:

$$\text{Need} = \text{Per capita service standard} \times \text{Population growth} \qquad 5.1$$

For example, if a city is expected to grow by 200,000 persons over a 20-year period, and water usage in 20 years is expected to be 100 gallons per person per day, then the additional water supply system capacity to be built to meet the expected demand in 20 years equals 20,000,000 gallons of water supplied per day. This algorithm, while common, gives short shrift to the many factors that need to be included in a needs assessment for sustainable infrastructure. See Box 5.3.

In lieu of the standard needs assessment calculus above, the preferred way to estimate life cycle infrastructure requirements in spatial terms is *demand-capacity analysis*. Demand-capacity analysis is as the heart of life cycle planning in a spatial setting, and is key to the approach presented here. It links the need for an infrastructure to not only to its population, but to its spatial service area, by considering two additional

> **Box 5.3 Limitations of Infrastructure Needs Assessments**
>
> The first infrastructure needs assessment that I read carried the ominous title *America in Ruins* (Choate and Walter 1981). Every one that I have examined since can be captured in three terms. First, dire warnings: of (in)adequacy, (lack of) capacity, and safety. Second, an off-putting number of zeros follows the dollar sign or other unit of currency. Finally, need always far outstrips supply, as well as funding. This persistent parade over the last 40 years suggests solutions to the problems that they bring to light have not really been forthcoming. There continue to be major funding shortfalls because we are still stuck in 'business as usual', in terms of planning, systems design, network integration, and in particular, financing. The message is to better link infrastructure assessments with actual funding mechanisms and spatial planning.

factors. These factors are 1) the capacity of the land and environment to support the population, the infrastructures, and their impacts, along with 2) the capacity of the jurisdiction providing the infrastructure in terms of economic (fiscal capacity), social (preferences of the population, community support and / or opposition), and political (political will) factors. The demand-capacity analysis is fully detailed in Chapter 6.

The capacity of the land and overall environment to support the infrastructure starts with a suitability analysis of the land and various habitats / ecosystems on it. Carrying capacity calculations stem from the method innovated by Ian McHarg in his book *Design With Nature* (McHarg 1969). These methods have become standardized via geographic information systems (GIS) coupled with environmental, public health, and other databases that yield the capacity of an area of land to support human development and occupation. An example is the amount of human waste a septic system can process without exceeding the capacity of the land to absorb it in a way that the land, soil, water, habitats, and species are not harmed by the effluent in the septic system's leach field. The factors to consider in this case include soil type and depth, hydrogeologic substrate, aquifers, surface waters, rainfall, climate, topography, and related items within the "impact range" of the leach field. Each type of infrastructure has an attendant capacity of its environs to support its presence. The capacity depends on the nature of its impacts and the way its network is distributed across the landscape. The intent is for the infrastructure not to exceed the natural carrying capacity of the land, water, and ecosystems needed to support it and remain healthy and functioning. That is, to maintain the ecological and functional integrity of the land.

One benefit of conducting the capacity analysis of the land is that it enables a more complete consideration of the possibilities of the land itself and its ecosystems to provide similar services that "hard" or built infrastructures would provide. For example, can a coastal wetland or marsh absorb hurricane or storm impacts cheaper and better than a concrete wall? Can an intact forest with its streams and lakes filter rainwater better and cheaper than a typical water supply treatment plant and a constructed reservoir? Can an inland marsh treat sewage better and cheaper than a standard sewage treatment plant consuming chemicals and electricity while producing CO_2, CH_4, and effluent? The advantages that methods such as these entail include lower costs, less environmental degradation, less habitat fragmentation, and less stress on species. Some of these services are called green infrastructures and ecosystem services or nature services.

Demand assessments can measure three categories of needs: deficiencies of existing systems to serve existing populations (backlog demand / need), the amount and type of infrastructure(s) to adequately serve population and economic growth at a specified time in the future (prospective demand / need), and changes in infrastructure requirements given new social and political norms, such as redressing equity imbalances, addressing climate change (mitigation, adaptation, resilience), and enabling new technologies (internet, streaming, artificial intelligence). These are covered in greater detail in Chapter 6. Box 5.4 spells out reasons for the incompleteness and inconsistencies of typical needs or demand assessments that are currently conducted. These obstacles need to be addressed in demand assessments in order to obtain comprehensive findings that guide policy and decision-making in an equitable and sustainable manner.

Planning

Life cycle *planning* implies long-term stewardship. Life cycle planning is a comprehensive system that covers the entire range of infrastructure planning, development, and operations; from the initial stage of demand assessment to the final stage of evaluation. What converts this sequence into a full cycle is the use of the final evaluation stage in the next iteration of the assessment stage, resuming the entire cycle.

Box 5.4 Reasons for the Incompleteness and Inconsistencies of Typical Needs or Demand assessments

1. Different time horizons: typically 5, 10, or 20 years, or an unspecified time
2. Lack of sufficient resources and staff to prepare assessments
3. Lack of adequate data and documentation
4. Lack of attention to a documented problem
5. Lack of a method to calculate needs, such as life cycle planning
6. New findings that change what we know, such as seismic stress models for structural safety, climate change modeling
7. Low levels of awareness that a problem exists or persists, such as lead paint and asbestos before the 1960s
8. No auditing of individual agencies' data by a coordinating authority
9. No provision in law or policy to mandate an assessment
10. No link to a spatial plan or planning process

Source: *Adapted from Neuman and Whittington 2000, 55*

The life cycle should not be restrictively interpreted to be followed only in a linear sequence. Combinations or mergers of stages are possible, such as design-build and build-operate-transfer.

Technology Selection

Choices exist from which to select infrastructure technologies or methods. They include built systems and networks, natural and ecological services, or a hybrid among them. These choices include the disposition or arrangement of a network in a city-region or rural landscape, such as centralized or decentralized, distributed or concentrated, modular or unitary, and so on. See Figure 0.3 in the Introduction for a comparison of dispositions and arrangements. The *technology selection* step is vital for the simple reason that it is often overlooked when making decisions. In that case, a dominant and accepted system type, a four-stage sewage treatment plant for example, might be so standard that its selection is ingrained and practically predetermined, even as it may be expensive and less sustainable. Yet as knowledge increases and options proliferate, evaluating options becomes increasingly important.

Often the choice is path dependent, meaning determined by prevailing institutions, professional standards, and financial risk models. Sometimes legacy infrastructure restricts the horizon of more sustainable infrastructure choices. When conducted over an entire cradle-to-cradle life cycle that incorporates both a demand-capacity analysis which assesses life cycle impacts of various technology options (see Chapter 6) and a rate process calculation that measures the energy and material consumption and byproduct production (impacts) of technology options (see Appendix 2), then a comprehensive sustainability evaluation can be made that can compare the pros and cons of those options. This type of comparative assessment requires collaboration across a range of disciplines and professions to assemble the data and methods (algorithms) needed in order to conduct it.

Programming

Programming is a subset of the planning function that assigns a specified amount of an infrastructure service to a defined user population. It converts a long-term demand assessment of ≥ 20 years into a medium-term program of ~ 5 years that indicates more specifically how much service is delivered to whom, how, where, and when. The purpose of programming is to provide more precise data for designers, cost accountants, and budgeters to proceed by preparing plans, designs, and budgets that permit construction.

The capital program serves as the quantitative basis for the physical planning and design of infrastructure networks and facilities. The capital program contains a composite listing of annual schedules and costs for the construction, overhaul, and / or expansion of infrastructure over a medium-term time horizon, typically four to six years. The capital program translates standard need or demand equations for an entire infrastructure network into a specific action agenda. When coupled with facility design, a capital program links the demand assessment to the annual capital budget. This intermediate term time horizon differs from a long-term plan with a twenty to fifty year horizon and an infrastructure budget with a one or two year horizon.

Programming entails a calculation of service delivery to the end user group that is more specific and precise compared to a long-term needs assessment done for an infrastructure system or network for an entire population. Service delivery can be measured for shorter time periods, such as what the infrastructure provides on any given day, week, month, or season. For example, a water supply system can be programmed to provide irrigation water in the crop growing season. It can also be programmed specifically to the periodic needs of a particular industry or other end user. Electric power grids have their particular programming characteristics because electricity is "live" and must be distributed and used as it is generated, or else it is lost, unless it can be stored.

Well-developed branches of programming exist for a range of infrastructures, notably electric power, transport, and schools. In the case of electricity, elaborate national (in some instances multinational) schemes coordinate the timed release of specified amounts of power into transmission networks according to mathematical models run by computer software programs in increments of minutes, in order to meet scheduled demand. This level of precision is required due to the quantities and geographic scales involved, and the criticality of assuring power delivery at multiple points of use, many of which have life or business threatening consequences if not delivered on time in sufficient amperage.

Public school districts' planning departments couple demographic projections with facility design and educational programming to determine accurate student counts, classroom capacities, teaching loads, and so on. Educational programming converts a long-term needs assessment, which specifies the number of schools and their buildings and associated land for an entire school district, into specific facility construction and personnel requirements, such as numbers of classrooms, desks, and laboratory spaces per grade level per school, numbers of teachers per grade level per school, numbers and types of athletic facilities, cafeteria and kitchen size, and so on. Programming determines the size, location, and service capacity of specific facilities in a network so that design, costing, and construction can proceed with reliable specifications.

Programming infrastructure involves decision-making according to selected parameters. Decision parameters are typically determined by policymaking processes that are political. There are several issues that highlight the need to reorient optimization models for sustainable programming. In spite of advances in multi-criteria decision modeling, the basic concern is that optimization models are usually optimized for one or a few variables. Optimizing for one or a few variables has led to imbalanced and non-judicious decisions that ensue from de-emphasizing of important social, economic, and environmental concerns. In a word, these concerns are political, and confound pure optimization theory and methods. This critique of mainstream optimization theory is not new (Tribe 1972). The aim here is for programming to account for multiple parameters according to sustainability principles.[1]

Design

Here, design deals with *network design*, which we distinguish from facility design. We will almost exclusively concentrate on the design of an entire network rather than an individual facility. Nonetheless, all infrastructure planning is executed on the ground through physical design, whether of networks or facilities. Network design concerns physical structure – the form, function, and distribution in geographic space of the entire infrastructure network. Network types include the electric power grid, water supply system, city street grid, metro or subway system, and the internet. Facility design for an individual infrastructure facility or node within a network pertains to engineering and architectural design. A facility can be a bridge, train station, sewage treatment plant, or a dam. A network is comprised of smaller networks, subnetworks, and facilities; and itself can be a subnetwork for larger ones. Nesting networks inside other networks synergistically adds value to each network. What we refer to as network design, some refer to as network planning. We use the term design to signify the creation of physical form, which we distinguish from planning, a term for the overall life cycle planning of a network, as presented in this chapter.

Physical design is a critical component of infrastructure planning because infrastructures are tangible physical objects that exert a fundamental presence in our lives, and because all urban planning, when implemented, is eventually executed on the ground through the design and building of structures of some sort. Design is a context-sensitive process that creates a time- and place-specific solution to a functional problem. This section presents general design principles that can be adapted to specific conditions in the creation of infrastructure networks. Design principles are general guides and not rigid rules. Local knowledge and cooperation during the design process supplements these principles and adapts them to prevailing conditions. The guidelines and principles which follow are suggestive rather than exhaustive.

Optimize the Number of Land Uses and Individual Users Served by Each Network

This fundamental principle of infrastructure design at the network level is a question of adding value through increasing the accessibility that infrastructure affords. Cities exemplify this principle, and city centers are the supreme example. Higher densities of activity are permitted by and in turn sow the need for more infrastructure – a city–infrastructure symbiosis. The goal of network design is to optimize connections. This principle applies to all human settlements, with differences in scale and extent of the infrastructure spelling the difference in the size of the settlement.

Facilitate Synergistic Co-location of Facilities

Synergistic co-location builds on the access optimization principle stated above. An example is to link modes of transportation at a commuting hub in a city center or edge city, or at a logistics hub like a seaport, airport, or railport. Doing so enhances accessibility and permits the optimal selection of transport modes in order to minimize energy use and pollution. It improves the chances to chain work, shopping, and other trips; and to share parking with other high-density, high-volume public, community, or commercial facilities. Designs that enable synergistic co-location also amplify the opportunities to share transportation rights-of-way with other infrastructure networks.

Share Rights-of-Way

Sharing rights-of-way affords numerous benefits and savings in the design of infrastructure networks. An infrastructure policy for sharing rights-of-way is critical outside urban areas for environmental preservation purposes – so multiple infrastructures do not chop up natural habitats so much. It is also critical inside urban areas, to save valuable land and to co-locate infrastructures. Sharing rights-of-way in rural areas along highways obviates the need to buy land for superfluous rights-of-way, maintain it, clear its vegetation, and secure its safety. It allows the safe passage of wildlife, keeps ecosystems intact, preserves the functional integrity of natural habitats, decreases wildfire danger from downed lines, and increases overall safety. Rights-of-way sharing can provide significant advantages if planned and designed properly. It takes unaccustomed foresight and collaboration among infrastructure entities that have had a historical tendency to plan and operate disjointedly. These interinstitutional transactions confer benefits well worth the costs.

There are limits to sharing rights-of-way, as seen in past mistakes. For example, in the 19th and most of the 20th centuries, storm sewers and sanitary sewers were designed to mix stormwater runoff and sewage in one duct. Combined water and sewer systems were the norm, in a misconceived effort to save costs. Over time, the mistake of this design became apparent in the aftermath of large rainstorms and floods. Combined systems overflowed because their capacity could not handle the rainfall from a large storm. Overflows contained large quantities of unprocessed sewage that spilled from the treatment plant, which backed up due to the excess flows. Since the environmental movement, many billions of dollars have been spent separating sewerage from stormwater runoff networks and cleaning up surface water and groundwater contaminated by these overflows. Another example is locating train tracks or roadways immediately next to rivers and other bodies of water, exposing them to flooding and cutting off the city or landscape from the water, and impeding natural flows vital to ecosystem function. Nonetheless, when properly planned and executed, sharing rights-of-way can confer many benefits.

Nest Networks Inside Other Networks

Nesting networks inside or alongside one another adds value to each network and the places and peoples they serve. In addition to the first three principles listed above – access, co-location, and sharing – which can be considered as specific types of nesting techniques, superposing infrastructure networks proffers other benefits. Enhanced economic innovation and productivity, cultural and artistic creativity, and unforeseen, unplanned opportunities are three key outcomes of skillful nesting. Often the best things happen by surprise, and these surprise chances favor the best prepared (by planning) and the best connected (by infrastructure). Civic engagement and civil society have been correlated with increased interactions that are afforded by infrastructure, including public gathering places.

Use Rate Process Criteria

Infrastructure networks are designed to transmit fluxes through conduits by definition. This essential nature of infrastructure brings into mind flow rates, which are expressed conceptually and mathematically using rate processes. Incorporating rate processes into infrastructure network design is essential to achieve sustainability.

Consider the free-flowing river. It is a transportation infrastructure, as well as a right-of-way that can be shared with other infrastructures, including properly sited roads, rails, electric power and telecommunications lines and towers, water conduits, recreation facilities, and energy-generating plants. Large dams that create reservoirs can be seen as synergistic, by providing recreational opportunities, large-scale power generation, and water storage. Yet the size of large dams inhibits the free flow of rivers and wildlife species dependent on them. In so restricting river flow and creating lakes, many infrastructure synergies are lost as a few are gained.

Now imagine a series of smaller scale turbines strung along the length of the river, each producing a fraction of the large-scale power station located at the large dam, yet maintaining free flow. Added together they can produce the same or even more power. Reconceiving the river as an integrated infrastructure system that maintains sustainable flow rates lets win-win designs prosper, obtaining power along with other benefits: least disruption to natural and cultural regimes (salmon runs, canoeing and kayaking, etc.), silt deposits that enrich agricultural bottom lands in the flood plain, natural flooding and cleansing regimes, irrigation that benefits from gravity flows, commercial river traffic, timber log floats, wildlife corridors, white water boating, canoeing and rafting, and fly fishing, to name just a few. Natural river flows sustain a prodigious number of processes that advantage humans as well as other species and ecosystems. This is a sustainable flow rate that requires no human inputs. No wonder smart planners have historically taken maximum advantage of the river's natural bounty.

Durability

What if we demanded that infrastructures last (only) twice as long as those built by our historical predecessors? That would halve construction costs and minimize impacts while increasing long-term sustainability. If aqueducts, canals, and buildings constructed 2000 years ago have lasted 500 years or more, then why do we accept 30 to one 100 year life spans today? For instance, solid natural stone in bridges, a meter or more thick, withstood the elements for a millennium or longer. When used in the walls of a building, thick stone afforded a type of insulation that permitted ambient cooling, heating, and ventilation instead of the massive, expensive, energy- and material-dependent, and unsustainable HVAC systems installed currently. The proper stone is well suited for building and infrastructure foundations as well, in addition to imparting an inimitable elegance and texture into appearance. Who can resist the warmth of granite in a public building or a bridge reflecting a glowing sunrise or sunset?

This principle calls for longer life spans for infrastructure in order to cut overall per annum investment costs, minimising impacts on the environment and population, and decreasing maintenance costs by investing in durable systems. Durability increases service reliability and decreases maintenance and replacement costs, and the disruptions they cause.

Permanence

Permanence has to do with the persistence of an infrastructure in its place, and the impacts it has on the place. In this way permanence draws upon physical durability, yet of course, differs from it as well. A ready example of permanence is the persistent use of travel paths by different species, and by different modes of motion by humans. Animal tracks and migration paths were transformed to human footpaths that followed the same route because it was a "natural" connection to vital elements such as sources of food and water, and places of shelter and gathering. A steady progression ensued, from footpath to vehicle path, from vehicle path to motorized vehicle path, from road to highway to multilane freeway, occasionally supplanted or adjoined by public transit and railways. Some of these paths-cum-superhighways have persisted for thousands of years, and will probably do so for thousands more, should we see that time.

Such persistence humbles transportation and infrastructure planning pretensions. It also provides a critical perspective on network design for sustainability. Permanence does not equal or assure sustainability – think of nuclear power plants. Yet factoring in permanence sharpens our sights on the consequences of the location and layout of infrastructure networks. A bridge over a river can fix the location of a city for millennia.

Permanence is not limited to transportation infrastructure. Some infrastructures endow permanence by protecting, like dikes and breakwaters. Another path to permanence by protection is to locate infrastructures and development away from the sources of natural hazards. This includes volcanoes, low lying coasts, flood plains, wildfire zones, and earthquake faults.

Infrastructure confers permanence in other ways. A coliseum, arena, auditorium, main public square, wide boulevard, central park, or any other prominent public gathering space not only confers place identity; it marks history by being the setting of historic events. Such public places not only imprint themselves on individual memory. They are the places in which collective memory is created and passed along through the generations. This vital function of infrastructure has gotten lost in efficiency paradigms along with cost-conscious and productivity-enhancing strategies prescribed by infrastructure financing and developing institutions. Historical analysis reveals that *genius loci* is conferred by the congenial design of public gathering places or other infrastructural monuments, and not only by the innate qualities of the place before settlement. The best places combine the two, marrying built and natural environments into an unforgettable and inspiring combination. This transcendental quality should be a common aspiration in infrastructure design.

Recyclability

Converting obsolete or otherwise unused infrastructure is an art of creative foresight. The creative redesign of an obsolete network or facility asserts its advantages when it is too costly, harmful, or otherwise unsuitable to dismantle or recycle it. The conversion of abandoned railroad tracks into hiking and biking trails is a case in point. Landfills converted to hilly parks, such as the many Mount Trashmores in the United States and Mount Junk (*Teufelsberg*) in Berlin, are other resourceful conversions. The *resourceful* conversion of what some consider waste is a prime exponent of what Kevin Lynch called "wasting well" (Lynch 1990).

Pragmatically, recycling cuts disposal costs, reduces toxics in waste streams that eventually end up in air, soil, or water sinks, reduces mining and material extraction costs, reduces manufacturing costs that use raw materials, and inspires creativity in infrastructure design, among numerous other benefits. Materials that have low embodied energy and are carbon balanced possess a greater degree of recyclability in that it costs less energy and other inputs (chemical, labor, machinery) to convert them or break them down. Using materials that are recyclable and creating designs that allow for easy dismantling and recycling comprise attractive challenges to gifted designers.

Wastability

Wasting is a natural process, and its product, waste, is a natural outcome. Everything inexorably and irresistibly turns to waste, as indicated by the laws of thermodynamics. Yet most Western societies do not tolerate waste and filth, often associating them with danger, illness, disease, and superstition. Elaborate rituals are employed to get rid of or avoid waste (Douglas 1966). Some of these attitudes are changing. Wasting has been embraced into design with profitable results (Hawken, Lovins, and Lovins 1999). *Wastability* refers to how a product or infrastructure wastes. It also refers to how much waste material there is and its degree of assimilability into natural and cultural environments. Wastability is a term that captures these characteristics (Lynch 1990).

Quality wastability can be illustrated by nature. The banana is touted as the perfect package. Its peel is the perfect packaging. The fruit is 100 percent edible. The packing is 100 percent degradable. No additional materials, processing, or cooking is required. The main sustainability concerns are its growing methods and transportation costs. Can banana principles be mimicked and applied to infrastructure design? A design that considers how waste will be absorbed into natural and cultural processes without disruption or harm, like a banana, is a sustainable design. The flip side of wastability is designing so there is as little waste in the future as possible. These are good starting points for sustainable infrastructure network design where the output of one process becomes the input to another. This integrates infrastructures sustainably.

Visibility

Why have infrastructures, or galleries that contain multiple conduits of infrastructures, been located underground? Why not transparent and above ground where possible? This way people can see the conduits, instead of being hidden underground. A good example is the Centre Pompidou museum in Paris. It might also inspire more aesthetic and visually pleasing designs. People would be exposed to and learn about the persistent presence, functions, and importance of infrastructure. This in turn aids the political process through more widespread understanding and acceptance, placing infrastructure higher on priority lists for funding and resources. Above ground exposure, or below ground if covered transparently, is more challenging in dense metropolitan areas. Beautiful bridges and dams, city halls, civic buildings and stadia, boulevards and waterfronts nevertheless are classic instances of the positive effects of visible infrastructures. Can pipes and wires be as beautifully designed and packaged?

Cost Accounting

Once a network or facility is designed, its construction costs can be calculated. Life cycle *cost accounting* goes to the heart of sustainable infrastructure planning in a capitalist economy, whether market based, centrally planned, or mixed social welfare in its form. In a capitalist economy, an economic calculus is the predominant criterion by which capital investment decisions are made. Finance capital is invested with the expectation of accruing future returns. Investment decisions are evaluated by the expected rate of return on the initial investment. For infrastructure investments, the amount of debt available for investors to purchase is based in part on the value of the infrastructure, for which accurate cost estimates are required. Consequently, how cost is calculated bears on investment decisions, and thus on their returns. By this logic, the method by which cost is accounted for becomes a de facto evaluation criterion. Under these conditions, an important avenue by which to introduce sustainability into capital investment decision-making is through cost accounting.

Life cycle costing introduces sustainability as a costing criterion across the entire life cycle of a network or facility. A life cycle costing approach goes beyond traditional cost accounting methods by expanding costing methods to include calculations for all costs over the entire service life. Also referred to as sustainability accounting techniques. See https://www.globalreporting.org and https://www.globalreporting.

org for example. Internationally it has various names, including full cost accounting (Bebbington, Unerman, O'Dwyer 2014), true cost accounting (Soil & More Impacts and TMG Thinktank for Sustainability 2020), and environmental-economic accounting (https://seea.un.org/). The common thread among the approaches is to account monetarily for as complete set of factors across each of the 15 steps of the life of an infrastructure, also incorporating embodied energy, materials, transport, and impacts. Life cycle costing is cradle-to-cradle accounting that more completely encompasses all the costs associated with an infrastructure network.

Life cycle cost accounting goes to the heart of sustainable infrastructure planning. Life cycle costs include all the expenses that are expected over the working life of the infrastructure. The benefit of life cycle cost accounting is that the resultant monetary costs, when fed into a capital budget, permit all activities over the entire life cycle to be anticipated, planned, funded, and managed. Life cycle costs become the basis of life cycle budgets, which permit the calculation of sustainable streams of revenue to be generated and allocated throughout the service life of the infrastructure system. This overcomes the limitations of current budgeting practices and financing based on it, which cover capital (construction) costs only, leaving the rest of the life cycle unfunded or reliant on discretionary income that can be unreliable. Thus, without knowing life cycle costs, revenues to fund the entire life cycle cannot be budgeted. This limits financing options and potential revenue sources.

Impact Assessment

Once an infrastructure system is selected, designed, and costed; then an *impact assessment* can be conducted. This impact assessment can also be comparative, by evaluating different options available. The impact assessment measures and evaluates the consequences the system has on its environments and socioeconomic groups in its service area and the broader spatial territory. This type of comprehensive impact assessment can be fed back into the technology selection stage of the life cycle planning process, providing more criteria for that decision. Impact assessment methods are common around the world, evolving significantly since being introduced in the 1970s. Most jurisdictions have laws that specify how they are to be conducted. Yet statutory assessments tend not to evaluate the entire life cycle, yielding opportunities for their improvement. Impact assessment is among the stages of life cycle planning that benefit greatly from increased stakeholder participation because diverse stakeholders can identify impacts related to their place, interest, and specialty, which otherwise may be left uncovered by routine assessment methods.

Budgeting

A vital link between infrastructure programs and their financing is the capital budget. In contrast to a typical capital budget, a *life cycle capital budget* details specific planning, design, construction, maintenance, and rehabilitation costs, along with environmental and social impact mitigation costs, throughout the entire life cycle. This is what sets life cycle budgeting apart from standard practices. It enables a more sustainable approach to be incorporated into organizational practices. For a comparison among Assessments, Programs, and Budgets, see Figure 5.2.

A capital budget is a management tool that tracks and guides the income and expenditure of funds to build capital projects on an annual basis. Capital budgets are distinguished from operating budgets for accounting convenience. Budgeting converts a medium-term program of about five years into a short-term budget of one to two years, depending on the budget cycle.

As an annual snapshot of the financial management for the infrastructure assets of an organization, annual budgets tend to dominate infrastructure decision-making in the public sector, instead of longer term capital plans or programs. Budgeting is conducted according to laws which vary place to place. In actual practice, most capital budgets are local blends of zero-based budgeting, prior-year-based budgeting, and performance-based budgeting. Nonetheless, a California observer characterized the process in this way: "Try as one might, the natural law that governs the budget process is: 'you get what you got in the prior year, plus growth'" (California Constitution Revision Commission 1996, 37).

Part of the reason for this is that sometimes bad economic conditions afford little discretionary funds to allocate in the capital budget. Another reason, regardless of the blend of budget types (performance, prior year, zero-based), is that the complexity, opacity, and low priority of the process give little incentive. Polity-wide budgets are often summed up from individual agencies' requests for specific facility projects, instead of a long-term plan. But does a wish list of projects make a good

---

Assessments of Demand
- Long term: 20 to 30 or more years into the future.
- Based on demographic projections for user populations: population, housing, employment, industry needs.
- Based on equations which a standard demand per capita is assumed: total demand equals the demand per capita times the projected future population.
- Also called Needs Assessments.

Capital Programs
- Medium term: four to six years into the future.
- Based on design cost estimates for specific facilities and networks.
- Also called Capital Plans, Capital Improvement (or Investment) Programs, Capital Improvement (or Investment) Plans, CIPs.

Capital Budgets
- Short term: one to two years into the future.
- Based on actual construction costs for specific facilities or networks.

Figure 5.2 Comparison Chart of Assessments, Programs, and Budgets

capital budget? Agencies use their own processes and criteria in determining their priority lists. Funding priority at the overall jurisdiction level is often determined by ranking dissimilar projects against one another, leading agencies to compete with each other on uneven footing. In addition, in a political environment, bargaining determines which projects obtain funding according to power and influence. A life cycle approach adopted jurisdiction wide can correct these deficiencies.

Financing

To be covered in Chapter 8.

Construction

This is not covered in this text, as it is specific to each type of infrastructure, and is more properly the province of engineering and technical specialties.

Operations

This is not covered in this text, as it is specific to each type of infrastructure, and is more properly the province of engineering and technical specialties.

Maintenance and Repair

For our purposes, we distinguish between *maintenance* and *repair*. Maintenance is the routine work that is done to keep a system operating in good order, to maintain service satisfaction among users, and to prevent deterioration that can be avoided with regular, quality maintenance. Repair is the one-off work done to fix a system once it fails or falls below service standards. The key here is to incorporate both routine maintenance and foreseeable (programmable) repair into the life cycle. This leads to incorporating both into planning and design, so labor and material costs are built into the system, rather than being an afterthought or reaction. Further, it leads to preparing programs and budgets that routinely account for all maintenance and repairs. It also means developing life cycle financing that incorporates repair and maintenance, so that their budgets are systemically funded and do not get cut in economic downturns or due to political whim.

Rehabilitation and Replacement

This stage in the life cycle planning process is treated lightly, as it is technical matter specific to each system or facility. While *rehabilitation and replacement* are addressed in engineering and management texts and professional standards, it is important to cost and budget for this stage and then to finance it in an ongoing way so that it does not get overlooked, as indicated above for maintenance and repair. By considering this and the prior stage along a continuum permits them to be better incorporated into the life cycle.

The Continuum of Maintenance, Repair, Rehabilitation, and Replacement

A common cause of infrastructure problems stems from deficiencies in maintenance, repair, and rehabilitation. Study after study has reported failures due to disrepair and deterioration; accidents leading to property loss, injury, and death; decreases in environmental quality, public health, economic output and productivity; as well as premature facility failure or retirement. By including these stages squarely in the life cycle, they receive greater attention in managerial and political agendas.

A well-developed Maintenance, Repair, Rehabilitation, and Replacement (MRRR) System, if implemented fully and correctly, can be expected to minimize physical deterioration and system downtime while it maximizes system performance and uptime. MRRR systems are types of Operational Support Systems (OSS) and Decision Support Systems (DSS). Texts going back decades indicate the data requirements and other parameters needed to develop the database for a life cycle infrastructure maintenance decision support system (Biondini and Frangopol 2019). Indicators used in MRRR databases serve as inputs into a comprehensive performance evaluation system. To improve MRRR system management in the context of spatial planning, and to integrate the two, the MRRR database can be linked with a geographic information system (GIS). This allows the physical and operating conditions to be correlated with the spatial location of the facilities and conduits of infrastructure networks in order to improve management. For an indication of the expected life span of infrastructures according to early 21st century criteria, see Figure 5.3. When planned, designed, and maintained in accordance with sustainable and life cycle criteria and methods such as those presented in this book, these can be doubled, tripled, or extended even further.

Evaluation

Evaluation tells any interested party how well an organization accomplishes its mission. This follows the old adage "you can't manage what you can't measure".

Airport buildings	50–70
Airport runways and aprons	40–50
Bridge decks	20–30
Bridge sub- and super-structures	50–100
Dams	80–100
Vehicle tunnels	80–100
Nuclear power plants	20–40
Ports, marine terminals	70–100
Public buildings	30–100
Transmission lines	50–100

Figure 5.3 Typical Expectations of Infrastructure Service Life in Years

Source: *Hudson, Haas, and Uddin 1997, page 172, Table 8.1*

Linking evaluation to the life cycle planning process provides a complete database that serves as an essential management tool for each stage of the life cycle.

For infrastructure, evaluation measures fall into three categories: monitoring the organization and its management, monitoring the physical condition of the infrastructure, and monitoring the services provided. Performance measures that use comprehensive life cycle sustainability criteria are best. The landmark impact analysis of the 1992 *New Jersey State Plan* was an early example that illustrates an application of these types of criteria (Burchell 1992). Internationally, standards have been developed by the International Standards Organization (ISO) and the World Bank, among others (ISO 14000 series for Environmental Management Systems and ISO 2018; Farvacque-Vitkovic and Kopanyi 2019). Comprehensive assessment models that employ a greater number and wider variety of criteria to evaluate performance have become more common.

In developing a life cycle-based evaluation program for infrastructure, first select what it is that you seek to evaluate. Second, select standards or benchmarks to measure the performance of these items. See Appendix 3 for a list of international institutional sources of sustainability indicators. Then, develop a database that arrays the items to be evaluated and their benchmarks according to a monitoring schedule over the entire life cycle. Next, conduct periodic field evaluations by checking equipment condition, service performance, and organizational effectiveness. Then, analyze and interpret the field data. Finally, results and consequences for practise should be recorded in the database if ongoing managerial and decision-making processes are to profit from the evaluation.

Conducting a life cycle evaluation performs a number of functions for the infrastructure agency. It provides greater accountability to politicians, managers, owners, users, citizens, and interest groups. It increases organizational effectiveness by providing a comprehensive assessment framework to improve processes and information. It helps the organization's staff to plan and manage by offering benchmarks to focus attention and priorities. Evaluation programs help legitimize and improve planning processes by providing performance targets. These targets apply internal discipline to the organization to hold management and employees accountable. Evaluation improves the communication of information by providing explicit goals, objectives, and performance measures. In addition to being the touchstone for democratic transparency by both publishing and making available to the public the evaluation process and criteria, it can include citizens, interest groups, and so on in participative, democratic processes. Evaluation programs are used to review and improve life cycle cost and benefit methods as well as MRRR budgets and programs. Robust and comprehensive evaluation programs help predict rates of equipment deterioration and possible failure, which assists MRRR scheduling (ISO 14000 and 9000 series).

Evaluating infrastructure is an activity waged on many fronts. Infrastructure can be gauged on the basis of service performance (on time, continuous availability, reliability), user satisfaction (ease of access and use, meets expectations, quality of experience), physical condition (structural integrity, load capacity, deterioration), safety (accidents, injury, property loss), and / or security (risk, vulnerability). Other criteria include contributions to society and the economy, its environmental, social, and other impacts on its surroundings, and the distributional equity of its accessibility. This list is suggestive, not limiting.

Reassessment of Needs – Return to the Beginning

As we have seen, fundamental to life cycle planning is to treat infrastructure as having a life span, also known as service life. Each type of infrastructure has its specific life cycle. This entails a long-term view of infrastructure networks and their consequences in urban spatial terms. Long term can mean hundreds of years. This goes beyond the time scales commonly considered for modern infrastructure systems, in which short term is one election or accounting cycle (usually one to four years), medium term is perhaps five to ten years, and long term ranges between ten and thirty years. Curtailing time horizons has led to the decrease of practices that are truly sustainable.

A dramatic example of the long-term consequences of infrastructure can be seen by comparing irrigation practices of Egyptian and Mesopotamian civilizations 5,000 years ago:

> Egyptians relied on [Nile River] basin irrigation, trapping flood waters behind dikes, letting the fertile soil settle on the land, and then allowing surplus water to run off downstream when it became time to plant. This prevented salt buildup, whereas in Mesopotamia salt accumulated year after year when irrigation water evaporated from the fields, since even fresh water contains a little salt. This process eventually turned the land of Sumer into the desert it is today. Egypt, however, remained fertile (McNeill and McNeill 2003, 52–53).

In other words, had the Sumerians used a sustainable irrigation (infrastructure) practice that considered long-term impacts, the once fertile Mesopotamian Valley might not have turned into a desert, and world history would likely have been altered significantly.

There are other notable instances of the long-term impacts of infrastructure. The walls and layout of the Forbidden City in Beijing determined the principles of physical urban planning throughout China for over half a millennium. Dikes and canals in the Netherlands not only carved out land for settlements from the sea, they also shaped urban form in cities such as Amsterdam, and have exerted their influence for upwards of five hundred years. Medieval and Renaissance city walls in Europe, now torn down but then serving defensive purposes, still delimit the historic urban centers, currently in vogue as cultural precincts and tourist destinations. Many Indian trails in the United States became pioneer trails, and in turn roads, turnpikes, highways, and / or railways. This pattern of succession in pathways, often themselves treading upon animal paths, has been repeated on every continent, with some paths cum roads thousands of years old. Through path succession, roads convey the longevity and *gravitas* of infrastructure. This characteristic makes planning decisions about roads extremely consequential for the long term, punctuating the importance of life cycle planning and taking the longest possible view of an infrastructure's "life" and its footprints.

Caveats to Keep in Mind

Life cycle assessment (LCA) is a performance-oriented method when linked to levels of service. LCA is also an analytical tool to measure long-term value. When referred to as "cradle to grave", "well to wheel", or "farm to table", for example, it imparts the sense of a long-term accounting of input and output factors, including upstream and downstream impacts and embodied energy. While different methods are emerging and applications are increasing, LCA is extraordinarily data intensive, limiting its use. Its greater employment in planning is hampered because most accounting and inventory systems were not designed with LCA data needs in mind.

Any valid life cycle approach for urban infrastructure and its planning must answer the following question: What are the most effective methods and models to measure and project future scenarios for the full sustainability of infrastructures, including embodied energy and carbon, comprehensive economic and environmental impacts, and social equity?

Some other infrastructure planning tools are antiquated, such as *cost-benefit assessment* (CBA) and *environmental impact assessment* (EIA). They are being replaced by new tools such as combined risk and cost-benefit assessment (National Research Council 2014). Even an analytical tool as ostensibly straightforward as cost benefit analysis is fraught with problems in application and limited in its capacity to inform decisions in a conclusive manner (Laird, Nash, and Mackie 2014). They are less applicable to complex networks that intersect with other networks. Moreover, as conditions change rapidly, such as costs skyrocketing due to unforeseen circumstances arising during the long periods for the design, approval, and construction of large infrastructures (CBA), or climate change, pandemics, disasters, etc. that complicate EIA calculations, these tools become more circumspect.

The question is not merely how to improve or better use these and other tools. The question is how to align these tools (or create new ones) with money and power. Tools are the province of technocrats and professionals, while power is the province of politics and finance. It is the latter who are the ultimate arbiters of infrastructure decisions. What values and methods are to be incorporated into planning without compromising the health, safety, and welfare values of the past and sustainability and equity values of today?

Linking Infrastructure Planning to Urban and Spatial Planning

What does life cycle infrastructure planning imply for city and regional planning? Due to their common threads, life cycle infrastructure planning is easily woven into urban planning techniques, like spatial planning, growth management, land use, urban design, urban regeneration, and community development. The life cycle approach is a primary tool that can link urban planning with infrastructure planning.

In the context of urban planning, linking the rate process to the life cycle method frames decisions regarding infrastructure, scale network arrangement, and connectivity. Further, rate process methods inform performance measures used in the evaluation stage of life cycle planning. Rate process measurements enable continuous monitoring and assessment of the sustainability of infrastructure throughout its life. Finally, the life cycle approach allows planners and managers to steward infrastructure sustainably over its entire working life.

Taken together, these techniques let planners integrate or consolidate the "layers" of settlements – natural systems, infrastructure systems, and superstructures (visible urban form) – through the practice of spatial planning that reflects the way we actually experience cities, towns, and suburbs in daily life: as a unified piece. To use an analogy:

> listening to music is a seamless experience. We hear the music and not the studio, the conductor, the score, and so on. We use infrastructure seamlessly as well. We do not necessarily know or care when a phone line becomes an optical signal, digital transmission, or microwave relay; or local street becomes a county road, state highway, or federal freeway. We just want to communicate and get there (Neuman and Whittington 2000, 81).

The process presented in this and the governance chapter enables the integration of infrastructure and urban planning in a way that results in more seamless infrastructures, and in cities that are more sustainable and more physically integrated.

Network Planning and Technology Selection

Networked infrastructures necessitate networked planning. Networked infrastructures, as city-region shapers, exert a two-sided influence. One side is the integrating influence of infrastructure on societies and economies, and its effect as an integrator of urban space. Infrastructure services such as public schools, libraries, water, roads, and sewage disposal that are designed to deliver the same or similar levels of service to an entire population in an area are integrators of urban space, by providing a degree of homogeneity and coherence. The same infrastructures can also splinter or fragment urban space physically as a barrier, and socially, by inequitable provision to different segments of a population. In this sense, the type of infrastructure technology and its geographic deployment and distribution determines whether it integrates or splinters urban space.

This double-edged sword can be seen in two different examples. One occurs in less industrialized economies, where potable water flowing through pipes directly into the home is reserved for developed urban areas inhabited by the wealthy, while poor residents of marginal slums and rural areas rarely have potable water piped to their homes. The poor may pay up to hundreds of times more for a unit of water which they buy in small quantities from private sources such as street vendors, which they then have to haul back to their home or business. In this case, differences in water provision result in splintered urban space, potential public health problems, and gross social inequities.

In another instance, in developed countries' urban areas, must a house or building be connected to infrastructure networks, such as the power grid, storm sewers, or water supply? Or may they be permitted to be more self-sufficient, using renewable services available on-site, such as renewable energy, natural drainage, and rainfall? Existing planning and building codes in many jurisdictions do not enable the off-grid option. As a result, development is automatically plugged into existing non-sustainable networks at great costs. Smaller scale networks have economic benefits. They allow easier producer entry into the marketplace, making it more competitive. Smaller plants increase the range of ownership options. They also allow production closer to end users, reducing reliance on transmission and distribution networks, thus undermining the natural monopoly characteristics of large networks.

These two cases illustrate the impact of network design and technology choice on infrastructure, and their links to sustainability. To handle these issues, network technology choices and the geographic layout of the networks should provide user options and flexibility so that long-term sustainability is explicitly considered. Otherwise, urban space can become splintered by infrastructures, so that the terms "the other side of the tracks" and "digital divide" reflect inequitable disparities. Often, financial-technological-professional complexes inhibit alternatives, and most consumers and even infrastructure and urban planners do not consider options outside path-dependent norms. Using the tools presented in this book provides infrastructurists with powerful methods for addressing the complex and interrelated conditions that infrastructure generates.

Selected Examples of Infrastructure Planning

Three examples of infrastructure networks in Barcelona, Spain illustrate good design and planning principles. They are highway planning, shared utilities tunnels, and an integrated megaproject.

In Barcelona's remarkable planning-led transformation for the 1992 summer Olympic Games, an overlooked aspect was that the transformation almost completely involved infrastructure, including critical underground infrastructure such as reconstructing stormwater drainage. We highlight two aspects of that infrastructure transformation, the new ring roads as they traversed the dense historic center and the multi-conduit infrastructure galleries placed underground.

Architects and urban designers worked with highway engineers to stitch the ring road into the urban fabric seamlessly, as a plastic surgeon stitches a face. Their designs minimized cutting into (tearing down) the existing city. In addition, the upper ring road was depressed below grade in U-shaped, open-air road beds or fully undergrounded in tunnels. (A lower ring road, near the sea, was also built below grade, yet open to the sky or tunneled along some stretches.) Over time, some stretches of the open-air roadway were covered with parks, recreational facilities, other buildings, and streets in places where they fit deftly into the adjoining urban tissue. This contrasts dramatically with the sledgehammer analogy used to describe the bludgeoning perpetrated on many historic North American city centers by urban freeways since the 1960s.

In Barcelona, below ground infrastructure "galleries" house a number of conduits – cables and pipes – that in other cities are separately placed in their own channels, if not directly in the dirt. Infrastructure galleries are tunnels located underground that afford easy access for expansion, maintenance, and replacement; with minimum disruption to surface activities or other infrastructures. The largest galleries, serving as collectors, are located alongside major highways and rail lines. Infrastructure galleries also allow easy field inspections. They permit planning to proceed with more certainty because nearly all infrastructures are neatly and orderly assembled in one maxi-conduit. The list of items in the gallery is long: electric wiring, cables for television, telephone, and the internet, water supply pipes, sewerage pipes, stormwater conduits, and anything else that can be delivered via wire, cable, or pipe. The infrastructure gallery is an evolutionary advance over the previous maze of poorly charted (in some places, uncharted) wires, pipes, and conduits. Integrated galleries do not hinder building construction, and in fact lower design and construction costs because their location is mapped with certainty, and because the galleries are out of the way rather than scattered and jumbled underneath the city. Another good example of sustainable urban district revitalization that included undergrounding of utilities in tunnels is the former harbor district in Stockholm, Hammarby Sjöstad.

Box 5.5 The Forum 2004 in Barcelona

A two square kilometer urban district on the shore of the Mediterranean was transformed from an ugly, smelly, noisy, polluting trio of metro-scale infrastructures – a solid waste incinerator, a sewage treatment plant, and an electricity generation plant – into a world's fair with a convention center, recreational boating harbor, two waterfront parks, a cultural event district, and a university sub-campus; while still keeping the three infrastructures *in situ* and operational, and making them more sustainable. How did they do it?

Barcelona turned the usual formula used to site waste infrastructures inside out by converting NIMBY infrastructures that repelled into attractive and productive destinations. Instead of a major blight, people were attracted to the formerly polluting infrastructures because of the quality of their conversion and their new uses in the district. The solid waste incinerator was converted into an electricity co-generating plant. Its effluent gases were cleaned up so much that a large new city park was placed at its base. The sewage treatment plant added tertiary treatment, eliminated sludge discharge into the sea, and employed a sludge drying plant that doubles as a co-generator, producing 25 megawatts of power. Fourth stage biological treatment was added. A combined sewer outfall was split into separate stormwater and sewerage systems, further enhancing water discharge quality. The place where the sewage treatment plant meets the sea is now a recreational marina and a public park with open-sea swimming. The preexisting power plant was converted from diesel generation to cleaner fuel sources. Finally, 17,000 square feet of new photovoltaic panels sit atop a sculptural pergola, generating 1.3 megawatts of power (Acebillo 2004).

These improvements converted hazardous and unsightly infrastructures into safe and sustainable ones, and created attractive public places. They spurred urban development nearby, including hotels, thousands of housing units, and a large park. It propelled the redevelopment of some of the poorest neighborhoods (including *La Mina*) just inland from the site. Instead of the usual NIMBY treatment, citizens are now lured to this former wasteland by exemplars of planning and design that combine beauty with biology in the treatment of everyday sewage and trash, and combine elegance and engineering in the generation of power.

Bringing it All Together

The life cycle method of infrastructure planning and management is structured to allow practitioners from any discipline to understand the complete life cycle from their discipline's point of departure. It situates professional practice in a long-term, comprehensive, and sustainable context. Thus, an engineer can consider the multiple impacts of a network on the landscape and adjust the design accordingly. An engineer can also evaluate the environmental and energetic costs and impacts of the materials used to build the infrastructure. A programmer for a school district can work with a land use planner to best locate school buildings in a community to encourage development where desired (and minimize auto trips to and from school), and work with parks and recreation planners to coordinate athletic field and playground use, and with civic officials to program activities that occur outside of school hours in school facilities. This has the added benefits of increasing civic involvement by community members who have more opportunities to interact, and saving money by the multiple programming of facilities. A budget analyst can collaborate with engineers to attain the lowest life cycle costs that consider the full ramifications of an infrastructure system's construction, operations, and maintenance – and not merely materials and labor costs. Moreover, budgeters can cooperate with urban planners to determine what the full range of cost and benefit assessment criteria should be. A financial manager or investment firm can work with budget analysts to fashion a life cycle financing process that provides a sustainable stream of money to pay for all the requirements of an infrastructure network throughout its service life. A politician can set the overall goals, general evaluation guidelines, priorities, and the legal-institutional framework for life cycle planning, and monitor them by legislative oversight. Urban planners can coordinate the entire effort by designing and managing processes that engage collaboration of all participants. Their knowledge of place and planning, of institutions and processes, along with their comprehensive and long-term outlook that evaluates the multiple future consequences of current decisions and actions makes planners suited for a coordinating role. Each participant and profession plays a role in the life cycle.

The knowledge needed to plan, design, and manage infrastructure fills shelves of books and technical manuals. This chapter focused on life cycle methods. Yet planning and design are not merely number crunching exercises. The chapter is a guide for the physical design of the infrastructure, the distillation and manifestation of planning. Design embodies and gives shape and meaning to the energy and materials extracted, fabricated, and recycled; bringing the life cycle to life. Design places infrastructure in the hands of the user, and shapes each user's direct experience of it. Infrastructure design, when coupled with urban design and physical planning, sews the facilities and networks into the fabric of the city and region. Fitting into place as hand in glove is what good physical design and planning seek to accomplish.

Note

1 Optimization theory is a broad field that has engaged mathematicians, statisticians, management scientists, computer programmers, engineers, operations researchers, and their counterparts in related disciplines since its founding during World War II. Optimization theory is robust, as is its offshoot, linear and nonlinear programming. As many physical and social phenomena have been reconceptualized as network phenomena over the last few decades, the new field of network theory was developed. In time, optimization methods were applied to network problems, including infrastructure. The merger of optimization and network theories gave rise to network programming, whose main intent is to optimize the performance of a given network according to a specified parameter.

References

Acebillo, J. (2004). Una nueva geografía urbana, *Arquitectura Viva*, 94(95): 44–53.
Altshuler, A. and Luberoff, D. (2003). *Mega-projects: The Changing Politics of Urban Public Investment*. Washington DC: Brookings Institution Press.
Bebbington, J., Unerman, J. O'Dwyer, B. (eds.) (2014). *Sustainability Accounting and Accountability*. London and New York: Routledge, 2nd edition.

Biondini, F. and Frangopol, D. (eds.). (2019). *Life-Cycle Design, Assessment, and Maintenance of Structures and Infrastructure Systems.* Washington DC: American Society of Civil Engineers.

Burchell, R. (1992). *Impact assessment of the New Jersey State Development and Redevelopment Plan.* Trenton, NJ: New Jersey Office of State Planning.

California Constitution Revision Commission. (1996). *Executive Summary: Final Report and Recommendations to the Governor and the Legislature.* Sacramento, CA: Author.

Douglas, M. (2003 [1966]). *Purity and Danger: An Analysis of Concepts of Pollution and Taboo.* London: Routledge.

Farvacque-Vitkovic, C. and Kopanyi, M. (2019). *Better Cities, Better World : A Handbook on Local Governments Self-Assessments.* Washington DC: World Bank.

Flyvberg, B., Bruzelius, N., and Rosengatter, W. (2003). *Megaprojects and Risk: An Anatomy of Ambition.* New York: Cambridge University Press.

Hall, P. (1982). *Great Planning Disasters.* Berkeley, CA: University of California Press.

Hawken, P., Lovins, A., and Lovins, L. H. (1999). *Natural Capitalism.* Boston, MA: Little Brown.

Hudson, R., Haas, R., and Uddin, W. (1997). *Infrastructure Management: Integrating Design, Construction, Maintenance, Rehabilitation and Renovation.* New York: McGraw Hill.

ISO (International Standards Organization). (2018). *The Integrated Use of Management System Standards (IUMSS).* Geneva: ISO.

Laird, J., Nash, C., & Mackie, P. (2014). Transformational transport infrastructure: Cost-benefit analysis challenges. *Town Planning Review*, 85(6): 709–731.

Lynch, K. (1990). *Wasting Away.* San Francisco: Sierra Club Books.

Lynch, K. (1981). *Good City Form.* Cambridge, MA: MIT Press.

McDonough, W. and Braungart, M. (2010). *Cradle to Cradle: Remaking the Way We Make Things, 2nd edition.* New York: Farrar, Straus and Giroux.

McHarg, Ian L. (1969). *Design With Nature.* Garden City, NY: Natural History Press.

McNeill, J. R. and McNeill, W. H. (2003). *The Human Web: A Bird's Eye View of World History.* New York: W. W. Norton.

National Research Council. (2014). *Reducing Coastal Risks on the East and Gulf Coasts*, Washington DC: Author.

Neuman, M. and Whittington, J. (2000). *Building California's Future: Current Conditions in California's Infrastructure Planning, Budgeting and Financing.* San Francisco: Public Policy Institute of California.

Soil & More Impacts and TMG Thinktank for Sustainability. (2020). *True Cost Accounting: Inventory Report.* Toronto: Global Alliance for the Future of Food.

Three Gorges Dam Project

Facts

- **Who:** The People's Republic of China, Three Gorges Corporation
- **What:** the largest, most expensive dam in the world
- **Where:** Yangtze River, near Yichang, Hubei province
- **Height:** 181 meters
- **Length:** 2,335 meters
- **Submerged rivers:** approximately 600 kilometers upstream
- **Number of laborers:** 1.13 million
- **Installed power generation capacity:** 22,500 megawatts
- **When:** approved in 1992, construction began 1994, completed 2006
- **Why:** Flood control, power generation, improved navigation
- **How much:** $32 billion, approximately

Planning and Sustainability

Yangtze River is the longest river in the People's Republic of China. The idea of building a gigantic dam in the Three Gorges area to harness the Yangtze River is not new. First talks began in the 1920s, and Mao Zhedong promoted the idea in the 1950s, resulting in initial planning. After a long time spent on meticulous feasibility studies, on April 3, 1992, the National People's Congress approved the construction of the project.

The Three Gorges Project has its main benefits in flood control, power generation, and navigation. Historically, the population is serious threatened by flooding. The project's reservoir has flood control storage of 22.1 billion cubic meters. The dam was designed to increase flood control capacity from the present 10-year frequency to

100-year frequency. With its total installed capacity of 22,500 megawatts, the Three Gorges Hydropower Station generates on average 85–105 TWH a year, one-ninth of the national total generated power at the time of its completion. Thirdly, the project enabled 10,000-ton ships to sail upstream 2,250 kilometers from Shanghai, as far as Chongqing City. The Yangtze's navigation capacity was increased significantly.

The project also presented daunting problems and undesired impacts. These included resettlement of a population of about 1.3 million from over 1,500 villages and towns. The destruction of scenic landscapes, unique habitats, heritage buildings, and archeological treasures were significant. Water pollution and deforestation along with coastal erosion and altered ecosystems endanger many species. A direct impact of the dam is erosion and huge landslides, which has led to significant silting of the river and the loss of fertile topsoil downstream.

Finance

The project is thought to have cost more than any other single construction project in history. The project was completed in 2006 after 12 years of construction. The total investment for the project amounted to 203 billion Yuan (US $32 billion). The funds come from several sources: the Three Gorges Construction Fund, revenues from the Gezhouba Sam Hydropower Plant, power revenues from the Three Gorges Project starting from the year 2003, loans and credits from the China Development Bank and other domestic and international banks, and corporate bonds. In spite of the above sources, it is estimated that there exists a funding gap of billions of dollars. This gap was made up through domestic loans, export credits, overseas commercial loans, and bond issuance.

Sources: Encyclopedia Britannica and Wikipedia

6
Demand-Capacity Management

This chapter lays out a spatial planning method by which to determine and distribute spatially the amount of infrastructure projected to be needed in a geographic jurisdiction at a specified future, so that policy and financing decisions can be made. This method is based on a comprehensive suitability analysis of the entire jurisdiction that takes in to account three factors:

1. Existing population, housing, and jobs; and their locations.
2. Existing infrastructures in place, including deficits in service quality and quantity of existing infrastructures, and
3. future projections for population, housing, and jobs; and their locations. This could incorporate scenarios that compare projections and locations.

Comprehensive *demand-capacity management* is designed to be integrated into planning processes that prepare a spatial plan. This chapter integrates several strands of infrastructure planning into an integrated and comprehensive approach applicable at any scale. Demand-capacity analysis involves two steps. First is to perform a demand-capacity analysis of the geographic area being planned, to determine the overall demand for infrastructure services needed at a specified future time in a geographic area, consistent with the ecological, social, and economic capacities of that area. The second step is to conduct a life cycle analysis of an infrastructure network, which assays its sustainable stewardship over the infrastructure's entire working life, as outlined in Chapter 5. These two steps link infrastructure planning with urban planning to provide a comprehensive evidentiary basis for sustainable infrastructure.

Infrastructure is a preeminent urban growth management tool. Infrastructure either can be withheld in order to stop or stifle development, or it can enable and encourage it. Simply put, no infrastructure means no urban development. Denying infrastructure in this way effectively protects and maintains rural and natural environments as they are. This approach can be used to great effect in low lying coastal areas subject to recurring severe storms, earthquakes, tidal waves, and other extreme natural events; saving lives, property, hardship, money, and insurance claims while maintaining the ecological integrity of habitats and the functional integrity of their processes. On the other hand, infrastructure can bolster the density and mix of people and activity, "supercharging" development.

A balanced growth management strategy for an urban area encompasses both ends of the spectrum and points between. It apportions infrastructure in a concerted manner over time to impulse growth where and when it is desired and reigns it in where and when it is not. This type of advance planning designates a graduated set of areas (districts, zones, tiers) in which the scale and timing of the primary growth-*inducing* infrastructures (water, sewerage, and transportation) and primary growth-*supporting* ones match planned development expectations. In this way infrastructure is built in outlying areas only after inner areas where infrastructure already exists are fully developed. This timing and sequencing of infrastructure development to stimulate growth uses the same principle as time-release vitamins. Infrastructure-based growth management, when properly conceived and applied, prevents hopscotch and leapfrog sprawl settlement patterns. It also limits squandering the existing capacities of capital facilities.

A hierarchical "tier" system of growth, future growth, limited growth, and no growth zones can be identified, mapped, and managed by using infrastructure as a king pin in the growth management process. Inner urban core areas receive a higher priority for growth, other urban areas and older inner ring suburbs a somewhat lower priority, new suburbs and exurbs even lower, and the lowest priority for urban infrastructure is in the rural, agricultural, and natural environments outside the urban fringe. Infrastructure-based growth management reflects the convergence of environmental protection and urban revitalization interests, who have realized that their aims are mutually compatible.

A more articulated version of infrastructure-based growth management is to structure additional priorities to target growth or no-growth spots within larger areas. Targeted growth sites include urban centers, towns, multimodal transport hubs, airports, seaports, logistic zones, and depressed areas seeking rebirth. A library, school, park, or conjunction of community facilities can do wonders for a neighborhood just as a sports arena, museum, high-speed rail station, or combination of facilities can do for an entire city-region. Infrastructures and the activities and access they provide can catalyze urban regeneration, when carefully planned with their urban context.

Demand-capacity management builds on this understanding of urban development as the sum of the interactions of a wide range of processes that have been deposited archeologically over time. It consists of integrating two analytical methods in a specific geographic area: carrying capacity analysis in the McHargian tradition, and comprehensive infrastructure needs assessments as outlined herein (McHarg 1969). The nine steps that guide the demand-capacity management for sustainable infrastructure are listed in Figure 6.1.

---

1. Establish carrying capacity levels of the natural environmental and human social systems to support urban development.
2. Establish levels of service standards for each infrastructure network and facility that define desired conditions at a specified future date.
3. Analyze the capacities of the existing and programmed infrastructure networks and facilities based on the levels of service standards established in Step 2.
4. Determine population, employment, and housing projections for a specified future date in the geographic area being planned.
5. Calculate the future demand for infrastructure using the population, employment, and housing projections of Step 4 and the levels of service desired in Step 2, according to the formula:

    Total demand = number of units × demand per unit

    units = population, jobs, households

    demand per unit (level of service) = amount of infrastructure per unit of service(for example, gallons per day per person)

    Total demand is measured for a given geographic area (city, metro area, region) at a projected future date, for example 20 or 50 years in advance.
6. Compare the anticipated future demand calculated in Step 5 to the existing and programmed infrastructure network and facility capacities calculated in Step 3 and the social and environmental carrying capacities calculated in Step 1.
7. If the anticipated demand for infrastructure exceeds existing and programmed infrastructure capacities, then calculate the environmental, social, and fiscal costs of expanding infrastructure capacity to determine whether the anticipated growth can be sustainably supported.
8. Based on the analysis conducted in Steps 6 and 7, adjust desired levels of service (Step 2) and population, housing, and employment projections (Step 4) to arrive at a politically acceptable and sustainable level of demand for each infrastructure network and facility.
9. Use the output of this demand-capacity analysis as input into the life cycle planning process, in order to prepare plans that manage population and employment growth and public investment in order to maintain a balance between the growth in demand and the capacity of the infrastructure, in the short and the long term. This typically means growth and urban development occur in existing or newly planned settlement centers where economies of scale vis à vis infrastructure are most readily achieved.

Figure 6.1 Demand-Capacity Management

The following pages present the demand-capacity management method step by step.

Step 1 Establish Carrying Capacity Levels

Establish carrying capacity levels of natural and social environments to support urban development. This analysis is based on the ecological planning principles identified by Ian McHarg in his book *Design With Nature* (1969), executed using GIS programs and readily available databases. Ecological carrying capacity is the ability of all the habitats in a region to support human settlement of a given size and density. It concerns surface and subsurface water supply (both quantity and quality), air quality, soil quantity and quality, the capability of the underlying hydro-geochemical substrate (the combined composition of soils, slopes, bedrock, and aquifers), the functional integrity of ecosystems, ecotones, and other ecological habitats, and the survival capability of individual species. This names just some of the factors to be assessed for their capacity to carry, or support, urban development.

For human settlements, carrying capacity techniques are adapted to measure the capacity of social, economic, and political systems to sustain urban development. This includes public health, crime, education, equity, community character, and other social factors. In an urban area, it considers the existing or planned / programmed capacities of schools, libraries, parks, health care, child care, police and fire departments, and other social services that are commonly provided via infrastructure.

In a metropolitan or regional scenario, a carrying capacity analysis would allocate total projected growth among its municipalities and counties (or other supramunicipal jurisdiction) after assessing the ecological and social capacities of three types of areas to support growth: 1) existing (built up) communities (cities, towns, and suburbs), 2) the planned capacities of all new communities, 3) and the capacities of the undeveloped or less developed environs (exurbs, farmlands, forests, other rural habitats). See Equation 6.1 for calculating sustainable population and job growth capacities.

$$\text{Total Projected Growth} = \text{Capacity of Existing Communities} + \text{Capacity of New Communities} + \text{Capacity of Environs} \qquad 6.1$$

Existing community capacity is calculated by determining the amount of growth that can be sustained in each existing (developed) community, based on infrastructural, environmental, social, and fiscal capacities to support it. The available development capacity in existing communities is located on infill, brownfield, greyfield, vacant, and otherwise open land; plus in the opportunities to redevelop existing buildings, structures, and places, such as rail yards, industrial districts, and other underutilized assets. If more intensive development is desired, multifunctional intensive land use (MILU) strategy optimizes development so that unused or underused land or spaces such as rooftops, parking, rail yards, and occasionally used spaces such as auditoria get used more frequently and more intensively. This entails a parcel-by-parcel, zoning district by zoning district tabulation for each jurisdiction in the metro area.

Once total growth capacity for existing communities is calculated, subtract it from the total projected growth in the metropolitan area to yield the amount of remaining growth that is to be allocated into new communities and environs, as locally determined by each municipality.

These calculations are then adjusted regionally by the metropolitan or regional planning agency in consultation with the municipalities and other intermediary political jurisdictions. This regional adjustment fine tunes the initial allocations determined at the outset.

New community capacity is calculated by determining the amount of growth that can be sustained in new communities based on infrastructural, environmental, social, and fiscal capacities to support it. This calculation occurs after subtracting the growth to be accommodated in the existing communities, calculated in the step above.

These calculations are then adjusted regionally by the metropolitan or regional planning agency in consultation with the municipalities and other intermediary political jurisdictions. This regional adjustment fine tunes the initial allocations.

Environs capacity is calculated by first determining the maximum (ceiling) capacity based on natural, agricultural, rural, infrastructural, and other systems' capacities. This carrying capacity is calculated as described above (establishing ecological carrying capacity), after subtracting the growth allocated to existing and new communities as calculated in the two prior steps.

These calculations are adjusted regionally by the metropolitan or regional planning agency in consultation with the municipalities and other intermediary political jurisdictions. This regional adjustment finetunes the initial allocations.

In sum, demand-capacity analysis matches projected population, employment, and housing levels with existing and projected infrastructural, environmental, social, and fiscal capacities to support growth. When combined with the rate process method outlined in Appendix 2 and the life cycle method outlined in the Chapter 5, it comprehensively integrates infrastructure and urban planning. It enables planners to allocate the locations and scale of growth sustainably by considering all factors, and to plan the amount and type of infrastructure needed to support that growth.

It is important to note that demand-capacity management does not limit growth, unless so desired. It can accept the total amount of projected growth as a given, if so determined. It merely allocates growth spatially in a sustainable manner consonant with the capacities of various systems to support it. Demand-capacity management enables planners and their constituents to choose growth allocations for existing communities, new communities, and environs explicitly. It also provides a basis to evaluate the costs and benefits of several differing growth scenarios.

This method reveals thresholds for the upper limits (ceilings) of densities and quantities of growth in environs for each major growth-determining factor – infrastructural, environmental, social, and fiscal. Environs are slated for lower densities, compared to existing and new communities. Conversely, the method reveals thresholds for the lower limits (floors) of densities, intensities, and floor area ratios for urban-scale development in existing and new cities and towns, where urban-scale development is desired and preferred, compared to the environs.

Community service areas are the areas within new and existing communities that mark the geographic boundaries for infrastructure, services, and utilities. Community service areas provide strategically targeted areas for the prioritization of urban infrastructure investments. In community service areas, specific *levels of service* are established and maintained for each infrastructure, service, and utility. These levels of service guide calculations in the demand-capacity method. An advantage of the demand-capacity method is that it permits planners to compare different scenarios by varying the factors used to evaluate anticipated growth and its impacts. Software programs exist to conduct comparative and comprehensive growth scenario impact assessments. These types of growth scenario assessment software programs are especially powerful when coupled with geographic information systems (GIS), so that scenarios can be compared visually and spatially in addition to quantitatively. Community service areas also can serve as the basis for growth management programs that are based on the progressive timing and sequencing of growth.

Step 2 Establish Levels of Service Standards

Establish levels of service standards for each infrastructure network and facility that define desired performance parameters. Levels of service indicate a minimum standard level to be maintained by an infrastructure or utility service provider. Traditionally, levels of service were expected to be supplied continuously, all of the time, at an unlimited quantity, as long as it is free to the public, such as a city street, or the user is willing to pay, such as a toll bridge. For some infrastructures, levels of service vary, depending on differences in demand over time or across space, such as public transit. For other infrastructures, levels of service can be completely demand based, as for electricity consumption.

Demand-based measures of service levels are gaining importance because they lessen the need for infrastructure services, lowering costs and impacts. See the section below titled Demand Management.

Levels of service standards are typically established by government or by professional or industry associations. Historically, these standards were based on safety, best engineering practices, and user satisfaction. Increasingly, sustainability and equity criteria are calculated to help determine levels of service.

Sustaining reliable levels of service that users can confidently depend on is the ultimate goal of any infrastructure service provider. Reliability itself is an important measure of service quality. Reliability of complex infrastructure networks is increasingly jeopardized as the result of hacking into proprietary or public computer networks (cybersecurity breechs), power grids that succumb to fires or freezes (extreme weather impacts), and infrastructures that get inundated by floods (service outages). In these and other cases, reliability becomes paramount, especially for critical infrastructures. Reliability and the built-in resilience needed to attain it are increasingly vital to the design and planning of infrastructures.

Equity considerations, for populations to be served fairly and equitably, are paramount because subconscious bias is built into accepted or traditional standards, and needs to be understood in order to be corrected.

Step 3 Analyze Capacities of Existing and Programmed Infrastructure

Analyze the capacities of existing and programmed infrastructure networks and facilities based on the levels of service standards established in Step 2. This is done by multiplying per unit (per person, household, etc.) levels of service by the number of units of infrastructure delivering the service (number of vehicles in a metro or subway fleet, number of lane miles of a street network, number of reservoirs and / or aquifers, each with its rated capacity, for example). The sum is the total capacity for each type or system of infrastructure. See Equation 6.2. This capacity is determined for all infrastructures in the area of the jurisdiction doing the planning. The calculation takes into account both currently existing networks or facilities, plus those that are definitively planned and programmed for the future (approved plans, budgeted programs).

Step 4 Determine Population, Employment, and Housing Projections

Determine population, employment, and housing projections for a specified future date in the geographic area being planned. These figures are usually aggregated from smaller units, such as municipalities and counties, into a larger geographic polity such as a metropolitan region. The projections can usually be obtained from the relevant government agency overseeing the jurisdiction being planned. Projections are usually calculated by government agencies.

A drawback of using official data projections is that they typically are projected only several decades into the future. This is less than the life span of infrastructure. The prudence of this limitation stems from the unknown and unpredictable factors that affect population, job, and housing growth. For example, average household size, used in calculating housing projections, varies according to long-wave social and economic tendencies and preferences, and is difficult if not impossible to predict with a degree of accuracy that supports infrastructure demand-capacity analysis. The relatively short-term time accuracy of these projections (short term, in view of sustainability, though long term, in view of contemporary political and economic time horizons) complicates the calculation of sustainable life cycles, keeping in mind that the service life of an infrastructure such as a sewer system, bridge, or road may be centuries long. In this regard, planning and designing extra capacity, while potentially more costly in the short run, can save significantly in the long run.

Step 5 Calculate the Future Demand for Infrastructure

Calculate the future demand for infrastructure using the population, employment, and housing projections of Step 4 and the levels of service desired in Step 2, according to the formula in Equation 6.2, taking into account any reductions due to demand management measures. See the section titled Demand Management, below.

$$\text{demand } d = \text{number of units} \times \text{demand per unit} \qquad 6.2$$

units u = population, or jobs, or households (u_p, u_j, u_h)
demand per unit (level of service) = amount of infrastructure service provided per unit (for example gallons per day per person)

Total demand d is measured for a given geographic area (city, metro area, region) at a projected future date, say 20 or 50 years in advance, by adding the demands for each unit of demand (population, jobs, housing) to yield the total demand.

Step 6 Compare Future Demand to Existing Capacity

Compare the anticipated future demand calculated in Step 5 to the existing and programmed infrastructure network and facility capacities calculated in Step 3 and the social and environmental carrying capacities calculated in Step 1.

Step 7 Determine whether Growth Can Be Sustainably Supported

Determine whether the anticipated growth can be sustainably supported, using the evidence-based comparison derived in Step 6. If the anticipated demand for infrastructure calculated in Step 5 exceeds existing and programmed infrastructure capacities calculated in Step 3, this means in principle that new infrastructure is needed to support the anticipated growth. Another option is to manage demand, or provide an alternative service(s). After demand management and other options are evaluated, and new infrastructure is determined to be needed, then analyze the environmental, social, and fiscal costs and impacts of expanding infrastructure capacity to determine whether the anticipated growth can be sustainably supported.

Step 8 Calculate a Sustainable Level of Demand

Calculate a politically acceptable and sustainable level of demand for each infrastructure network and facility. Based on the analysis conducted in Steps 6 and 7, adjust desired levels of service (Step 2) and population, housing, and employment projections (Step 4) to calculate a politically acceptable and sustainable level of demand for each infrastructure network and facility. This entails combining political and professional judgment with the technical analysis obtained using the demand-capacity method. Constraints and opportunities are applied to the technical analysis at this point. Here we witness how infrastructure planning emerges as an art and craft informed by science and politics.

Step 9 Use Outputs of Demand-Capacity Analysis as Inputs to Life Cycle Planning

At scheduled, periodic moments in the planning process, assemble performance data of all phases of the life cycle and use them as inputs into reevaluating the infrastructure system *de novo*.

> O, reason not the need: our basest beggars
> Are in the poorest things superfluous:
> Allow not nature more than nature needs,
> Man's life is as cheap as beast's.
>
> (Shakespeare, *King Lear*)

Demand Management

Demand-capacity management assumes that the amount of growth – population, jobs, housing – that will occur in the future is determined by the usual combination of forces: market, demographic, social, and government policy. Official policy itself can change market and social force and movements, and thus future projections in a number of ways. However, government policy notwithstanding, demand-capacity management does not assume that the level of growth will be limited by policy. This assumption holds true for most nations. Nonetheless, infrastructure planning based on demand-capacity management accepts the "natural" amount of growth as a given, and does not manage that number. Instead, it manages the location, density, and timing of the projected amount of growth.

Demand management, by contrast, manages consumption by infrastructure to attain more sustainable cities and societies. The infrastructure planning technique of demand management seeks to limit or otherwise control user demand of infrastructure and its services. Demand management shifts the focus of infrastructure from the provider to the consumer, and has been developed in most infrastructure fields, notably water, energy, and transportation (Ghalehkhondabi et al. 2017).

> Most policy assessments focus on the supply side of infrastructure planning. A common misstep is to prepare forecasts of need based on per capita estimates of consumption. These per capita indicative standards largely ignore price elasticity of demand, the effects of conservation, and technological change.

> In addition to estimating demand, state policymakers should consider how demand management strategies can be applied to infrastructure services.... These strategies include using facilities more efficiently and raising prices to reduce demand for scarce infrastructure resources. If widely implemented, demand-management strategies can significantly reduce the cost of new infrastructure investment (Dowall 2000, ix).

Demand management poses a basic question: Are there ways to meet infrastructure needs without investing in new capital facilities? It is possible to manage the demand for existing infrastructure in ways that encourage its most efficient use and thereby minimize the need for new investment. Demand management contrasts with traditional approaches, which focus almost exclusively on increasing the supply of infrastructure. In its baldest form, supply-oriented planning forecasts infrastructure needs based on per capita estimates of consumption. These per capita estimates, in turn, are based on historical patterns of infrastructure use. Demand management, in contrast, begins with consumers' willingness and ability to pay for services. It recognizes that the demand for infrastructure is dynamic, and it seeks to control the key drivers of that demand to make the most efficient use of existing resources.

Managing the demand for infrastructure effectively, requires planners to understand what drives demand. Key drivers include:

Growth and Composition of the Population

As supply-oriented planners understand, the state's infrastructure must expand as the population increases. However, the composition of the population is also an important factor in infrastructure demand. For example, age profiles determine schooling and corrections needs, and the demand for some infrastructure services may vary across ethnic groups.

Level of Economic Activity

Economic expansion generates increased demand for infrastructure services such as energy, transportation services, and water supply.

Income

As income rises, the demand for infrastructure services tends to increase. These trends are found for water, electrical power, recreation, higher education, and vehicle miles traveled.

User Fees

Consumers will economize on their use of services as prices increase. Forecasting methods that ignore the potential effects of pricing will routinely overestimate capacity requirements.

Tastes or Preferences

The demand for certain services can change as social groups develop new preferences.

Availability of Alternative Services

Consumers have increasingly sought out alternatives to such public goods as schools, roads, police enforcement, and parks. For example, private schools have proliferated, gated communities have provided their own roads and security services, and new partnerships between park districts and local organizations have formed to improve park management and operations.

Technology

Changes in technology are likely to affect the demand for and supply of infrastructure services. For example, distance learning technologies have drastically shifted the demand for all levels of education, as the Covid-19 pandemic of 2019–2021 has shown.

Conservation

Utilities have introduced a range of energy conservation programs that have altered the demand for electricity and other forms of power. More recently, urban water districts have offered incentives for low-flush toilets, drip irrigation systems, and drought tolerant landscaping. Agricultural water users have also lined canals and sold their surplus water to metropolitan markets (adapted from Dowall and Whittington 2003, 125–126).

For further details, there are ample literatures on demand management, both scholarly and professional, that contain a wealth of principles and practical examples.

Infrastructure Demand Assessment

The basic rule governing infrastructure demand (sometimes referred to as "need", a distinction explained below) was succinctly stated in an aphorism by Diane van Maren, Associate Secretary for Health and Human Services in the state of California: "There is always more need than funding, by far" (Neuman and Whittington 2000, 53). Given this operative reality, the strategy of preparing a long-term infrastructure demand assessment nonetheless offers the advantage of creating a baseline data set to guide management decisions regarding financing, funding priorities, growth strategies, safety, health and other performance factors, and tradeoffs among repair and new construction. A long-term infrastructure demand assessment is the base of life cycle planning, a fact which cannot be stressed enough.

The basic algorithm for conducting an infrastructure demand assessment is represented by Equation 6.2 presented in step 5 of the demand-capacity section above:

$$\text{demand } d = \text{number of units} \times \text{demand per unit} \qquad 6.3$$

This formula assumes a clean slate, as it calculates new demand. Yet infrastructure planners rarely operate with a clean slate. Demand assessments measure two types of demand, new facilities and existing facilities. The demand for new facilities uses the formula above. Existing demands can be organized into two categories: repairing and rehabilitating, and bringing up to acceptable service standards. Assessments of existing infrastructure entail field surveys conducted by technical experts who know the equipment and its structural and operating characteristics. Our integrated assessment model includes these three types of demand: *new infrastructure, rehabilitation,* and *backlog.* The three categories – new, rehab, backlog – are identified below.

1. New infrastructure covers new facilities and networks, and the capacity expansion of existing infrastructures, that serve new growth and development. In practice, investments made to upgrade existing infrastructures to satisfy new growth demands tend to also satisfy rehabilitation demands and existing populations.

2. Rehabilitation of existing infrastructure includes recurring periodic activities to replace or improve existing infrastructure in order to keep it in service at specified levels of service standards. It includes routine scheduled maintenance and repair in addition to overhaul and rehabilitation. This category is for actions necessary to maintain the original design capacities of existing infrastructures. It does not include the expansion of existing facilities and networks to support enhanced levels of service, extended capacity, or new growth. A distinction we make here from common definitions of rehabilitation activities is that we include routine maintenance and repair, which are typically contained in operating budgets and not capital budgets. We include them together to maintain the integrity of the life cycle method, and to compensate for the fact that maintenance budgets are among the first to get cut or eliminated in tight fiscal conditions. These cuts, when persistent, hasten deterioration and lead to more expensive repairs or replacement in the long run.

3. Backlog expenditures correct existing deficiencies to serve the existing population. They may include upgrades to infrastructure capacity to fill unmet needs resulting from past growth or other increases in infrastructure consumption patterns. An example would be road widening or mass transit expansion to relieve traffic congestion on an existing roadway network. Filling backlog demand also raises deficient levels of service to minimum desired or mandated levels. Examples include bridge improvements to meet national structural safety codes and improving sewage treatment so that effluent meets environmental standards.

In practice, many factors shape needs determinations, including policy, headlines, and politics along with professional standards, growth projections, and service deficits. But most importantly, dollars drive needs. Available funding determines more than any single factor what can and will be built. Most needs assessments are reactions to perceived conditions, especially those that were politically driven. Neuman and Whittington (2000, 55) identified a host of reasons for the incompleteness and inconsistency of typical assessments that added distinct service providers' data into an aggregate one. This underscores the imperative to conduct a comprehensive assessment using a uniform demand-driven protocol.

Former California State Treasurer Phil Angelides summed up the disconnection between needs assessments and comprehensive planning this way: "Current needs assessments are not based on a comprehensive plan of investment, nor are they designed to achieve the goals of ensuring sustained economic growth, environmental preservation, equality of opportunity, and livability" (Angelides 1999, 5).

The concept of needs itself contains a value judgment as to what society or a subset of society "needs" to survive, stay healthy, be productive, enjoy a certain level of welfare, and so on. These and other important observations and criticisms are contained in an insightful analysis of needs as a base for development strategies (Brundenius and Lundahl 1982). The term needs is often used in infrastructure assessment literature. I use instead the term demand. While the concept behind demand is not value free, demand varies according to actual individual preferences and behaviors rather than to politically or professionally determined levels of need.

An example illustrates the distinction between need and demand:

> A need projection for schools multiplies the projected enrollment increases over a given period of time by the standard amount of space needed per student. This simplification does not assume other needs and demands, such as modernization, life safety improvements, class size reduction, and so on. A demand projection for schools is illustrated by [various universities' "compacts"] to increase the number of science and engineering graduates [and increase enrollment by underrepresented populations]. The demand-based approach responds to the demands of society ...
>
> In the past, needs assessments based on standard parameters and user growth projections have been the norm. The very term "needs assessment" is a carry-over from that mode of thinking. ...
>
> Whether a need or demand approach is used, one trend common to all agencies is their use of decentralized methods, where projects are solicited from as close to the actual user or customer as possible. This approach solicits direct user feedback and data to determine actual levels of use rather than projections based on professional standards (Neuman and Whittington 2000, 57–58)

There is also the issue of supply-driven versus demand-driven needs or demands. Each is an extreme on the spectrum of infrastructure consumption. Actual conditions lie in between. Supply-driven consumption is determined by the service provider. The user does not have much influence on the service being provided. Demand-driven consumption is determined by the end user. Infrastructure provision has historically favored supply-side management, for example water, electricity, telephone, and commuter rail; whose use parameters were fixed by the provider, who offered inflexible conditions. This has changed in the last decades, fueled by the breakup of government and private monopolies, by aggressive privatization and decentralization campaigns by national governments and international development organizations, and by the technology purveyors themselves, most noticeable in the rapidly expanding markets created through the convergence of formerly separate telecommunications media.

Bibliography

Angelides, P. (1999). *Smart Investments*. Sacramento, CA: California State Treasurer.
ASCE (American Society of Civil Engineers). (2021). *2021 Report Card for America's Infrastructure*. Washington DC: Author.
Brundenius, C. and Lundahl, M. (eds.). (1982). *Development Strategies and Basic Needs in Latin America: Challenges for the 1980s*. Boulder, CO: Westview Press.
Carmona, M, and Sieh, L. (2004). *Measuring Quality in Planning: Managing the Performance Process*. London: Spon Press.
Del Borghi, A, Gallo, M, Del Borghi, and M. 2009. A survey of life cycle approaches in waste management. *International Journal of Life Cycle Assessment* 14: 597–610
Dowall, D. (2001). *California's infrastructure policy for the 21st century: Issues and opportunities*. San Francisco: Public Policy Institute of California.
Dowall, D. E., and Whittington, J. (2003). *Making Room for the Future: Rebuilding California's Infrastructure*. San Francisco, CA: Public Policy Institute of California.
Flyvberg, B, Bruzelius, N, Rosengatter, W. (2003). *Megaprojects and Risk: An Anatomy of Ambition*. New York: Cambridge University Press.
Ghalehkhondabi, I., Ardjmand, E., Weckman, G., and Young, W. (2017). An overview of energy demand forecasting methods published in 2005–2015. *Energy Systems* 8:411–447.
Government Accounting Standards Board (GASB). (2021). *Technical Plan for the First Third of 2021*. Norwalk, CT: Author.
Government Accounting Standards Board (GASB). (1999). *Basic Financial Statements for State and Local Governments*. Norwalk, CT: Author.
International Standards Organization. (2000). *Environmental Management – Life-Cycle Assessment – Life Cycle Impact Assessment International Standard 14042*. Geneva: Author.
Lynch, K. 1990. *Wasting Away*. San Francisco: Sierra Club Books.
McHarg, I. (1969). *Design with Nature*. New York: Natural History Press.
McNichol, E. (2019). *It's Time for States to Invest in Infrastructure*. Washington DC: Center on Budget and Policy Priorities.
Neuman, M. and Whittington, J. (2000). *Building California's Future: Current Conditions in California's Infrastructure Planning, Budgeting and Financing*. San Francisco, CA: Public Policy Institute of California.
New Jersey State Planning Commission. (2001). *The New Jersey State Development and Redevelopment Plan*. Trenton, NJ: Author.
World Bank. (2004). *Reforming Infrastructure: Privatization, regulation, and Competition*. Washington DC: Author.

MANAGEMENT

7
Governing Institutions

How do we transform infrastructure governance? To achieve the book's vision requires governing across sectors – governance. The challenge is the institution of governance itself. Its "sunk costs", its inertia, like those of infrastructure, work against the urgent and bold transformations needed to tackle the crises confronting humanity. The term *transform* here is literal, to trans-form, not merely change. How to transform governing institutions that are large, complex, slow, rigid, and messy, with the weight of history and tradition – path dependence – bogging them down? Governance across public, private, nonprofit, and citizen sectors multiplies this challenge. The modus operandi of any institution is to perpetuate itself compounds the task. This chapter takes this conundrum on.

At the same time, the benefits of institutions, especially government, are many. They provide stability and assurance, especially in tough times. Stability opposes our chaotic, crisis-laden era. Crisis is the inability of a system to reproduce itself using its existing means. Crisis unresolved ends the system. If instability is a sign of crisis, then the current era of multiple crises is one of radical instability. Yet institutions, which can crumble rapidly under certain conditions, tend to remain stable by perpetuating established norms expressed in charters and laws through structures and procedures. This duality (opposition) of stability and need to transform pinpoints the crux of the challenge (Neuman and Gavinha 2005).

To solve this dilemma is a tall task when confidence in government is at an all-time low (Saad 2020; IPSOS 2018). "This looming disequilibrium between existing and future challenges and the ability of institutions and systems to respond is likely to grow and produce greater contestation at every level" (National Intelligence Council 2021, 1). As a result,

> politics within [nations] are likely to grow more volatile and contentious, and no region, ideology, or governance system seems immune or to have the answers. ... Large segments of the global population are becoming

wary of institutions and governments that they see as unwilling or unable to address their needs. ... These challenges will repeatedly test the resilience and adaptability of communities, states, and the international system, often exceeding the capacity of existing systems and models (National Intelligence Council 2021, 3, 8).

Some suggest that a rupture occurring in which citizens do not trust politics and therefore government. As a result, they advocate a break with the past and its institutions in order to attain meaningful progress (Castells 2018). This is daunting because of all the social, political, intellectual, and economic capital invested in creating and perpetuating existing institutional orders. These "sunk capitals" are inscribed in their norms, traditions, symbols, and meanings; as well as laws, rules, and structures. They anchor the institutions' (former) stability. Yet sociopolitical orders are breaking down rapidly. Now, precisely because trust is low and order is breaking down, there exists an opening for true transformation.

This opening takes advantage of the huge opportunities that the current crises offer. These opportunities are signaled by the Chinese character for crisis, *wei ji*, composed of two individual characters: danger and opportunity. They suggest tipping points that are strategic yet not without risk: the ability to inject new norms and forms into governance institutions that break from the past. They include collaboration instead of competition, cooperation rather than conflict, co-creation in lieu of winner take all, and co-production, not zero sum. These approaches mirror aspects of emerging realities afforded by new technologies, applications, and social media that, on the one hand, seeded and sewed the divisions and unrest that prevail today. Thereby a risk. On the other hand, movements that they spawned, including equity, justice, and climate movements such as MeToo, Black Lives Matter, and Extinction Rebellion, possess the potential to bring together, reconcile, and heal. Social movements are a start yet not enough. Transforming governing institutions is a critical task for lasting progress. For our purposes, it points to productive roles for infrastructure because they serve all people in vital ways, transcending divisions.

On top of these issues, the crises are accelerating in pace and in complexity. They compound the challenges to act, and to reform governance. Challenges to reform are especially acute in the legislative branches of Western democracies now, polarized as they are. A more fruitful avenue of reform is in the executive branches. According to Leon Fuerth, "To deal with acceleration, we must begin installing new approaches to organization that feature much greater sensitivity to faint signals about alternative futures, and which enable us to respond to these with increased flexibility and speed" (Fuerth 2013, 33). Flexibility and speed can be improved by the principles of governance put forward in this chapter.

Fuerth goes on:

> Modern policy issues are complex phenomena, not linear. Linear problems can be broken down into components, and then sequentially

administered and resolved. Complex problems are the result of concurrent interactions among multiple systems of events. They do not lend themselves to permanent solutions, but instead tend to morph into new problems, even as the result of our interventions to deal with them. They do not automatically move toward stable outcomes, but instead can exhibit highly disproportionate consequences in response to relatively small changes of condition. Complex challenges cannot be permanently resolved because they continuously mutate. Instead, they must be constantly monitored and managed (Fuerth 2013, 33).

How to transform governance to deal with these challenges? Infrastructures provide the media that enable and propel transformational processes. Government guides society towards the public good – a more perfect union. Infrastructures also serve common societal goals, because as public goods they benefit all. They cut across interests and demographics, and even serve to coalesce them. (Infrastructures divide, too.) We know that infrastructure is essential for virtually every facet of contemporary society. In this way infrastructure can be marshalled by those who seek to transform governance to be more effective. Two strategies to achieve this are by employing practices such as coordination and integration, and by retooling the institutions to be more agile, in line with the right-hand side of Figure 7.1. This helps institutions respond to the acceleration of phenomena and their complexity using adaptive and anticipatory governance. As current institutions tend not to be designed to operate in these ways, but rather in linear, hierarchical ways ill-suited to today, much less tomorrow.

Coordination and its deeper counterpart integration are as essential to effective governance as they are to sustainability. Fragmented organizations and institutions, as sole-purpose and / or sole-discipline "silos", hamper solutions to complex problems. Rather, coordinating them by linking policies and practices, budgets and laws; integrating them through common plans and strategies (including government-wide), and consolidating them into larger units takes positive steps toward effective governance.

To integrate infrastructure networks to attain sustainability, as highlighted in the preceding chapters, integrating their governing institutions is a prerequisite. Common capital budgets and plans across ministries and departments are another. They can go as far as coordinating across levels of government (de Roo and Boelens 2016).

Is this scale of integration and coordination possible? Yes, says Naomi Klein in *This Changes Everything*. Look at the success of globalization. She asks why can we coordinate globally such complexities as global trade and the global political economy, but not other complexities such as climate change, injustice, inequity, poverty, and hunger (Klein 2014). Similar to the urgent, large-scale changes needed to deal with the climate crisis, itself directly related to infrastructure, massive changes are needed to governance. These stem, as lasting government and governance initiatives do in representative democracies, from changes that people institute in their lives (Mau 2020).

Institutional integration wrought by the globalization of the political economy since World War II began with Bretton Woods, the IMF, the World Bank, and the Common Market. It evolved into the EU, the WTO, free trade agreements, and so on. Institutional integration par excellence on this level took decades.

Global integration has been accelerated by the ICT revolution, itself the result of complex integrations at multiple scales of multiple institutions, technologies, standards, processes, etc. It is further accelerated by the transport revolution, which has followed suit. Transport of people and goods is increasingly integrated globally through logistic supply chains and travel protocols. Together, they led to the global economy, global cities, and globalization itself, with both beneficial and drastic, unsustainable consequences. These prime examples of successful infrastructural integration represent a marriage between institutional and infrastructural integration. We can, and must, mirror these achievements in the realms of governing sustainable infrastructure and urbanism. There are two lessons here. One is that institutions matter and shape society, not merely reflect it. The second is that the type of integration and the type of institution matters.

Institutional change is critical to the effectiveness of policy change. The efficacy of policy change is limited when the institutions don't change along with them, because policies can be overturned by an incoming regime of a different political party. But how does lasting, massive institutional change occur in governing structures that we have inherited from the 18th century (nation-states) and the 12th century (municipalities)? Are they up to it? Haphazard reform is not enough. Piecemeal incrementalism, typically addressing policy alone, is the modus operandi of business as usual. We need new, truly transformed institutions that collaborate, that cooperate, that reflect the new needs of societies changing at lightning speed. Policy change alone is not enough. Transformed institutions that nurture new policy are needed.

Following this analysis, and the next section on institutional networks, this chapter highlights four themes: governance, design, leadership, and principles. They address key issues such as devolution and subsidiarity, public versus private versus partnership, and centralized, decentralized, or networked management. Specific tools for governance could also be mentioned. However, they are beyond the scope of this chapter. (Financing tools are covered in Chapter 8, planning tools are listed in prior chapters.) Emphatically, specific tools (methods, practices) need to be custom-made to fit the complexities of any specific place and time. "One size fits all" – the indiscriminate transfer of tools from one place to another inappropriately – often creates more problems than it solves. Crafting tools that affect many need to be shaped collaboratively and consensually using the principles presented here.[1]

Given the fact that each nation and smaller political subdivisions have their own particulars derived from history, this exposition will not elaborate the "nuts and bolts" of specific governance arrangements in any place and time. General principles are presented instead. The focus on principles becomes apparent when considering the complicated context surrounding the many factors linked to large infrastructure networks. These principles, by their nature, can be adapted to meet the demands of varied contexts.

Institutional Networks

"Civilizations, like sand dunes, are firmly anchored to the hidden contours of the earth; grains of sand may come and go, blown into drifts or carried far away by the wind, but the dunes, the unmoving sum of innumerable movements, remain standing." This evocative analogy, by historian Fernand Braudel, in his magisterial *The Mediterranean* (1992), could have described institutions instead of civilizations. Institutions contain paradoxes, a sure sign of the complexity and contradiction attendant to any institution, making attempts to reform and redesign them difficult. Designing institutions to account for human complexity and paradox goes beyond typical institutional design parameters that are based on rational action. Creating capacity to deal with complexity means designing for flexibility, redundancy, and overlap in terms of institutional structures (Landau 1969).

In addition, research shows that decisions are behavioral and contextual rather than cognitive (Kahneman 2011). Fear and greed, emotion and intuition, guide more than rationality. These considerations need to be applied to institutional processes. Adding institutionalized capacity for negotiation in informal processes in addition to structured, formal ones is also key (Neuman 2010).

Multi-Scalar Large Institutional Networks are the new forms by which infrastructure policy and planning is, or should be, conducted (Neuman 2007a; Brenner 2019; see Deutsch 1963 for a primordial view). They are "large" because city-regions can extend over thousands of square kilometers. State and national networks are larger. Their tentacles extend beyond the geographic bounds of any particular region, owing to globalization. Large institutional networks entangle multiple levels of governance. In the past, governance scholarship centered on the distinction among levels and among scales. For years, this distinction tended to focus on one scale. Now barriers among scales are being broken down, yet they still exist. As each level of government has its own elected and appointed officials, budgets, and laws, it is easy to fathom why separation persists.

New large-scale networks have emerged, and built bridges ad hoc to span separations. They promote more interaction and integration among government levels and geographic scales. Multi-scalar approaches more accurately portray current territorial realities. Within these networks, each entity (agency, organization, institution) is a single node in the overall network. The Multi-Scalar Large Institutional Network (MSLIN) is the emerging form of these interactive webs. Progressive institutional design for infrastructure governance would do well to establish formal arrangements of MSLINs to enhance their effectiveness.

The governance of infrastructure decision-making processes deals with who governs, how, and for whose benefit. Furthermore, infrastructure and its service provision has wide-ranging impacts, positive and negative, on physical space, individual persons, and social groups outside the boundaries of any given delimited jurisdiction. This illustrates the complexities and challenges confronting infrastructure leaders and managers, and the need for retooling institutions and their relations.

Governance Institutions

The very possibility of governance — providing robust human rights, meaningful participative democracy, equitable distribution of wealth, goods and services, and strong protection for health, safety, welfare and the environment — is being severely tested in this neoliberal age. Many large popular movements as well as small-scale local initiatives are bubbling up to fill the voids resulting from multiple failures of mainstream institutions to maintain longstanding social contracts to protect individuals from harm and to advance the public good. The panorama is far more complex than these lines suggest. Some institutions, particularly but not only smaller or local ones, are doing better at maintaining trust. And some popular movements and initiatives are retrogressive. Nonetheless, governance institutions need much work to improve, keep pace with rapid change, and anticipate and shape a future that is livable and equitable.

What are the sources of inadequacies in infrastructure governance institutions? Robust scholarship suggests they include: 1) fragmented and uncoordinated processes due to overlapping jurisdictions of governmental agencies and quasi-governmental authorities, districts, and utilities; 2) shortsighted financing for building of individual projects instead of long-term funding for the life cycle of entire systems or networks; 3) lack of comprehensive plans and strategies to guide management and budgets; 4) limited and improper metrics for measurement of performance; 5) two generations of neoliberalism that continues to diminish governments' capacities and budgets; and 6) zero-sum and winner-take-all politics of conflict. Naming them takes the first step in surmounting them.

One way to address these is to design and redesign institutions. While the design of governance institutions is not a panacea to all infrastructure challenges, it is key for *sustaining* advances in policy, funding, and leadership. Moreover, institutions shape decision-making. The approaches presented here are designed to deal with inadequacies in institutions.

First, brief definitions of institution (vs. organization) and governance (vs. government). Strictly speaking, institution is an object of the verb to institute. It stems from the Latin *institutum:* plan, design, purpose, ordinance, instruction, precept. These early meanings were directly related to the giving of form and order, the established order that is regulated by a constitution. What distinguishes an institution from a "mere" organization or system of organizations is its persistence over time and extension through space (Giddens 1984), its history of affiliation among its members (Steinmo, Thelen and Longstreth 1992), and its embedded norms that are manifest in common practices and traditions (Bellah et al. 1991). Not all institutions are organizations, strictly speaking (handshake, marriage, environmental impact statement), nor are all organizations institutions. Norms that express values are at the heart of all institutions. This draws on a long line of public philosophy in affirming "institutions are normative patterns imbedded in and enforced by laws and mores (informal customs and practices)" (Bellah et al. 1991, 10). "The only idea common to all usages of the term 'institution' is that of some sort of establishment of relative permanence of a distinctly social sort" (Hughes 1936).

We distinguish governance from government. It is not just the designated government agency. Nor is it the executive branch or the entire level of government containing that agency. Instead it is a multiorganizational construct. It is all those organizations, public, private, and mixed, that are implicated in infrastructure. It includes interest groups such as those who plan, design, and build (utilities, government, developers, builders, unions), those who finance (investors, banks, insurers, government, utilities), and others (neighborhood associations, environmental groups, citizens, property owners). It can go as far as to span all branches at each level of government and all sectors of society. This is particularly applies to infrastructure at the city-region or larger scale, even more when integrating many types of infrastructure.

Understanding institutions and governance in this way situates policy and planning more clearly, enabling more fruitful interventions and change. It also gives a stronger grasp of and context for the vast number of organizations at all levels of government – typically uncoordinated and often competing – that complicate strategy formation, policy planning, and service delivery. Consider the outtake, below, from a book-length report to the California governor and legislature that shows how infrastructure insiders see their own institutions. It is not a pretty picture. It underscores the need for coordination and integration.

> Providing infrastructure to the seventh largest nation[2] in the world is a very complex and tough task. Accordingly, and not surprisingly, we have found that the complete picture of the infrastructure system at the State level is not fully understood by any single person or agency. Some have described it as a black box. Others have used the classic metaphor of the blindfolded person and the elephant. Both of these characterizations refer to the density, complexity, and opacity of the panoply of infrastructure management institutions. It was hard for them to get a handle on the whole. Some did not even believe a whole exists.
>
> A few recognized there is a system of sorts, and used other metaphors to describe it, typically a wheel or puzzle. Those who thought of a wheel saw the rim as the framework, the hub as the control center, and the spokes as the line agencies. Most often, they perceived the infrastructure system wheel as having no hub or rims, or flimsy ones. Those who

thought of a puzzle said that they know their own piece, perhaps a few adjoining pieces, and perhaps some other scattered ones. They were not sure how the pieces fit together into the whole because they did not know where the frame is, and had no overall picture to guide which pieces fit where.

Regardless of which metaphor that long time state government insiders used, the fact that they invariably settled on one of them shows how poorly understood the system is, and how it is missing some fundamental components (Neuman and Whittington 2000, 4–5).

Institutional Design

Institutional design assembles the building blocks of the institution itself. These "blocks" are three: the structures, processes, and norms that undergird its rules and traditions. Key fact: institutions *are* designed, always. The structures in large-scale governance are comprised of multi-scalar large institutional networks of agencies at each level of government, and entities from other sectors of society – quasi-public, private, and nonprofit. To better manage these large networks, institutional design assembles these building blocks into a stable composite.

> "Too often, services fail poor people."
> (James Wolfensohn, President, World Bank
> *World Development Report 2004)*

When infrastructure services fail, in the end it is the result of institutional failure. Yes, individuals were involved, who made political decisions that caused poor service delivery. Yet these individuals and the decision-making processes which involved them are housed in and carried out by institutions and their rules. "Path dependence" stemming from institutional histories, cultures, and trajectories work to condition individuals' actions (David 1994). The long arc of institutions infuses our thoughts and acts, whether consciously or not.

Only institutions can amass the capital and other wherewithal to build and operate large infrastructures and networks. The question is: How do we design new or redesign existing institutions to meet the demands for infrastructures to be sustainable? The answer is largely found in the "new infrastructure characteristics" for institutional design, listed in Figure 7.1. They apply to a new design out of whole cloth, with a written constitution setting forth norms, structures, and processes; and to redesign out of incremental evolution, where the norms, structures, and processes are tinkered with.

Design principles for institutions must match solutions to the sources of the problem. For example, historical dependence on large-scale, centralized infrastructure was identified as a key source of problems. Large, centralized systems led to incremental, cumulative, cascading, and non-dissipative impacts following from that design. Institutional design solutions can be addressed with the same perspective. Infrastructure networks and their governance institutions can be transformed or reshaped so that their impacts are not negative. The choice between these two design paths depends on context. In my view, smaller scale, modular, and distributed yet highly connected institutional networks increasingly form a key part of design principles for governance. How then do we translate these principles for governance? What are the levers that we can manipulate to accomplish this?

The answer is to apply new design principles to the three building blocks of institutions: structures, processes, and norms. For institutional structures, Figure 7.1 suggests new characteristics of infrastructure governance networks. No longer monolithic institutions, rather they should take on forms that fit large-scale institutional networks: distributed, flexible, adaptable, smaller scale, modular, and integrated with other components of the institutional network. In practice, this means reorganizing old institutional structures, an act of governance, so that the reformed institutions realign with new and future conditions. It places a premium on more and better coordination, and rewriting laws and regulations to enable it. It requires broad-minded leaders that are farsighted, cooperative, and inclusive.

A fundamental precept for the design of institutional networks stems from a basic law of networks: the more connections a node has in a network, then the more important that node is, and the more it is subject to failure or attack (Albert, Jeog, and Barabasi 2000). Their research was about tumor genes in the human body and illness, yet we can extend it to risk and vulnerability in physical infrastructure as well as institutional design. An implication is that redundancy and overlap (more nodes, create extra links among nodes, distribute importance among nodes) in network design is good (Landau 1969), and should be built into institutions' structures and processes.

Other structural reform issues include centralized versus decentralized forms. Centralization causes standardization, perhaps suitable for a world of great certainty and authoritarian control – but not today. In the times of the Roman Empire and its colonies and armies, the Spanish Empire and Law of the Indies, and similar edicts ascribed to other empires and their institutions, centralization may have served well. Decentralization couched in the context of subsidiarity is better suited for the complexities and rapid changes that prevail today. Decentralization requires significant coordination and communication, thus some standardization. Think of standardized computer codes and internet protocols that are required to manage the massively distributed and decentralized internet.

At the same time, decentralization can oblige destandardization, or modifying standards to be adapted flexibly according to circumstances. New types of standards for infrastructure institutions (that conduct design, planning, budgeting, financing, and regulating) can be analogous to genetic code, by which species evolve and adapt according to local environmental conditions to assure long-term survival according to evolutionary theory. The structures (and processes) that develop and apply standards for infrastructure and its institutions need to be evaluated and adapted continually, in an evolutionary way that incorporates learning and improvement, in order to be up to date and meaningful. This is an essential principle for design for institutional transformation.

For institutional processes, transformation means mutual understanding and learning to support a new mode of governance. Rewiring processes for them to happen means reciprocal interactions instead of one-way command and control. Feedback loops that continually incorporate and analyze data, create and explore options, reinforce learning, strengthen communications, and build confidence and trust are needed to more effectively manage institutional performance and infrastructure service delivery. Better still in real time, with a range of means to visualize, extended to the entire institutional network, even when mobile. Transforming processes in this way makes individuals more knowledgeable and capable. This empowers them, enhancing individual delegation and institutional subsidiarity. It makes the institutional network more agile and resilient. Increased devolution to those closest to the action / decision enables this level of agility. Improved coordination and cooperation become the norm through procedures redesigned in this way.[3]

For norms, we refer to institutional norms rather than societal ones, recognizing that society's norms are embedded in them. Old or current norms can be found in the left-hand column of Figure 7.1. These norms were inherited from a distant and profoundly different past. They tend not to serve the current and prospective needs of institutional networks that govern infrastructure.

These norms, however, are embedded in habitual thinking, ways of working and living, including academic and professional education and training. They are enshrined in doctrine (Faludi and van der Valk 1994). They are the explicit (encoded) and implicit (intuitive) rules and models that guide institutional action (Choay 1996). They are embodied in images, slogans, and memes that perpetuate institutions easily and rapidly (Neuman 2012). Thus images, slogans, and memes need to be changed along with the institutions and their norms. Taken altogether, breaking from the past is no easy task. It requires significant will, resources, and persistence. To be sure, these norms are already changing toward the right-hand column in Figure 7.1.

OLD / CURRENT	NEW / FUTURE
centralized	distributed / networked
fixed-in-place	mobile
inflexible	flexible
rigid	adaptable
large scale	small scale
unitary / indivisible	modular
expensive	inexpensive
risk prone	resilient
isolated	integrated

Figure 7.1 Infrastructure Institution Characteristics

The key precept to keep in mind in institutional design / redesign is that all three parts – structures, processes, and norms – must be taken into account concurrently. Structural reform alone, for example, is not enough. A supremely illustrative example of the need to work all three components together is the case of the privatization of British Rail under the Thatcher government. This story was told convincingly in the "12:10 to Leeds" by Ian Jack (Jack 2001). It concerns the import of institutional cohesion, as the opposite – institutional fragmentation – steered the dissolution of British Rail, whose institutional "train wreck" led to the literal and deadly train wreck reported by Jack. See Box 7.1.

> **Box 7.1 The 12:10 to Leeds**
>
> Ian Jack (2001) and a government investigative panel (Independent Investigation Board 2006) dissect the remnants of the former and formidable institution British Railways, an icon of the glory days of Great Britain. Their analyses uncover every aspect of the institution of British rail transport and its multiple failures revealed by the Hatfield rail crash of 1999. The title of Jack's story, "The 12:10 to Leeds", referred to the time the train left London's Kings Cross station. Jack digs deep by beginning his hunt for clues in the 18th century origins of the institution that became British Rail, broken up by the Railways Act of 1993, in his search for those responsible. He concluded that the clumsy break-up of the institution into parts, each blind to the other parts, is largely to blame. That is, a failure in institutional design.
>
> Briefly, the train derailed on the down east line (going north) as it travelled through the Welham Green curve. The high rail fractured into over 300 pieces over a distance of 35 meters. Four people were killed, many more injured. It was one of the many public sector privatizations and breakups initiated during the government of Prime Minister Thatcher in the 1980s that continued through the 1990s. British Rail had been the vertically and horizontally integrated owner and operator of all of Britain's rail infrastructure and services. Its formerly unified (integrated) institutional structure and services were split apart into an array of smaller private companies, each responsible for a piece of the pie. Some of the new, smaller entities are / were:
>
> - The Great North Eastern Railway: a train operating company and operator of the train that derailed.
> - Network Rail: owner of rail infrastructure, including the railway tracks, signals, overhead wires, tunnels, bridges, crossings and most stations, but not the rolling stock. Established in 2002 in the wake of the derailment.
> - National Rail: a brand used to promote passenger railway services and to harmonize passenger ticketing.

(*Continued*)

- Train Operating Companies: 22 companies that operate passenger train services. Defunct, functions transferred to the Rail Delivery Group.
- The Rail Delivery Group: a rail industry membership body that brings together passenger and freight rail companies, for marketing, licensing, communications, and policy.
- Railtrack: a group of companies created as part of the privatization of 1993 that owned rail infrastructure, including the railway tracks, signals, overhead wires, tunnels, bridges, crossings, and most stations from 1994 until 2002.
- The Office of Passenger Rail Franchising: a statutory office created in 1993 to sell passenger rail franchises to private sector companies participating in the privatization of the British railway industry. In 2001, its functions were transferred to the newly created Strategic Rail Authority.
- Strategic Rail Authority: provides strategic direction for the railway industry. It was abolished in 2006, its functions being absorbed by the national Department for Transport or the Office of Rail Regulation, the latter now the Office of Rail and Road.
- National Rail: the trade name of the Rail Delivery Group, an industry membership group whose members consist of the Train Operating Companies (TOCs). The TOCs run the passenger services previously provided by the British Railways Board, from 1965 using the brand name British Rail.
- Rolling Stock Companies: owners of passenger trains (rolling stock) formerly owned by British Rail, and passed to three private companies.
- Balfour Beatty Rail Maintenance Limited: a company responsible for maintenance on the East Coast Main Line, the tracks of the crash.
- Office of Rail Regulation: the independent safety and economic regulator for Britain's railways. It is responsible for ensuring that railway operators comply with health and safety law, regulating Network Rail activities, funding, and access to the railway network, and licensing the operators.
- Rail Accident Investigation Branch: an independent investigator of accidents, which informs the industry and the public.
- Health and Safety Commission: a non-departmental national government body that advised and informed all agencies regarding its remit. It merged with the Health and Safety Executive in 2008.

While the stated purpose of the 1993 Railways Act was to promote competition and improved performance, the actual result was the opposite, resulting in numerous reorganizations, continuing inefficiencies and poor performance, and in some cases, ridership drops. Ever since, there have been numerous reviews, white papers, reports, and reorganizations; a continuing saga of poor institutional design.

Finally, success in institutional design requires savvy and timing. Savvy because when the stakes are as high as they are with large, expensive, and consequential infrastructure, politics and finance are involved. Timing because institutions, once established, do not go on without end or without change. At times they shrink, break apart, or collapse. Institutions, like organizations and infrastructures, have life cycles (Neuman 2010). Instrumental for institutional reform is recognizing where in its lifecycle an institution finds itself. That way, the proper tools can be used in a timely way to more effectively transform it. Knowing the stages of institutional transformation suggests both the best timing for and the appropriate mode of intervention for each stage in the life cycle. Change cannot be continuous, regardless of its type.

In the evolutionary view of institutional change, institutions progress through a life cycle from birth to death or complete rebirth, phoenix-like. Figure 7.2 identifies five types of institutional change, with each type corresponding to a stage in the institutional life cycle. The first stage in the institutional cycle is creation. The institution is constituted by an act of political will and institutional design. The second stage of institutional change is through gradual evolution. The third stage occurs by reform, understood as a non-incremental jump that fully transforms the institution. The fourth stage is degradation or destructuring, in which there is a loss of faith in the institution. Finally, there is demise, which can be planned or be the result of "natural" extinction.

Type of change	Stimulus for change	Change to constituting image	Outcome of change
Creation	Dissatisfaction with status quo	New image	New institution
Evolution: incremental change	No stimulus, or stimulus to maintain or improve slightly	Maintain existing image stability	Stability within existing societal frame
Reform: major change	Internal or external recognition that major conditions are changing, thus institution must too	New image coexists and / or competes with existing image, and may replace it	Stability-preserving change within new societal conditions, or instability (unintended result)
Decline / destructuring	Internal disregard, external threat	Decline of faith in existing image	Atrophy, decline
Demise	External threat, internal disregard	No image, loss of image	Extinction

Source: Neuman (2010)

Figure 7.2 The Life Cycle of Institutional Transformation

Principles

Peter Hall's landmark book *Great Planning Disasters* chronicled classic episodes of planning failures. Each was about infrastructural and institutional failure (Hall 1982). A myriad of books, articles, and reports from around the globe have documented similar infrastructure failures that in the end are governance and institutional failings (Flyvbjerg, Bruzelius, and Rothengatter 2003; ASCE 2020). There are important lessons to be learned from these experiences. Yet a significant drawback occurs when specific rules, policies, procedures, or structures are transferred directly to other places and cases, without adjusting for context, whether cultural, historical, political, or institutional. This has led to continuing failures. A better approach is to understand fundamental, underlying *principles* of why and how, and then adapt them as appropriate. Doing so can address and correct the governance issues identified previously, along with others:

1. Fragmented and uncoordinated processes due to overlapping jurisdictions of governmental agencies and quasi-governmental authorities, districts, and utilities
2. Shortsighted financing for building of individual projects instead of long-term funding for the life cycle of entire systems or networks
3. Lack of comprehensive plans and strategies to guide management and budgets
4. Limited and improper metrics for measurement of performance
5. Two generations of neoliberalism that diminishes governments' capacities and budgets
6. Zero-sum and winner-take-all politics of conflict

Coordination

Coordination is key for infrastructure governance. The primary goal of any infrastructure provider is to satisfy users. Each provider is responsible for deploying services within its specified jurisdiction. For example, a city streets department is responsible for keeping its surface streets in sufficient operating condition to permit smooth traffic flow as they host numerous modes of motorized and people-powered vehicles. Yet county, state, and national highways flow through the city, and need to be connected seamlessly to local roads under the purview of the locality. The streets also provide multiple functions: travel, public spaces, parking, access, light and air, stormwater management, and rights-of-way for other infrastructures. Sidewalks, street furniture, trees, parking, and more find their home adjacent to urban streets. Underneath are mass transit, pipelines, wires, cables, and so on. We see how a city streets department must interact with numerous other agencies. This is one of the prime reasons why some streets departments have evolved into public works departments, housing many, but not all, infrastructures related to streets. Yet a not insignificant number of these other agencies are private companies or other levels of government, or neighboring jurisdictions of the same level. Without coordination, individual efforts are compromised.

Coordinating infrastructure activities goes on at every level of government. Within each level, nearly every department affects or is affected by infrastructure and participates in its planning and budgeting decisions. To hint at the enormity of the task, consider the state of California. In the year 2020, its state government had 64 agencies serving a population of 40 million. Plus, there were 53 regional infrastructure entities, 58 counties, 482 municipalities, 1,037 school districts, and over 3,300 special districts with infrastructure responsibilities and taxing powers (water service, sewer service, parks, fire protection, etc.). In the San Francisco Bay Area alone, there are 27 different transport planning agencies. This fragmentation is at the core of transport planning problems there. These numbers give a glimpse of the scale and complexity involved in infrastructure governance.

Methods of coordination include jurisdiction-wide plans and strategies to guide policies, budgets, construction, and operations. A budget itself is a tool to coordinate. For infrastructure, the capital (long-term) budget coordinates investments into facilities and networks. The short-term budget coordinates operations and maintenance, and is particularly effective when the life cycle is incorporated. Maintenance, Repair, Rehabilitation, and Replacement (MRRR) programs are another tool to coordinate stages of the infrastructure life cycle. Flexible standards that are evaluated and adapted continually, in an evolutionary way that incorporates learning and improvement, are another method. Critical to coordination is the co-production / co-generation and sharing of data and knowledge via ICT platforms. Visualizing data, models that project trends, and scenarios that can compare and evaluate options for action that are shared on open-source, free, and public platforms go a long way in coordination. A distinction to keep clear is the coordination of long-range decision making through plans and strategies, and the coordination of ongoing operations and performance via budgets and other tools.

Coordination is an important matter across the board, for all stages of the life cycle. Coordination is essential to the accomplishment of each entity's mission. Coordination with others helps them achieve their own missions as well as common ventures with their counterparts.

Collaboration

Collaboration differs from coordination, even as it is a way to attain it. Collaboration is among individual persons conducting infrastructure management tasks. Collaboration among individuals within an organization as well as among other organizations involves a range of activities, including but not limited to communication, understanding, negotiation, and mutual action. Collaboration engages stakeholders so they commit to focus over the period(s) of time needed to transform the institution or parts of it, and attain their aims. This strains most participants' time budgets, and necessitates a feasible vision and strong leader / facilitator to keep the collaborative process on track. Collaboration is more personal than coordination.

An exemplary case of collaboration involves green infrastructure in the Okavango River delta in Botswana. It was led by the three nations involved, Angola, Botswana and Namibia, in collaboration with numerous partners to protect the delicate and critical ecosystem. Partners included local governments, industry, the academy, and NGOs such as the Namibia Nature Foundation, the Nature Conservancy, National Geographic, Conservation International, World Wildlife Fund, and the Peace Parks Foundation. Important was the selection of motivated and interested partners willing to play the long game. The intense interest was clear because the delta is a UNESCO World Heritage Site home to more than 700 species, diverse critical habitats, and vital natural resources.

A decisive element of the collaborators' strategy was to replace a hydroelectric dam with small-scale solar and other modular green infrastructures. Their multi-partner, multi-interest collaborative governance process – typical of large-scale infrastructure – entailed considering small-scale and low impact energy generation sources in lieu of dams and irrigation in order to protect the river delta. Their evolving success is based on several factors common to effective collaborations, including locally focused initiatives that mattered to survival, livelihoods that were dependent on a positive outcome, and the co-development of a common plan of action. Those most directly affected by the outcomes took more ownership of the process. This led to multiple gains for all the parties (Nature Conservancy 2019). Adapting and applying these tenets of collaboration enabled the participants to negotiate terms amenable to all parties (Moore 2014).

Integration

There are several types of *integration* that apply to the institutional take on governance. One is vertical integration. In an industry, for example electric power, it refers to the ownership of all levels of operations – generation, transmission, distribution, customer – in one company. In automobile manufacturing it refers to the entire supply, manufacturing, marketing, and sales chain: the suppliers, sub-manufacturers, assembly in several places, final assembly in one place, headquarters, sales outlets, and so on. Vertical integration occurs among levels of government as well as across multiple sectors. One example of the latter is the *New Jersey State Plan*. It integrates policies, plans, programs, and capital budgets of local, county, regional, state agencies using the State Plan itself and a legislated collaborative process used to prepare it: "cross-acceptance". Cross-acceptance of the first State Plan adopted in 1992 took four years and engaged thousands of government entities and tens of thousands of their employees, citizens, and interest groups (Gualini 2001; 2004). Full-scale integration takes time and resources.

Horizontal integration in an industry, for example consumer electronics, means that ownership for all four layers or levels – production (including parts, components, and subassemblies), distribution, sales, repair – is distributed among many different companies. Horizontal integration within a level of government, such as a local urban general plan (master plan, comprehensive plan, city plan), coordinates infrastructure, land use, environmental, housing, and related policies for one jurisdiction over a specified time horizon, say 20 years.

A singular example of infrastructure integration at the municipal level occurred in Stockholm's Hammarby Sjöstad district. There, the city redeveloped a former industrial port district into a new community by starting with a foundation of new infrastructures, each integrated with the others so that the outflows of one became the inflows of another. This circular infrastructure approach integrated each network with the others to create an integrated assemblage. Further, they were integrated into the natural environment for a sustainable foundation for the district (Iveroth et al. 2013). It was an example of multisectoral integration, both horizontal and vertical, in that the national government was involved.

The New Jersey and Stockholm examples can be translated into metro-, city-region-, and national-scale infrastructures via comprehensive planning and policy using collaboration and coordination. When multiple networks (electric, water, sewerage, etc.), multiple jurisdictions (local, regional, national), multiple sectors (private, public, non-profit, citizens), and multiple disciplines are involved; these processes take levels of resources and time well beyond routine governance. Yet this is what is required to govern complex and integrated infrastructures effectively.

Integration is enhanced and made easier when nodes in both the institutional and infrastructural networks are modular, small scale, and plug-and-play. This makes them more adaptable to other circumstances and transferable to other nodes. In this context, modular means a component such as a process that fits readily into another. Small scale refers to subsidiarity – matching the scale of the decision-making institution to the scale of infrastructure. Plug-and-play means operating a modular piece easily, once it has been inserted into the larger network. These characteristics are designed into the institution from the start, or retrofitted into a redesigned institution.

Flexibility

In the tripartite framework of structure, agency, and doctrine, two essential principles stand out that need be incorporated into both infrastructure and their governance institutions: *flexibility* and *adaptability*. They derive from the analysis represented in the right-hand column of the infrastructure characteristics outlined in Figure 7.1.

Infrastructure strategies, policies, plans, and the institutions that govern and finance them must be redesigned to implement these principles. Given the variety and complexities among cities and nations, there is no one-size-fits-all, no one silver bullet. In fact, universal, one-size-fits-all "silver bullets" propagated by large-scale and centralized institutions are a main source of our current predicaments. Institutions must be redesigned creatively to be adaptable and flexible in accord with their contexts. Switzerland, for example, approximates the conditions referred to, in that it has a highly articulated and interconnected federal network in which many small units of government are coordinated and integrated, more or less. We have also seen this type of integration at a much larger scale in Europe, operating for quite some time now, in the European Union.

Partnership

Partnerships entail collaboration, yet differ in that they often result in a legal, contractual relationship. They tend to involve fewer partners. Common partnerships are PPPs – public–private partnerships. A downside is that they can exclude others from the process and therefore the outcome, with potential suboptimal results. While partnerships in principle can result in positive outcomes, the disparities in power between them can benefit one partner over others. This has been documented to favor private sector partners (World Bank 2004b; Sclar 2000; among others).

Consider the evolution of governance institution. Their complexity, owing to the increasing intricacy of infrastructure networks themselves and their elaborate governance arrangements, is greater than ever (World Bank 2020). How is this complexity specified and codified in contractual agreements that govern PPPs for infrastructure? How again, when government and / or private sectors are corrupt or otherwise lacking capacity? The rapidly emerging role of the private sector in infrastructure worldwide is welcome due to infusions of capital and expertise. Yet they impose other costs that pose questions. Chief among them: Do current norms and practices in multisector partnerships safeguard the public interest?

Yet PPPs have multiple advantages *if* prepared and executed properly, and consider all the factors facing infrastructure managers. The research on actual practices, while heterodox, nonetheless suggests that partnerships can bring more benefits to the process if each partner exercises mutual respect and restraint, and allows for multiple win outcomes. This ideal is strained in the real world (World Bank 2019).

Privatization

Privatization involves the shifting responsibility from the public to the private sector. Historically, in many nations, infrastructure as a public good was the responsibility of the public sector. Robust research has long tested the effects of privatization on performance, and analyses found mixed results: some efficiency gains, some efficiency losses, and increased cleavages among sectors and levels of government. Tellingly, privatization studies typically focus on economic and service performance, with the recent addition of equity, and less on distributional, social, and environmental consequences. A landmark global assessment on privatization has revealed more problems than benefits, especially social inequity and negative environmental impacts (World Bank 2004b). Its findings are largely replicated by more recent studies, and still hold today.

Box 7.2 The World Bank

The operative word in World Bank is *bank*. It is an institution designed for the creation of financial wealth. In this it protects its investors and increases their earnings and assets. It was created as an outcome of the Bretton Woods Conference in 1944 as part of a global group of new institutions to extend "Western" institutions to the "developing world". Its modus operandi was financing the construction of large infrastructure projects to raise standards of living in poor nations. Hence its official name, the International Bank for Reconstruction and Development. Its report *Reforming Infrastructure* (World Bank 2004a) is indicative of its financial bias to concentrate wealth in private hands. The report is written by an economist, under the supervision of another economist, "with guidance from an advisory board" comprised of economists, with a forward written by economists, and peer reviewed by economists (World Bank 2004a, xv). It should not be a surprise then that its principal recommendations are those pertaining to the decrease in government regulation to enable increased private sector participation in the ownership, operation, and management of infrastructure. This 40-year worldwide strategy has involved deregulation and privatization, a strategy clearly signaled by the subtitle of the report: *Privatization, Regulation, and Competition*. The World Bank was a handmaiden to and simultaneously a generator and arbiter of the current neoliberal order. To quote from the report's forward: "effective regulation … is the most critical enabling condition for infrastructure reform. Protecting the interests of both investors and consumers is crucial to attracting the long term private capital needed … (World Bank 2004a, xii). The first sentence of the forward could not have more explicitly signaled the bank's bias: "Infrastructure industries and services are crucial for generating economic growth, alleviating poverty, and increasing international competitiveness" (World Bank 2004a, xi). Not only are the three principal objects of infrastructure all related to mainstream economic activities and indicators, the term infrastructure itself modifies "industries", a combination rarely seen in the literature. Instead, infrastructure almost always modifies networks, facilities, systems, or projects – instead of a blatantly economic word such as industries. This textual analysis of a few key portions of the book is merely indicative. The entire book is an instructive primer on these topics, vital for cautionary lessons for infrastructurists of all persuasions.

Anticipatory Planning Using the Life Cycle

Anticipatory planning may seem to be a pleonasm. In fact, much planning is reactive. Anticipatory planning is prospective, forward looking, and reasoned, taking the long view. Anticipatory governance in a new mode adapts the life cycle approach to infrastructure by providing a template for institutional design that is transformative. It starts with assessing how existing structures and processes correspond to the "old / current" column of Figure 7.1, followed by scenario testing for how to change them to correspond to the "new / future" column. This would continue by incorporating the stages of the life cycle (see Chapter 5) into the new structures and processes, as adapted for institutions. Thus: institutional technology selection, institutional design, costing the transformations, impact analysis, budgeting and financing that is continual and sustainable, instituting the actual reforms, life cycle management, training and recruiting, performance evaluation, and finally, reassessment via continual monitoring.

Leadership

Former mayor of Atlanta, Georgia Shirley Franklin called herself the "sewer mayor". Since when do American mayors unabashedly align themselves with infrastructure, especially one as unsexy as sewers? She was not just any mayor. *Time*, *U.S. News and World Report*, and *American City and County*, among others, awarded her honors.

Was it for her "pothole posse"? The ability to bring contentious actors together and fund a $3.9 billion "Clean Water Atlanta" program to clean up local waterways and sewage systems? Her administration linked infrastructure to development in other ways, including the Beltline Project, a 27-mile circular green transit corridor ringing Atlanta. Perhaps her biggest infrastructure achievement was to reinstate public sector leadership and funding for infrastructure. She got a 50 percent increase in property taxes and a one percent voter approved sales tax dedicated to infrastructure. She recognized that systemic underinvestment in infrastructure exacts a big toll in the long run. According to Franklin, "The biggest challenge is to make decisions today that would be beneficial 150 years from now" (Pomerance 2007, 57).

Mayor Franklin provides a sharp counterpoint to local governance in nations where neoliberal and austerity policies hold sway, when states and local governments have been systematically cutting spending on both capital and operational (including repair and maintenance) items in many but certainly not all jurisdictions. She knew that infrastructure investments guide growth and revitalization, and do so without regulations. In times of globalization and heightened competitiveness in which the best networked prevail, infrastructure does the networking and confers significant value to places and processes alike. In times when the call of sustainability animates responsible policy and investment decisions across all sectors of society and in all nations, leaders are progressively turning to infrastructure as a fundamental solution.

Other leadership exemplars include the legacies of the former American Secretary of State George C. Marshall, New York City and State official Robert Moses, and four-term Barcelona mayor Pasqual Maragall. The Marshall Plan, also known as the European Recovery Program, to reconstruct Europe and its cities after World War II was largely an infrastructure rebuilding effort. It won Marshall the Nobel Peace Prize in 1953. This use of infrastructure investments in a leadership capacity was paralleled in the institutional formation that accompanied the foreign aid, establishing the World Bank and the International Monetary Fund.

Robert Moses was arguably the most effective American planner – or more accurately, city builder – of the 20th century, in terms of getting projects built. His means were infrastructure. He was responsible for many parks, recreation areas, roadways, bridges, electric power infrastructures, and other projects. The political and institutional circumstances attending to his exploits are probably not replicable today, because he amassed a vast array of power, tools, and resources under his control. While his means and outcomes were questioned (Caro 1974), his profligate construction spree implemented in part another paragon of American planning, the Regional Plan Association's *The Regional Plan of New York and Environs*, itself in large measure an infrastructure plan (Regional Plan Association 1929).

Mayor Maragall was instrumental in bringing the 1992 Olympics and the Forum 2004 to Barcelona. Both massively transformed the city and the metro area, largely through infrastructure networks. He forged multisector and multilevel collaborations to design and build them, and designed responsive new institutions to govern them. His visionary leadership and ability to assemble and inspire individuals and interests to attain his transformative vision enabled the city to emerge as an exemplar.

Leadership that goes beyond the day-to-day back-and-forth of bureaucracies is needed. This is why infrastructure planners have an advantage that is well suited today. It is:

> leadership of the collaborative and visionary type [that] emerges readily in a strong planning culture. Planning is a leadership profession. This is due to the set of skills and knowledge that planners bring to their offices, including, a long-term horizon, a sense of the broader good, comprehensive consideration of the inter-relationship of complex and dynamic activities and their impacts, an inter-disciplinary perspective, and the ability to reconcile conflicting interests. This set of skills also serves, in part, to articulate what characterizes a strong, positive planning culture (Neuman 2007b: 162).

There are five general elements of leadership for infrastructure governance. These principles underlie the practice of leadership in planning, that is, the debating forums and decision arenas in which planning takes place. This often occurs outside the spaces of planning practitioners' offices and planning commissions. It happens in the halls of leadership, including those settings in which stakeholders and citizens take part. The five general elements of leadership are (Neuman 2019; see also Neuman 2009):

1. *Future orientation* – goals, objectives, strategies, plans
2. *Situational awareness* – place knowledge, context, complexity
3. *Cultural awareness* – place cultures, organizational cultures, interpersonal differences
4. *Communications* – listening, dialogue, understanding, evidence, images
5. *Greater good* – public interest, commonwealth, general welfare

Note that these elements are about people, and about the relations among people and among organizations. Thus, *relational* leadership approaches become critical if not paramount in a globalizing world where networked societies flourish. By contrast, *technocratic* approaches address performance outcomes. In principle, focusing on and measuring performance is fine, and complements relational approaches. However, when performance is paramount, people are subordinated to abstract criteria. Long-term consequences of a technocratic focus can lead to deteriorating performance of the governance institution. Its criteria, however, need to be aligned with the ways and means of finance and politics.

To close, what are the most effective structures and processes in governance institution to allow for the innovation, financing, and building of infrastructures that perform sustainably, equitably, and affordably? What are the barriers to their adoption? These are essential questions for institutional reformers and transformers.

The long trajectory of changing structural features of society, triggered by the advent of postindustrial globalisation and the networking of society, has yielded the global economy. Along with it, a genuine transformation of cities and how they are designed, built, and managed. These changes are especially notable in the infrastructure sectors. Yet our governance structures have not kept pace, and by and large remain conditioned by centuries old institutions, such as the municipal corporation and the nation-state. Is it any wonder that we are now saddled with crumbling infrastructure and declining service levels? This question underscores the urgency to transform governance.

Notes

1 This brings to mind the adage attributed to Mark Twain: "When all you have is a hammer, all your problems look like nails." – a condemnation of the inappropriate use of tools.
2 As of 2000, if California's GDP were counted as a nation. In 2020, per the IMF WEO (International Monetary Fund World Economic Outlook), California's state GDP would rank fifth in the 195 nation WEO database. https://www.imf.org/en/Publications/WEO/weo-database/2021/April/weo-report?
3 Here I use the term "process" instead of the social scientific term "agency". This is because agency as a verb typically (but not exclusively) refers to action by an individual (Giddens 1984). In the cited book, Anthony Giddens introduces the concept of "structuration", somewhat akin to my use of the term process, as structuration pertains to structuring the institution through an accumulation of individual agency and group process over time.

Bibliography

Albert, R., Jeog, H., and Barabasi, L-A. (2000). Error and attack-tolerance of complex networks. *Nature*, 406: 378–382.
ASCE (American Society of Civil Engineers). (2020). *America's Infrastructure Report Card*. Washington DC: Author.

Bellah, R., Madsen, R., Sullivan, W., Swidler, A., and Tipton, S. (1991). *The Good Society*. New York: Alfred Knopf.
Braudel, F. (1992 [1949]). *The Mediterranean and the Mediterranean World in the Age of Phillip II*. New York: Harper Collins.
Brenner, N. (2019). *New Urban Spaces: Urban Theory and the Scale Question*. New York: Oxford University Press.
Castells, M. (2018). *Rupture: The Crisis of Liberal Democracy*. Cambridge: Polity Press.
Caro, R. (1974). *The Power Broker: Robert Moses and the Fall of New York*. New York: Alfred A. Knopf.
Choay, F. (1996 [1980]). *The Rule and the Model: On the Theory of Architecture and Urbanism*. Cambridge, MA: MIT Press.
David, P. (1994). Why are institutions the "carriers of history"?: Path dependence and the evolution of conventions, organizations and institutions. *Structural Change and Economic Dynamics*, 5(2): 205–220.
de Roo, G. and Boelens, L. (eds.) (2016). *Spatial Planning in a Complex and Unpredictable World of Change: Towards a Proactive Co-evolutionary Type of Planning*. Groningen: Coöperatie In Planning UA.
Deutsch, K. (1963). *The Nerves of Government: Models of Political Communication and Control*. New York: The Free Press.
Faludi, A. and van der Valk, A, J. (1994). *Rule and Order: Dutch Planning Doctrine in the Twentieth Century*. Dordrecht, Netherlands: Kluwer Academic Publishers.
Flyvbjerg, B., Bruzelius, N., and Rothengatter, W. (2003). *Megaprojects and Risk: An Anatomy Of Ambition*. Cambridge: Cambridge University Press.
Fuerth, L. (2013). Operationalizing anticipatory governance. *Prism*, 2(4): 31–46.
Giddens, A. (1984). *The Constitution of Society*. Berkeley, CA: University of California Press.
Gualini, E. (2001). *The Intelligence of Institutions*. Aldershot, UK: Ashgate.
Gualini, E. (2004). *Multi-level Fovernance and Institutional Change: The Europeanization of Regional Policy in Italy*. Aldershot, UK: Ashgate.
Hall, P. (1982). *Great Planning Disasters*. Berkeley, CA: University of California Press.
Healey, Patsy, 2010. *Making Better Places: The Planning Project in the Twenty-First Century*. Basingstoke: Palgrave-Macmillan.
Independent Investigation Board. (2006). *Train Derailment at Hatfield: A Final Report by the Independent Investigation Board*. London: Office of the Rail Regulator.
Innes, J. and Booher, D. (2010). *Planning with Complexity: An Introduction to Collaborative Rationality for Public Policy*. London: Routledge.
IPSOS. (2018). *Beyond Populism?* Paris: Author.
Iveroth, S., Vernay, A., Mulder, K., and Brandt, N. (2013). Implications of systems integration at the urban level: The case of Hammarby Sjöstad, Stockholm. *Journal of Cleaner Production*, 48: 220–231.
Jack, I. (2001). The 12:10 to Leeds. *Granta*, 73: 67–105.
Kahneman, D. (2011). *Thinking, Fast and Slow*. New York and London: Penguin.
Klein, N. (2014). *This Changes Everything: Capitalism vs. the Climate*. New York: Simon and Schuster.
Landau, M. (1969). Redundancy, rationality, and the problem of duplication and overlap. *Public Administration Review*. 29(4): 346–358.
Mau, B. (2020). *MC24: 24 Principles for Designing Massive Change in Your Life and Work*. London and New York: Phaidon Press.
Moore, C. (2014). *The Mediation Process: Practical Strategies for Resolving Conflict*. San Francisco: Jossey-Bass.

National Intelligence Council. (2021). *Global Trends 2040: A More Contested World.* Washington DC: Author.

Nature Conservancy. (2019). *Connected and Flowing: A Renewable Future for Rivers, Climate and People.* Washington DC: Author.

Neuman, M. (2019). Leadership. In Green Leigh, N., French, S., Guhathakurta, S., and Stiftel, B. (eds.), *The Routledge Handbook of International Planning Education.* New York: Routledge, 174–183.

Neuman, M. (2012). The image of the institution: A cognitive theory of institutional change. *Journal of the American Planning Association,* 78(2): 139–156.

Neuman, M. (2010). *The Imaginative Institution: Planning and Governance in Madrid.* Aldershot, UK: Ashgate.

Neuman, M. (2009). Spatial planning leadership by infrastructure: An American view. *International Planning Studies,* 14(2): 201–217.

Neuman, M. (2007a). Multi-scalar large institutional networks in regional planning. *Planning Theory and Practice,* 8(3): 319–344.

Neuman, M. (2007b). How institutions and individuals use plans: Planning cultures and images of futures. In Hopkins, L. D. and Zapata, M. A (eds.), *Engaging the Future: Forecasts, Scenarios, Plans, and Projects.* Cambridge, MA: Lincoln Institute Press, 155–174.

Neuman, M. and Gavinha, J. (2005). The planning dialectic of continuity and change: The evolution of metropolitan planning in Madrid. *European Planning Studies,* 13(7): 985–1012.

Neuman, M. and Whittington, J. (2000). *Building California's Future: Current Conditions in California's Infrastructure Planning, Budgeting and Financing.* San Francisco: Public Policy Institute of California.

Pomerance, R. (2007). A cool hand leads Hotlanta. *Pennsylvania Gazette,* 105(6): 56–57.

Regional Plan Association. (1929). *Regional Plan of New York and its Environs.* New York: Author.

Saad, L. (2020). *Trust in Federal Government's Competence Remains Low.* Washington DC: Gallup Organization.

Sclar, E. (2000). *You Don't Always Get What You Pay For: The Economics of Privatization.* Ithaca, NY: Cornell University Press.

Steinmo, S., Thelen K., and Longstreth F. (eds.). (1992). *Structuring Politics: Historical Institutionalism in Comparative Politics.* Cambridge, UK: Cambridge University Press.

World Bank. (2020). *Enhancing Government Effectiveness and Transparency: The Fight Against Corruption.* Kuala Lumpur: Author.

World Bank. (2019). *Technical Brief on Resilient Infrastructure PPPs – Contracts and Procurement.* Washington DC: Author.

World Bank. (2004a). *Reforming Infrastructure: Privatization, Regulation, and Competition.* Washington DC: Author.

World Bank. (2004b). *World Development Report 2004.* Washington DC: Author.

8
Financing and Budgeting

Financing and budgeting are the crux of infrastructure in practice. They form its realpolitik. If there is no money to pay for it, it does not get built. First and foremost is funding infrastructure across its life cycle. Second is to link financing to the budget. This goes for both the capital and operating budgets. Third is to link the budget to the plan or strategy. This way, life cycle financing and life cycle budgeting based on long-term plans and strategies can become the norm. The goal is that the identification and sources of monies are as reliable and as sustainable as the infrastructure. These precepts will be explored in this chapter.

Political and economic leaders across the globe have taken notice of current failings and future challenges. Many places suffer from the inadequate planning, overburdened systems, and limited revenues that define the state of infrastructure today. There is a widespread recognition that it will take a *sustained* financial commitment to reverse the effects of past inaction.

Life cycle funding is the single most important missing link in solving the infrastructure finance conundrum. History reminds us that the role of finance in infrastructure and city building is always foundational. For example, along the path to its evolution as a global city, in London we see the pivotal confluence of finance capital with infrastructure. Just as in Rome two millennia ago, all roads led to London, as well as rails and ships. London was where the greatest merger of finance and transport made its mark in transforming London into the first global city. Prominent financiers such as Frankfurt banker Nathan Mayer Rothschild, who arrived in London and set up a banking house in the city in 1798, propelled the "marriage of two capitals" approach. Rothschild did so with a large sum of money given to him by his father, Amschel Mayer Rothschild. This bank financed numerous large-scale projects, including railways and the Suez Canal (Ferguson 1998).

London was not alone. New York and Chicago followed as first in the New World to apply this "tale of two capitals" formula. The two capitals being finance and facilities, always married. Historian William Cronon's magisterial *Nature's Metropolis* described how the marriage of these two capitals made Chicago, and transformed much of the American continent besides (Cronon 1991).

Today, society demands new types and arrangements of infrastructure to correspond to new needs like mobility, speed, agility, big data, the cloud, virtual reality, and so on. Is it not time to employ our intellectual capital to truly innovative thinking for infrastructure capital? As one of the biggest, fastest growing, and most lucrative sectors of the economy, surely infrastructure finance merits our best thinking. The European Union sees this as the future of the European economy. "The financial system should be a vehicle for promoting these objectives by embedding social and other sustainability considerations into capital allocation, and by promoting more socially sustainable approaches to finance" (EU High-Level Expert Group in Sustainable Finance 2018, 85).

The obstacle here is history. Infrastructure finance capital worldwide has historically been only to pay for the capital costs of construction. Taxes, tolls, and user fees were presumed to take care of operations and maintenance. Some were dedicated, many were not. Most did not keep pace with inflation, much less demand. Expenditures beyond operations and maintenance fell outside of standard funding mechanisms. This prevented any chance of cradle-to-cradle life cycle funding. The inevitable result was massive backlogs in infrastructure, for both construction (capital costs) and repair (operating costs). Funding the capital costs is only now in question. No matter the source, the amount needed and what it is needed for must be calculated in an entirely new way. Business as usual for infrastructure finance only digs the holes – infrastructure backlogs – we have dug even deeper.

One of the problems stems from the privatization of infrastructure and its financing. It has continued the focus on upfront capital costs. It is easy to grasp why the private sector, particularly finance, has muscled its way onto infrastructure turf. The increasingly superior returns on finance capital compared to other types of capital, on top of multitrillion-dollar worldwide infrastructure spending, go a long way in explaining the ascendance of infrastructure in equity arenas. Infrastructure investments are returning the solid and low risk yields compared to traditional alternatives. The old situation of government paying for infrastructure is gone. What will replace it that will be both sustainable and equitable in serving the public good?

To make sure that the public interest remains served, value capture, tax increment financing, and other new tools for infrastructure finance become paramount. This applies even more as governments have become more tax averse. Yet value capture is a tall order in debilitated government regimes. Private equity prefers government's hands-off infrastructure, especially now that bond and cash yields are nearly nonexistent and equities are increasingly risky. This is paradoxical, as private equity and real estate developers at the same time seek certainty, which in large part is guaranteed by strong and stable government, and an economy bolstered by reliable infrastructure. Can society have it both ways?

It is not only a matter of *how* financing is obtained. *What* it pays for, *who* pays for it, and *how* those decisions are made are also of import. What does not mean which systems or projects, like which airport will get a third runway or which type of energy will be funded. Existing mechanisms have those decisions more or less sorted, though we can always do with more transparency, evidence and civic input. Instead, we need to devise new financing decision criteria based on the cradle-to-cradle life cycle, equity, and sustainability. This represents a break from past practices, that have been fixed in law and professional codes. And hard to change.

The fixed costs of sunk capital and the fixed facilities it builds determine urban form and function, as they have for millennia. Sunk capital refers to non-recoverable funds that were invested in built infrastructure. Fixed facilities, such as roads and rails, ports and parks, and so on, are priceless assets of the public trust, and civic works of art at their very best. Can we transform equally fixed and discipline-bound methods to finance infrastructure? Professional habits die hard. Who would have thought Bruce Willis to be a philosopher of infrastructure?

Revealing are the terms in use today to call infrastructure, especially in finance circles. Public *capital, asset,* and *investment* have replaced what long ago was called the "public trust" and the "commonwealth". The terms have changed over time so that private sector language dominates now. Restoring a better balance of funding, so that all sectors and interests pay their fair share, is an aim of this chapter.

Why Infrastructure Budgets and Finance are Often the Cinderella of Governance

Any government manager knows that infrastructure is vital. The question then becomes: If it is so important, why are infrastructure deficits so large? Why is infrastructure in such bad condition? Of course the answer is there's not enough money. Why not? Who cut taxes, again and again? Who trims budgets year after year? What is often the first budget item to get cut? Infrastructure repair and maintenance. "We'll do it next year", we hear over and over. Next year never seems to roll around, until the bridge falls, the water main bursts, the levee breaks. Capital spending gets deferred, too. Infrastructure is prone to the double slash – in both capital and operating budgets.

Why do governments get seduced into not providing sufficient funds? In this era, political leaders are precluding, repealing, or otherwise turning back and scaling down government, regulations, and taxes. This stems from a worldwide neoliberal dynamic of deregulation, privatization, and decentralization. A healthy aim of these efforts is to increase accountability and responsibility at the most appropriate levels. Yet as the citizenry, media, and governments themselves awaken to the mounting evidence of the effects of the increasingly unfettered market, there is a new demand for government to reclaim more of its dominion over the public good in affirmative and proactive ways. Need it be regulatory, should it be strategic, or are there new ways? Regardless, financing infrastructure will take center stage.

The relation of infrastructure finance and politics has undergone a revolution in recent decades. The ascendance of finance capital in global cities and the networks that link and support them is one factor that conditions this relation (Sassen 2001). Other factors include the neoliberal shift transforming governance and the consequent changes in funding sources for and ownership of infrastructure – privatization and partnerships being their most predominant forms. This shift has complicated the governance of infrastructure, once a more straightforward public sector enterprise, easier when cities were smaller and comprised a much higher portion of the metropolitan population. These changes have been occurring for quite some time, and are not new (Neuman 2014, 799).

Infrastructure Finance Issues

In the United Kingdom, a recent case illuminates finance concerns. The high-speed rail (HSR) (300 kph) extension from London to northern England has become controversial for several reasons. One is endemic to large and complex projects – cost overruns (Flyvbjerg, Bruzelius, and Rothengatter 2003). Estimates suggest that over £100 billion will be spent on HS2 by the time it is completed. Is that amount better spent on high-quality fast rail (200+ kph) in northern and central England? Especially when travel time saving are in the order of minutes, due to the island's short distances. Is that amount better spent on smaller, distributed, multimodal systems throughout the UK? Existing mechanisms rely on politics to adjudicate such decisions. Are political decision criteria based on cradle-to-cradle, life cycle, equity, and sustainability factors? Are these criteria etched into institutional procedures? Are they fully transparent, evidence-based, and responsive to civic input? This discussion applies to HSR in the USA as well, to projects in Texas, California, and Florida, as well as the conversion to HSR of the Northeast Corridor between Boston and Washington. The UK and US cases raise broader issues, identified below.

1. *Funding is as critical as financing*
    Greater attention must be paid to the long-term (life cycle) funding of large-scale projects, rather than the short-term financing to get them off the ground.
2. *Project appraisal criteria must be objective, systematic, and long term*
    Methods of project appraisal need to take greater account of the long-term and wider economic, social, and environmental costs and benefits of infrastructure investment. Modeling of comparative options and scenarios needs to be able to account across the entire cradle-to-cradle life cycle for both positive and negative externalities, as well as for induced demand.
3. *Subsidiarity and trust are central to good investment*
    The governance of infrastructure investment decision-making needs to correspond to the criteria and principles of good governance outlined in the prior

chapter – the trust factor. More decision-making concerning the funding and financing of infrastructure should be devolved to subnational bodies at all scales, along with greater fiscal powers to unlock funding sources – the subsidiarity factor.
4. *Infrastructure often leads to significant political conflict*
   Conflicts are manifest in several ways. One is local opposition to large systems with big impacts. Another is competition between the public and private sectors. Yet another includes competition among service providers. The conflicts arising from political competition within a jurisdiction for projects due to the scarcity of funding is all too common. Multisector governance needs to account for these types of conflict fairly and as objectively as possible, while recognizing that they are inherently political.
5. *Multi-profession collaboration is essential to effective financing*
   Financing tends to be little understood by planners, designers, and engineers. Understanding and strengthening the links between financing and planning enables planners, designers, engineers, financiers, and policymakers to be able to be more effective when they collectively unite their respective expertise. They enlarge each other's scopes and extend each other's time horizons. Planners and designers add spatial and equity perspectives, the life cycle method, and the analysis of multiple impacts to the private sector's financial knowledge. Working together rounds out simple cost-benefit, efficiency, and environmental criteria that are commonly used. This is done best in an open, public arena with civic participation, transparency, and accountability because it inserts local knowledge into the process and enhances the trust that government needs to act.

Private Sector Benefits and Costs

Lest these paragraphs be misunderstood, there are advantages to private sector investments and financing:

> In the best resilient infrastructure projects, investors benefit because these projects provide portfolio diversification, mitigate the future climate risks that traditional infrastructure is exposed to as long-term assets, enable more efficient projects from design through approval, ensure operational continuity and thus ongoing revenue generation, even in the case of shocks or stresses, and provide environmental and social impact benefits (Coffee 2018, 4).

For example, reflect on the small portion of overall budget given to capital outlay expenditures by many governments. They can be less than 1 percent, which pales in comparison to robust private sector capital expenditures, not to mention research and development outlays. A business or government cannot succeed over the long term by investing so frugally. It is a matter of "penny wise, pound foolish".

The State of California is indicative. The total value of state-owned infrastructure in California is likely upwards of a trillion dollars. It consists of 20,000 owned and leased structures, 200 million square feet of built space, and two and one half million acres of property (Department of General Services 1999, Neuman and Whittington 2000). The state has added to this massive inventory by spending $2.83 billion annually (not all from state revenues) on capital facilities, averaged over the past decade (Department of Finance 1999, 42).[1] Thus California has been replenishing its stock of public works at an average annual rate of far less than 1 percent. While accounting categories prevent the calculation of an exact figure, we estimate that the state has been spending on the order of several billions of dollars annually to maintain its infrastructure, averaged over the last ten years.[2] In other terms, each year California spends a small fraction of the total worth of its public works on the maintenance of infrastructure (Neuman and Whittington, 2000). Is it not wiser to invest more in infrastructure? Private sector attitudes and practices can help in this regard.

Caution and balance must be applied. Infrastructure facilities and social services that are also infrastructures, such as education, health care, libraries, police and fire protection, and related ones, are in the end public services for the benefit of all in society. They are public sector responsibilities. This impinges on any privatization scheme or proposal. Why change to a system whose first priority is profit, not serving a broad public via the delivery of a service? Privatizing costs more because profits must be added (15–35 percent are typical industry profit margins, often much higher), insurance must be added, and taxes must be added. The latter two vary significantly, yet together can total at least another 25 percent. These costs are not borne when the infrastructure is fully built and operated by the public sector.

Moreover, there are questions of risk (will aggrieved parties be compensated, will aggrieving parties be held accountable), reliability (will environmental and social impacts be prevented or mitigated), equity (will the poor or otherwise differently abled have access, will livable wages be paid), accountability (can private entities – by definition more opaque and closed than government – become fully transparent to the public), and so on. Sometimes an industry or corporation providing infrastructure services becomes an out-of-control force with which governments and citizens grapple. These are critical matters that need to be resolved during discussions about privatization proposals.

Life Cycle Financing

A life cycle approach to infrastructure planning and financing as advocated in this book is the main method to get sustainable infrastructure. Let's compare the two life

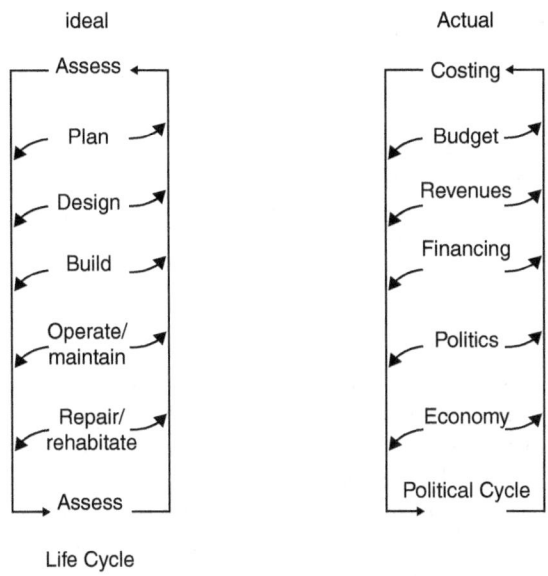

Figure 8.1 Life Cycle of Infrastructure – Ideal versus Actual

cycle methods in Figure 8.1. On the right side you see the current, "business as usual" approach. It is a politically driven, capital cost-based model that at best funds new infrastructure in line with the debt ratings of the jurisdiction as determined by financial institutions and markets. Do you want your future subject to a distant and impersonal number cruncher who doesn't know the local community and its aspirations? On the left is a truncated version (7 instead of 15 stages) of an ideal life cycle.

While the left side of the diagram is a general model, it can be adjusted to local realities. Its most important contribution is the recognition that infrastructure not only has a service life that is the actual life span of the physical infrastructure system or facility itself. Most "life cycle" approaches to infrastructure have stopped here. But the infrastructure life cycle as presented here is more than merely the life span of the bridge or road network. It takes into account the entire set of interrelated processes for getting infrastructure from the mind to the ground, and beyond.

Perhaps the most critical link in the life cycle chain, at least in places that put heavy reliance on long-term debt to pay for capital facilities, is finance. The debt accounting process in these polities does not enable two critical functions. The first is an *automatic funding mechanism* that provides for consistent and routine revenue flows for the entire life cycle of infrastructure. The second is a type of *sinking fund* and / or *revolving fund* that pays for continual maintenance and upgrades over a facility's or a network's lifetime. A dedicated percentage of debt service could automatically be deposited into this fund. The first of these functions has been discussed above. The second will be outlined below, in the next section.

Financing Mechanisms

Financing mechanisms mobilize funding for sustainable infrastructure. The list below refers to the more common existing means of securing revenue, and is not complete. Given the range of options for financing infrastructure services, policymakers must decide which of these methods are most appropriate. Innovations in finance are constant, and can be a major contribution of the private finance sector to infrastructure and its financing.

Bonds

Two categories of *bonds* are *general obligation bonds* and *revenue bonds*. A general obligation bond means that the issuer is guaranteeing repayment of the bond using any means necessary. The full faith, credit, and taxing power of the issuer are backing the bond. Revenue bonds distinguish themselves from general obligation bonds through their method of repayment. Unlike general obligation bonds that rely on taxation, revenue bonds are guaranteed by a specific revenue stream generated by the issuer. The most common issuers of revenue bonds, at least in the United States, are transportation, hospitals, power systems, and sewer and water systems. The capacity to issue debt bonds is conditioned by three factors: the financial markets, the preferences of voters, and the economic cycle. The latter two factors have the greatest influence on voting for bond referenda.

Indirect Methods and Subsidies

Indirect methods, such as pricing, subsidies, taxation, and fiscal policy, help reduce investment risks, thus enhancing levels of investment. They should be appropriately priced to guide demand. Policies and regulations are needed to set price signals. In this regard, fiscal measures include pricing of externalities such as carbon emissions, congestion, and phasing out fossil fuel subsidies. Structural policies that support investment in sustainable infrastructure include tax reform, subsidies, and other investment incentives (IMF 2019).

Sinking Funds or Revolving Funds

A *sinking fund* or a *revolving fund* is established to pay for continual maintenance and upgrades over a facility's or a network's lifetime. A dedicated percentage of debt service is automatically be deposited on a periodic basis into the fund. A sinking fund is a fund containing money set aside or saved to pay off a debt or bond issued to finance infrastructure. A government or company that issues debt will need to pay that debt off in the future, and the sinking fund helps to soften the hardship of a large outlay of revenue at the outset. A sinking fund is established so the issuer (government or company) can contribute to the fund in the years leading up to its maturity date. By contrast, a revolving fund is a type of sinking fund in which the original sum is continually replenished as withdrawals are made, instead of being gradually being drawn down. This makes a revolving fund more sustainable and long-lasting compared to a sinking fund.

Joint Development

Joint development projects involve the partnership of public and private entities for mutual gain, which would not be possible for either acting alone. A common example is for transport, allowing the integrated development of public transport and private commercial improvements, with transport physically or functionally related to commercial, residential, or mixed-use development. Public and private investments are coordinated between transit agencies and developers to improve land owned by a transit agency, with mutual benefit and shared cost among all parties involved. Joint development is a form of value capture, as a transit agency captures some of the economic value created by its transit system and uses the funds to help finance expenses.[3]

> For example, a transit agency may partner with a developer to lease property owned by the transit agency near a transit station to build office space or residential units, thereby raising revenue (via the rent payments) for the transit system in the process. Another example of a joint development is the coordinated construction of an underground transit station and a mixed-use development above it in the air rights (FTA 2020, 1).

Public–Private Partnerships[4]

A popular model for improving the quantity and quality of services is a partnership between the public and private sectors. Partnerships can also be forged between government and nonprofit groups. *Public–private partnerships* have been formed at all levels of government. Many partnerships revolve around the joint development of real estate, such as redevelopment around multimodal transport terminals, or transit-oriented development. Here value capture and tax increment financing play key roles. They typically involve arrangements in which a private entity leases or purchases assets to develop and operate them. These partnerships provide significant benefits to government by providing revenue and bringing technical and entrepreneurial talent to a project.

National Subventions and Transfers

The national and regional / state governments transfer considerable monies to smaller jurisdictions on an "earmarked" (dedicated to a specific use or purpose) and revenue-sharing basis. In the United States, the bulk of the transfers for "hard" infrastructure are linked to transportation infrastructure development and maintenance. For example, the states each receive annually millions or billions of dollars to build highways, bridges, and related infrastructure from the federal government via its highway trust fund. Social infrastructures such as health and welfare also have large transfers of funds to smaller jurisdictions.

General Taxes

All levels of government can impose taxes on citizens for the purpose of financing services. *General taxes* include income taxes for individuals, businesses, and corporations, and sales (value-added) taxes. General taxes pertain to general government services and special taxes pertain to taxes levied for specific purpose. General and special taxes can be used to finance infrastructure services when the distribution of benefits is disbursed across the public, but not when they target limited or specific groups.

Special Taxes

Special taxes include but are not limited to property taxes, fuel taxes, consumption taxes, and real estate transfer taxes. These are sometimes called "dedicated revenues". Other examples include licensing fees, airport use taxes, landing fees, and tolls for roads, bridges, and ferries. According to some charters and constitutions, however, the imposition of such taxes requires voter approval. Dedicated revenue streams are increasingly being diverted the general fund to pay for general expenses in times of austerity and government budget deficits (DuPuis and McFarland 2016). This subverts the law and intent of special taxes and dedicated revenues. As a result, the infrastructure it was dedicated to suffers.

Special Assessments

Some infrastructure investments (such as such as flood control, streetlighting, and underground utility service) produce spillover benefits to a spatially targeted population called a district. Special assessment *districts* are designed to levy taxes on property owners that directly benefit from this category of infrastructure investment. Voters or property owners must approve these *special assessments*, as provided for in local laws. Tax increment financing (TIF) is a subcategory of special assessment that provides another vehicle for financing infrastructure investments that enhance property values by capturing part of this gain and using it to pay debt service. Like many special assessments, tax increment financing is applied in special districts specified by law.

Developer Exactions

Developer exactions, also called *impact fees*, are levies on new development or redevelopment. They are one-time collections that are part of the building approval process. Impact fees are levied to cover the infrastructure costs associated with new development, such as school and library construction, sewer and water infrastructure construction or connection to an existing system, and road construction. Such fees are not viewed as special taxes if they reasonably reflect the cost of providing service and if the revenue is not placed in the general fund. This is referred to as "fair share" apportioning that covers the cost of new facilities and services directly attributable to the new development or redevelopment. The proliferation of developer fees and exactions has led, in some jurisdictions, to legislation designed to limit further increases in fees, whether in absolute or relative terms (adjusted for inflation, for example).

User Fees

User fees and *charges* are levied on the use and consumption of infrastructure services. Revenues generated by user charges can be used to finance the construction, operation, and maintenance of facilities. User charges can also be used to control demand, for example to avoid or limit congestion by varying the prices according to the level of demand during peak and off-peak periods. User fees and charges can be structured in a variety of ways. Fees can vary according to the level of consumption (as with water and electricity) or remain a flat monthly charge (as with garbage collection). User fees are not considered special taxes if they do not exceed the reasonable cost of providing the regulatory service or activity for which they are charged, and if they are not levied for general revenue purposes.

User fees can be levied by either a public or private entity. In the case of a government provider, fees need to reflect the costs of services to avoid voter disapproval. Also, the fees must be channeled into infrastructure service. If the service is privatized, the private provider is free to levy fees on users. If the provider is granted a utility franchise for which there are no alternative service providers, the government must regulate pricing and service provision to protect the public's interests.

Beneficiary Charges

Beneficiary charges are levies that are based on the beneficial effect that an infrastructure service has on properties and businesses. They are not associated with actual consumption but rather with the benefits generated by the infrastructure service. An example of a beneficiary charge would be a levy for street lighting or flood protection. On the other hand, public parks and squares, which increase the property and use values of those buildings surrounding them, do not impose beneficiary charges.

In Closing

In the end, questions of infrastructure boil down to money. As indicated in prior chapters, the deteriorating conditions of infrastructure in most countries, and the persistence of unsustainable, large-scale centralized systems, has been a long time in the making, largely due to structural factors pertaining to the economy and to governance in the neoliberal era.

These reasons are principally threefold: the impotence of and thus less confidence in the public sector, consequent decreases in tax revenue and regulation, and concomitant increases in deficits and debt. As a result, the complexity and escalating cost of infrastructure, along with other factors, have put politics and finance at the fore (Neuman 2014).

This panorama is highlighted by the fact that the capital costs of large-scale infrastructure systems are often referred to in financial and infrastructural spheres as "sunk costs". That is, once they are spent, the fixed nature of a given infrastructure system does not allow for that system or its cost to be recovered, other than as return on investment. Given the nature of infrastructure, mostly underground and completely unrecoverable, we see how ironically appropriate the term sunk cost is. How to invert this equation so that infrastructure revenue raising and expenditures are not one-time sunk costs, but continual and replenishing? These are political questions.

> While the politics-finance conjunction is easy to identify, current practices of infrastructure finance are beginning to tackle thorny issues such as public risk and value capture … While there is an abundance of ways to finance infrastructure when they are single projects and / or have limited time horizons, new types of financing are needed that are sustainable financially and economically over the long run (50 years and more).
>
> They need to answer some fundamental questions, until recently foreign to standard infrastructure finance decision processes. What aspects of private risk assessment can be adapted for the public sector and public-private partnerships that are not indebted to the pure profit motive? What are the most effective mechanisms to finance infrastructure in a tax constrained environment? Is there a life cycle approach to financing that goes beyond the traditional financing that is largely limited to the initial capital investment, to fund the entire life-cycle over the long term? (Neuman 2014, 806).

Notes

1. The total value of the state's capital assets has never been quantified. Such a calculation would require an appraisal of every property in state ownership. The cost and time to obtain this type of valuation is considered prohibitive by the Department of General Services.
2. From the *Governor's Budget Summary* (State of California 1999); and *Capital Outlay and Infrastructure Report* (California Department of Finance 1999).
3. Adapted from FTA Circular C 7050.1B of August, 2020
4. The remainder of these financing mechanisms are adapted from and closely follow Dowall (2000), for which the author is grateful.

References

California Department of Finance. (1999). *Capital Outlay and Infrastructure Report*. Sacramento, CA: Author.

California Department of General Services. (1999). *Statewide Property Inventory*. Sacramento, CA: Author.

Coffee, J. (2018). *Money for Resilient Infrastructure: How to Finance America's Climate Changed Future*. Chicago, IL: Climate Resilience Consulting.

Cronon, W. (1991). *Nature's Metropolis: Chicago and the Great West*. New York: W. W. Norton.

Dowall, D. (2000). *California's Infrastructure Policy for the 21st Century: Issues and Opportunities*. San Francisco: Public Policy Institute of California.

DuPuis, N. and McFarland, C. (2016). *Paying for Local Infrastructure in a New Era of Federalism*. Washington DC: National League of Cities.

EU High-Level Expert Group in Sustainable Finance. (2018). *Financing a Sustainable European Union*. Brussels: European Commission.

Ferguson, N. (1998). *The House of Rothschild: Money's Prophets 1798–1848*. New York: Viking.

FTA (Federal Transit Administration). (2020). *Joint Development Guidance*. Washington DC: Author. www.transit.dot.gov/JointDevelopment, accessed 2 March, 2021

Flyvbjerg, B., Bruzelius, N., and Rothengatter, W. (2003). *Megaprojects and Risk: An Anatomy Of Ambition*. Cambridge: Cambridge University Press.

IMF (International Monetary Fund). (2019). Sustainable finance. In *Global Financial Stability Report*, 81–92. Washington DC: Author.

Neuman, M. (2014). The long emergence of the infrastructure emergency. *Town Planning Review*, 85(6): 795–806.

Neuman, M. and Whittington, J. (2000). *Building California's Future: Current Conditions in California's Infrastructure Planning, Budgeting and Financing*. San Francisco: Public Policy Institute of California.

State of California. (1999). *Governor Gray Davis, Governor's Budget Summary 1999–2000*. Sacramento, CA: Author.

9
Future Directions

Whither Infrastructure?

> The point of the report is simply this: The world's economic systems teeter atop "backward-looking risk assessment models that merely extrapolate historical trends." But the future will not be like the past. Our models are degrading by the day, and we don't understand – we don't want to understand – how much in society could topple when they fail, and how much suffering that could bring. One place to start is by recognizing how fragile the basic *infrastructure* of civilization is even now, in this climate, in rich countries (Klein 2021, emphasis added).

The report noted above is *The Green Swan: Central Banking and Financial Stability in the Age of Climate Change* from the Bank for International Settlements (Bolton et al. 2020). When a conservative institution like the Bank for International Settlements sounds the alarm, the world's central banks, governments, monetary experts, and policymakers notice. And act. Even recent methods like risk assessment and much economic and scientific modeling cannot keep pace with the accelerating and cascading changes fueled by the climate crisis. This report like so many others makes clear that business as usual only digs our graves even deeper. Yet this should not be surprising. Conservative financial institutions take the long view, just as the principles and practices in this book. We must respect and regenerate nature, and cities, and their interaction – largely via infrastructure – in wholly new ways.

One way is to connect dots thought never before possible. An example is the Resource Renewal Institute's Fish in the Fields initiative. Fish in the Fields targets California's 500,000 acres of flooded rice fields to produce a new source of protein while cutting methane emissions from rice cultivation. This work has uncovered key discoveries that could have a large-scale impact on global health and climate (Resource Renewal Institute 2021):

- Tons of fish protein can be sustainably grown in flooded rice fields feeding solely on naturally occurring plankton to ease the pressure on ocean forage fish.
- Plankton, the natural food source for growing fish, sequester carbon at 20 to 50 times the rate that trees capture carbon.
- New scientific research demonstrating that the introduction of small fish can drastically cut methane released from freshwater.

While this is not infrastructure, commonly conceived, it is a new vision of productive green infrastructure that serves multiple purposes, like many national parks. It can start to shape a new economy, once scaled up. Many other examples exist worldwide where previously unconnected infrastructure dots come together in novel and sustainable ways. Connecting dots is a form of integration that is the soul of this book.

Infrastructure has always been essential to the well-being and prosperity of cities, regions, nations, and their inhabitants. Historically, urban planners assumed the role of planning and locating infrastructure, even as others designed, built, and managed it. Today, as we have argued, the planning profession's interest in infrastructure has declined in deference to specialists, such as engineers, other public work officials, and financiers. While this is true, it is only part of the story.

As the pace of technological innovation speeds up, new technologies place extraordinary demands on society to integrate them into the ever more complex webs of life. Not the least of these demands are urban complexes made possible by infrastructure networks. Megacity-regions exceed 25 million, urban complexes in China, Japan, and the United States exceed 50 million. These new technologies, including infrastructure, have required extensive planning, mostly done by the private sector in the gulfs opened by deregulation. I believe city-regions and their infrastructures require an entirely new type of planning due to the substantial changes wrought by the global economy, rampant inequality, and the climate crisis.

Relevant to these contemporary concerns are approaches that consider the networked nature of cities and society.[1] The internet continues to reshape both global and local geographies. This has accelerated and become abundantly clear in the light of work and life disruptions owing to the Covid-19 pandemic. Far from leading to the demise of cities and the "death of distance", new forms of communications and transport have enabled new phenomena, the global city and the global economy, to rise to dominance precisely because of the advantages networked infrastructures have conferred.

Furthermore, earlier infrastructures have caused impacts whose severity now wreak havoc, sometimes uncontrollably. They have produced longstanding impacts that continue to accumulate and fester. Most energy-producing infrastructure still falls into this category, particularly those using nonrenewable energy sources. So does private automobile infrastructure, with its insatiable appetite for fossil fuel, asphalt, and concrete. Water supply, wastewater and stormwater infrastructures tend to rely on old, centralized technologies such as dams, sewers, concrete drainage channels, and storm sewers. They also have extensive financial and environmental costs and impacts that are not sustainable (UNCHS 2020; Mehrotra et al. 2020).

Joining the combined forces of global technological change and its impacts is the decline of the public sector, especially its exercise over infrastructure. Under sustained attack since 1980 by the political right in many nations, the corrosion of belief that government can do good for the public has permeated institutions across the spectrum. The welfare states in Europe and North America have cut or weakened government programs, or deregulated, privatized, or decentralized them. As a result, most if not all data confirm that social and economic inequities continue to escalate, and environmental degradation and resource depletion accelerate, albeit with improvements in some places.

These trends are growing with the spread of wealth and personal consumption across the globe. For instance, China and India, with a combined population approaching 3 billion, and Africa, whose 2021 population of 1.4 billion is projected to reach 2.5 billion by 2050 and 4.4 billion by 2100 (UN, Department of Economic and Social Affairs, Population Division 2019), will begin to consume at per capita levels nearing those of OECD nations. In this setting of increased stresses coupled with decreased capacities for governments, new directions are paramount to transform infrastructure to be a force for the greater good once again. First is to boost public capacity. Another is to accelerate collaborations among sectors and disciplines. An early form, public–private partnerships, has raised capacity somewhat, yet not without costs. When executed poorly, they work to decrease public capacity and favor private markets. In this institutional milieu, efforts to manage infrastructure amount to staking out turf on terrain that is shifting seismically. These challenging times mandate new approaches and serious transformation.

This is why devolution and subsidiarity, not just in governance institutions and the private sector (read: less consolidation), but in infrastructure itself, is critical. Smaller scale, local, modular, distributed, networked, and inexpensive infrastructures can not only be more sustainable. They enable devolution and decentralization in governance, and thus greater participation by citizens, nongovernmental groups, and localities. This can lead to increases in local control and democracy. In this way, the new forms of infrastructure advocated in this book have big benefits to society not usually ascribed to them.[2]

The size and complexity of infrastructure and the cities that they support bear directly on the very possibility of their sustainability. As Eric Schneider and Dorion Sagan wrote in their monumental book *Into the Cool*: "That the open systems persist and grow in complexity reflects their ability to gather information to obtain energy" (Schneider and Sagan 2005, 60). This crucial gathering of information, whether DNA or digital bytes, takes intelligence and energy, and lots of both. This is what sets apart open living systems from inanimate ones, both still being subject to the laws of thermodynamics. Thus, smart grids and smart cities can only lead to the consumption of even more energy. Increases in the complexity and size of cities and economies further increases energy use. This understanding has profound consequences for infrastructure and cities. Can we design infrastructures intelligently, to take this into account? Can we design cities to be as smart as nature?

The meaning for cities and sustainable infrastructure could not be more clear. Letting nature be a guide, we build open and interconnected infrastructure networks that link infrastructures and buildings into a new and full conception of the built environment, reconsidered as networks of processes and not just forms. Otherwise, questions that vex our societies will continue to loom without answer. The answers are not more energy, more money, more technology. Together, they will dig the hole we have put ourselves in ever deeper.

Simplicity based on thermodynamics that calls for simple structure and simple order needs less energy and less information to keep it together and alive. Is any large object simpler than a star, mostly hydrogen and helium, the simplest atoms? Is anything older? On earth, the oldest living organism is the simplest – the microbe. They will be around long after we are gone. They also are the most extensive, making up 80 percent of earth's biomass. Natural materials are simple materials that let evolution imprint information and embody energy for free, making them innately sustainable. Old infrastructures and buildings have proven it.

We can go further and bring the emergent circular economy into the realm of infrastructure via the sharing economy. The sharing economy trades on use value, not exchange value. Use value as an underlying principle places sharing properly in the realm of ecology instead of economy, notwithstanding their common root in Greek, *oikos*. The sharing economy is part of a greater sharing ecology we simply call society.

We can craft multiple roles for new infrastructures in the sharing society. The new vision of smaller, modular, decentralized and distributed networks suits the interpersonal nature of caring and sharing. This form of infrastructure, digitally enabled, helps bring out the best in us. What's more, this type of infrastructure goes a long way in gaining greater social equity and distributive justice. Let us not overlook that sharing is caring. We can also grasp the benefits to democracy that stem from developing the sharing society. This is because cooperation is a key precept in society, heightened by caring and sharing.

The challenges outlined here have been so great that they have prompted a transformation of thinking in planning and governance that engages a diverse range of stakeholders in collaboration and consensus-building (Webb et al. 2018; Hasselberger 2017). To this call and many others like it, we can intuit that a full revival of the public sector ideal will occur once it fully incorporates sustainable infrastructure.

In light of this onslaught of challenges, the effective management of expensive and extensive capital investments now more than ever requires extensive collaboration, coordination, and integration. The wise use of infrastructure can aid us to solve vexing problems: sustainable urban development and redevelopment, social and economic inequity, the climate crisis, and others. Universal access to facilities and services that were (are) skewed towards the wealthy not only serves cities and societies. It preserves rural and natural environments, including the oceans and seas. Extending the scope of infrastructure to solve social, economic, and ecological problems in sustainable ways requires foresight and collaborative creativity. No single discipline has a unique hold on knowledge. Fortunately, it is widespread knowledge that these issues cannot be addressed by acting alone.

Over a century ago, British planning pioneer Patrick Abercrombie called for cooperation among areas of planning (Abercrombie 1912. Indeed, in that golden age of planning, engineers, landscape architects, and architects *were* urban planners. They routinely collaborated to solve problems and set new agendas. Shortly thereafter, however, Alfred Bettman's address to the 1935 Public Work's Congress, "City Planner and City Engineer Relationships", decried the inefficiency of infrastructure provision when coordination did not prevail (Bettman 1946). Today, we add that professionals and scholars, bureaucrats and business persons, however united collectively, must act in concert with society and its leaders to secure lasting improvements.

In the end, the evolving city-region in global society is a transaction-maximizing system fully dependent on interlinked telecommunications and transportation networks operating in real time across the globe at multiple scales (Meier 1970; Castells 1989; Sassen 2001). This new reality has made obsolete many old notions of cities, infrastructure, and their governance. As systems theorists, ecologists, ethnographers, city planners, and others who have studied whole systems have shown, parts of a system interact to endow it functionality and meaning greater than the mere sum of its parts. Thus, it is folly to separate components from a system, one infrastructure from a network of networks, or infrastructure from a city and its planning. This book presents a new vision for *integrated* infrastructure planning, management, and financing, backed by a set of analytical tools and methods. Together, they can forge a renewed link between infrastructure and cities in the professions, in government, and in the academy. It is a critical task in order to make city-regions more sustainable and resilient using infrastructure.

Cities cannot even exist without infrastructure. The path to sustainable cities is through sustainable infrastructure. These facts are complicated by two others: climate change and the very nature of infrastructure. Because of the way we have built infrastructure since the industrial revolution, many cities won't exist in a foreseeable future. This is due to the sunk costs – to use a term from finance – embedded in these large technical systems. Soon, in many places, these will become sunk costs literally, as rising seas swamp cities along coasts. Some estimates suggest that upwards of hundreds of millions of people will be displaced and become climate refugees.

What this means for infrastructure and the cities that they serve is that they must change, rapidly and massively. No longer can they be the infrastructure of your parents. No longer can they be fixed in place, centralized, massive, and "too big to fail". Too big to fail is an unfortunate euphemism for throwing unconscionable sums of money away on systems that are unsustainable. These same old systems keep us set in our ways and set in our cities that are both soon to disappear forever, at least as we know them now. Thus, we must design cities in a totally new way and retrofit existing ones so we can make them resilient and able to adapt to rapidly changing climate futures. Our futures depend on it.

Notes

1 Tarr and Dupuy 1988; Dupuy 1991; Graham and Marvin 2001; and Castells 2000; 2001 were early shots across the contemporary bow. Anticipating them all and still relevant today is Ildefons Cerdà (1867) – see Neuman (2011).
2 A litany of infrastructure mega-disasters have wreaked havoc on their locales, revealing the continuing folly of investing in large-scale projects that, when they fail, have devastating consequences that go far beyond the numbers of the many lives lost and affected. Whether nuclear: Chernobyl and Fukushima; oil: Deepwater Horizon and Exxon Valdez; hurricanes: Katrina and Mitch; tsunamis: Banda Aceh (Boxing Day) and Sumatra Strait; wildfires: Australia 2019/2020 and California 2020; power grid failures: Texas 2021 and New York City 1965 – this list could go on – the impacts on or by large, fixed-in-place infrastructures show their lack of resilience in the face of inevitable disasters. With the climate crisis accelerating, the question is why are we still building these behemoths when we know that they will fail?

References

Abercrombie, P. (1912). Town planning in greater London: The necessity for cooperation. *Town Planning Review*, 2(4): 261–280.
Bettman, A. (1946). *City and Regional Planning Papers*. Edited by Arthur C. Comey. Cambridge, MA: Harvard University Press.
Bolton, P., Despres, M., Pereira Da Silva, L., Samama, F., and Svartzman, R. (2020). *The Green Swan: Central Banking and Financial Stability in the Age of Climate Change*. Basel: Bank of International Settlements.
Castells, M. (1989). *The Informational City: Information Technology, Economic Structuring, and the Urban-Regional Process*. London: Blackwell.
Castells, M. (2001). *The Internet Galaxy: Reflections on the Internet, Business, and Society*. Oxford: Oxford University Press.
Castells, M. (2000). *The Information Age: Economy, Society and Culture I: The Rise of the Network Society*. Oxford: Blackwell, 2nd edition.
Dupuy, G. (1991). *L'Urbanisme des Reseaux: Theories et Methodes*. Paris: Armand Colin.
Graham, S. and Marvin, S. (2001). *Splintering Urbanism: Networked Infrastructure, Technological Mobilities, and the Urban Condition*. London: Routledge
Hasselberger, B. (ed.). (2017). *Encounters in Planning Thought*. London: Routledge.
Klein, E. (2021). Texas is a rich state in a rich country, and look what happened. *New York Times*, February 25.

Mehrotra, S., Lewis, L., Orloff, M., and Olberding, B. (2020). *Greater Than Parts: A Metropolitan Opportunity.* Washington DC: World Bank Group.

Meier, R. (1970). Cities as transaction maximising systems. In Meyerson, M. (ed.), *The Conscience of the City.* New York: Braziller.

Neuman, M. (2011). Ildefons Cerdà and the Future of Spatial Planning: The Network Urbanism of a City Planning Pioneer. *Town Planning Review*, 82(2): 117–143.

Resource Renewal Institute. (2021). *Fish in the Fields.* Mill Valley, CA: Author. https://www.rri.org/fish-in-the-fields/

Sassen, S. (2001). *The Global City: New York, London, Tokyo.* Princeton, NJ: Princeton University Press, 2nd ed.

Schneider, E. and Sagan, S. (2005). *Into the Cool: Energy Flow, Thermodynamics, and Life.* Chicago, IL: University of Chicago Press.

Tarr, J. and Dupuy, G. (eds.). (1988). *Technology and the Rise of the Networked City in Europe and America.* Philadelphia, PA: Temple University Press.

UN, Department of Economic and Social Affairs, Population Division. (2019). *World Population Prospects 2019, Volume I.* New York: Author.

UNCHS (United Nations Centre for Human Settlements – Habitat). (2020). *World Cities Report: The Value of Sustainable Urbanization.* Nairobi: Author.

Webb, R., Bai, X., Stafford Smith, M., Costanza, R., Griggs, D., Moglia, M., Neuman, M., Newman, P., Newton, P., Norman, B., Ryan, C., Schandl, H., Steffen, W., Tapper, N., and Thomson, G. (2018). Sustainable urban systems: Co-design and framing for transformation. *AMBIO*, 47(1): 57–77.

Appendix 1

Appendix 1

Column1	NAICS CODE	Sector Title	Paid employees May 2020 (rounded to 100)
Utilities and Public Works	22		541,300
Construction	237	Utilities and Public Works Construction	1,070,700
	238210	Electrical and Wiring Contractors	932,900
	238220	Plumbing and HVAC Contractors	1,109,700
Transportation and Warehousing	48 + 49		6,353,500
	481	Air Transportation	
	482	Rail Transportation	
	483	Water Transportation	
	484	Truck Transportation	
	485	Transit and Ground Passenger Transportation	
	486	Pipeline Transportation	
	487	Scenic and Sightseeing Transportation	
	488	Support Activities for Transportation	
	491	Postal Service	
	492	Couriers and Messengers	
	493	Warehousing	
	517	Telecommunications	692,200
	562	Waste Management	443,800
Education	61		12,741,000
Hospitals	622	Hospitals	6,104,700
	623	Nursing and Care Facilities	3,267,500
Museums	712		144,500
Public Administration	999223	State Government Legal	92,300
	999233	State Government Protective - Police, Jails, Fire	384,200
	999323	Local Government Courts	100,900
	999333	Local Government Protective - Police, Jails, Fire	1,381,700
Total			35,360,900

Appendix 2
Rate Process Theory and Examples

The fundamental concept of the *rate process theory* of sustainability is that the rate of any process must be able to be sustained over time without exceeding the innate and "natural" ability of its surroundings to support it. This definition goes beyond existing formulations of the carrying capacity approach pioneered in different realms in the 1960s and the 1970s by Ian McHarg, and by Donella Meadows and her colleagues (McHarg 1969; Meadows et al. 1972). These traditional views of carrying capacity dealt with a specific place at a specific point in time. Neither was process oriented, nor did either account fully for the dynamic nature of the systems they measured. Nor did they consider the co-evolutionary character of human interaction with ecosystems. Another flaw in the applications of these two carrying capacity approaches and derivatives of them is that they did not pay close attention to the surrounding environment and the definition of the boundary between the activity system under study and its surroundings. The rate process theory adds the dimension of time to the dimensions of space that prior carrying capacity approaches employed.

Common functional definitions of sustainable activity assumed "no net loss" as a guiding principle. This principle holds that sustainable activities are ones which do not result in a net loss of resources, energy, diversity, and the like. The net loss approach, while valuable, is concerned with a specific place at a fixed moment in time. Besides not admitting a dynamic conception of natural processes, it does not take into account the starting point, which may not be sustainable. The rate process formulation offers a useful tool, which, when properly applied, overcomes these objections.

We develop the rate concept for sustainability in five categories: rates of consumption, rates of production, rates of accumulation, rates of depletion, and rates of assimilation. The theory can be applied to any factor within these categories. For example, for consumption rates we can use energy and materials use. For production rates we can use goods, services, and wastes. For accumulation rates we can use wealth and poverty, and debt and profit – whether personal, corporate, or governmental. For accumulation we can also use nitrogen fixation, atmospheric carbon dioxide and nitrogen oxides, global climate change, aquifer contamination, and so on. For depletion rates we can use atmospheric ozone, aquifer recharge, desertification, biological diversity, habitat loss, language and cultural loss, and the like. For assimilation rates we can use water quality, atmospheric fluorocarbons, the introduction of invasive and exotic species into an environment, etc.

In terms of infrastructure and cities, rate processes can be calculated for solid waste reconversion and absorption (the ways we need to rethink "disposal" in order to be sustainable), aquifer and surface water extractions and recirculation into the hydrological cycle, energy production and consumption, and transportation. Transportation is complex in that it engages energy usage, pollution production, embodied energy in the physical plant, and social and economic equity considerations. These examples demonstrate a few ways that the rate process theory of sustainability applies to infrastructure.

The general theory of sustainability is based on the first and second laws of thermodynamics, expressed as rate processes. This basis derives from the biochemical and biophysical microfoundations of life processes. The theory must be generalizable across physical-metabolic and social-economic phenomena. As we have defined sustainable processes having rates of regeneration equaling or exceeding the rates of consumption and byproduct absorption, rate processes are an appropriate mathematical form to model the sustainability of a process.

Rate is defined as a unit of a process per a unit of time. Rates describe continuous rather than batch (all at once) processes. For example, heating a volume of air in a building can be described by the amount of energy to heat a specific volume in a unit of time, such as calories per cubic meter per day. The process in this case is the heating of air in calories per cubic meter, and the unit of time is one day. Combining the two yields a rate process.

The rate process can be applied to just about any phenomenon for which determining the degree of sustainability is desired. The sustainability of water usage may be described as the volume of water withdrawal from an aquifer (say) per unit of population per unit of time: liters per person per day. The degree of sustainability is measured by comparing withdrawal and recharge rates. The mathematical formulae for the rate process theory and several examples illustrating its application are presented in the following section.

Two scientific laws underlie rate process theory in general, and rate process theory for sustainability in particular. First is the first law of thermodynamics, which states that matter and energy are conserved. Second is the second law of thermodynamics, the entropy law, which states that energy tends to flow in one direction, from being concentrated in space to being diffused in space, over time.

We can rephrase the second law, roughly, to suit our purposes for deriving a general theory of sustainability as follows: whatever you use and then eject into the environment is of equal of poorer quality than that what you took from the environment. This form of the second law of thermodynamics refers strictly to a matter and energy perspective.

The Rate Process Equation for Sustainability

For a process to be sustainable, the rate of production must equal or exceed the sum of the rates of consumption (extraction), plus the sum of the rates of waste byproduct generation. See Equation A.1.

$$\text{rate of production} \geq \text{rate of consumption} + \text{rate of waste generation} \quad \text{A.1}$$

We can rewrite Equation A.1 as an equilibrium equation according to the second law of thermodynamics, dealing with the conservation of matter and energy. See Equation A.2.

$$\text{rate of production} - \text{rate of consumption} - \text{rate of waste generation} \geq 0 \quad \text{A.2}$$

We can further rephrase Equation A.2 by referring to rates of production (or regeneration) as output factors, and rates of consumption (or extraction) and rates of pollution and waste generation as accumulation factors. See Equation A.3.

$$\text{outputs} - \text{inputs} - \text{accumulations} \geq 0 \quad \text{A.3}$$

We can express Equation A.3 in simple mathematical terms, which sums all the rate processes related to an activity whose degree of sustainability we seek to measure. See Equation A.4

$$\sum j = 1, z_o \; \partial x_o/\partial t - \sum k = 1, z_i \; \partial x_i/\partial t - \sum a = 1, z_a \; \partial x_a/\partial t \geq 0 \quad \text{A.4}$$

$j = 1, z_o$ refers to the number of output factors of sustainability
$k = 1, z_i$ refers to the number of input factors of sustainability
$a = 1, z_a$ refers to the number of accumulation factors of sustainability
x_o refers to output (production or regeneration) factors of sustainability, expressed in a per unit basis, where the unit could be person, volume, area, ...
x_i refers to input (consumption or depletion) factors of sustainability, expressed in a per unit basis, where the unit could be person, volume, area, ...
x_a refers to accumulation or absorption factors of sustainability, expressed in a per unit basis
t refers to the unit of time for the sustainability factor, establishing it as a rate process

In its most universal mathematical formulation, a solution to the rate process theory is expressed in Equation A.5, for a batch (confined, unsteady-state) process.

$$\frac{1}{L}\frac{dx}{dt} = \sum r_i \qquad \text{A.5}$$

x = an extensive quantity such as mass
t = time
L = a measure of the extent of the system
r_i = represents various rate mechanisms,

Rate mechanisms r may be positive (inputs) or negative (outputs). A positive value for the right-hand side of Eq. A.5, namely $(dx/dt)/L$, represents the rate of accumulation of the quantity x and a negative value its rate of depletion, in both cases by the sum of the rate mechanisms r_i. In either event a finite value of $(dx/dt)/L$ indicates a deviation from sustainability that must be compensated for by some other rate mechanisms. Thus, Eq. A.5 is only one component of an expression for sustainability.

Let us illustrate Equation A.5 with the example of heating a building. Define q as the heat per volume (of the building). Inputs are denoted by the subscript k. Outputs are denoted by the subscript j. Start with a basic energy balance where accumulation equals input minus output, per Equation A.6.

$$\frac{dq}{dt} = \sum_{k=1}^{z_i} \frac{dq_k}{dt} - \sum_{j=1}^{z_0} \frac{dq_j}{dt} \qquad \text{A.6}$$

If the temperature of the system (or building) is to remain constant, then the accumulation term should be equal to zero, yielding Equation A.7.

$$0 = \sum_{k=1}^{z_i} \frac{dq_k}{dt} - \sum_{j=1}^{z_0} \frac{dq_j}{dt} \qquad \text{A.7}$$

Now, break up the inputs and outputs into terms that are easily identifiable, as in equation A.8.

$$0 = \frac{dq_{heat\_from\_furnace}}{dt} + \frac{dq_{radiant\_heating\_through\_windows}}{dt} + \frac{dq_{generated\_by\_occupants}}{dt} - \frac{dq_{lost\_to\_surroundings}}{dt} \qquad \text{A.8}$$

From the first law of thermodynamics, Equation A.8 is true. From the second law of thermodynamics, we know that we will never be able to recover all the heat lost to the surroundings into usable energy. Therefore, for sustainability purposes, we need to minimize the heat lost to surroundings, which then should also minimize the heat needed from the combination of active and passive heating sources. In this example, we equate input to the heat gained and generated by passive and active sources, and by the occupants and indoor activities. We equate output to heat gained by the volume of air in the building which we desire to maintain at a constant temperature. We equate accumulation to the heat lost to the surroundings. One convenient measure which allows comparability across buildings, locations, and seasons is to measure the rate process in units of heat per volume per degree day. Units could be expressed as BTUs per cubic foot per degree day or as kilojoules per cubic meter per degree day. Using the rate process method we can compare passive solar heating with conventional heating by convection, conduction, or radiation; or any combination of passive and active energy sources and fuels.

In another example, water consumption, one can compare a low flow, recycling water system against a conventional water purification and wastewater treatment system. Start by saying that accumulation of water is equal to zero, in Equation A.9. Define w as the volume of water usage per person, in liters or gallons.

$$0 = \sum_{k=1}^{z_i} \frac{dw_k}{dt} - \sum_{j=1}^{z_o} \frac{dw_j}{dt} \qquad A.9$$

w_k = water input (consumption) in volume per person
w_j = water input (consumption) in volume per person
t = time

$$0 = \frac{dw_{individual\_usage}}{dt} - \frac{dw_{to\_waste\_treatment}}{dt} \qquad A.10$$

The water balance equation (A.9) is rewritten explicitly in terms of inputs and outputs in Equation A.10.

From the second law of thermodynamics, we also know that Equation A.11 is true.

$$\frac{dw_{recovered\_from\_waste\_treatment\_for\_reuse}}{dt} \leq \frac{dw_{sent\_to\_waste\_treatment}}{dt} \qquad A.11$$

Therefore, since you can at best recover water of the same quality as you reject (and it takes energy to do the recovery), then the goal for sustainability is to minimize the rate of water sent to waste, which would then have three benefits:

1. minimize the amount of water extracted,
2. minimize energy and material inputs required to purify wastewater, and
3. maximize water quality, as there is the least amount of contaminated wastewater produced.

In this example, the more sustainable water treatment system is the low flow system. A fully sustainable water system would recover for productive ecological and economic purposes the wastes generated by a sewage treatment system, including the sludge and the output waters.

Telecommunications networks offer another example of the use of rate processes in infrastructure systems performance measurement. Data transmission costs have fallen sharply as technology has progressed. Bond developed a transmission cost index whose units are bits of information per second per kilometer. He found, in a sort of parallel to Moore's law regarding the decrease in the cost and increase in the speed of computer microchips processing power over time as technology improved, that between 1975 and 2000 transmission costs dropped by a factor of ten thousand (Bond 1997). This has enhanced the sustainability of telecommunications by offering more choices and increased portability to consumers, as well as made institutional monopoly management structures more flexible in both their internal operations and their management of telecommunications networks.

Some of the most intractable and persistent problems related to sustainability are social, not ecological. Social inequalities and armed conflict preceded environmental degradation by millennia. Devising sustainability measures for forms of social inequalities can provide useful tools and indicators for managing societal processes. One of the most visible and measurable forms of social inequity is the disparity of wealth. To aggravate matters, disparities of wealth generate or are at the root of many social conflicts, regardless of whether they are played out in political, military, cultural, religious, or ethnic arenas. We present a first approximation to measuring disparities of wealth accumulation as a proxy for other social sustainability measures. There are other social indicators that can be devised by using the principles of the rate process theory.

Leaving the accumulation term in Equation A.12 immediately below allows for different economic conditions. Under certain economic conditions, no wealth is created and accumulation is zero. In other economic conditions, such as a depression or recession, total wealth in the system decreases. In a growing economy, total wealth increases.

$$\frac{dW}{dt} = \frac{dW^r_{wages}}{dt} + \frac{dW^p_{wages}}{dt} - \frac{dW^r_{taxes}}{dt} - \frac{dW^p_{taxes}}{dt} - \frac{dW^r_{debt,insurance,etc.}}{dt}$$
$$- \frac{dW^p_{debt,insurance,etc.}}{dt} \qquad \text{A.12}$$

Let W define the wealth of the population.
Superscript p defines the poorer population.
Superscript r defines the richer population.

Social policy can be designed to create equity among social groups by selectively reducing housing costs, insurance costs, and other costs for population group p; or by reducing taxes for population group p. Social policy can also increase minimum wages, which should increase overall wages for population p.

Equation A.12 above depicts a particular balance for a population group per time. However, we could also sum over all the individuals in the population, yielding terms similar to those depicted in Equation A.13. This would allow an explicit accounting of the fact that population p and population r are of different sizes.[1]

$$\sum_{r=1}^{r_n} \frac{dw^r_{wages}}{dt} \qquad \text{A.13}$$

The general nature of the rate process theory allows it to be applied to the life cycle of all these processes – that is, for their assessment, planning, design, construction, management, maintenance, operation, repair, replacement, and funding. The rate process theory is fully consonant with the multitude of life cycle methods that are being instituted in realms as diverse as industrial ecology, social service delivery, infrastructure provision, building design and construction, public sector fiscal management, and ecosystem and natural resource management. The rate process theory also allows comparisons among different types of processes.

The fluxes conveyed through infrastructure networks are perfectly suited for measuring their degree of sustainability using the rate process theory. We can, for instance, measure the percentage of transmission of a flux through a network, in terms of what percentage of electricity that makes it from generating station to an appliance in the home. We can also measure the percentage of water lost in a water supply pipeline network. Another case could be the rate of pollution production, such as the amount of CO and NO_x emitted per automobile per distance or time (tons per mile or tons per day).

Finally, the analogue of Equation A.5 for a process carried out in *continuous flow* through a tube of cross-sectional area A is shown in Equation A.14

$$\frac{wdX}{Adz} = \sum r_i \qquad \text{A.14}$$

z = the distance along the tube
w = the mass rate of flow through the tube
X = the extensive quantity of concern per unit mass

Note

1 The author thanks Theresa Good and Stuart W. Churchill for their insights in this section.

References

Bond, J. (1997). *The Drivers of the Information Revolution: Cost, Computing Power, and Convergence. Viewpoint.* Washington, DC: World Bank.
McHarg, I. (1969). *Design With Nature.* New York: Natural History Press.
Meadows, D. H., Meadows, D. L., Randers, J. and Behrens, W. (1972), *The Limits to Growth. A Report for the Club of Rome's Project on the Predicament for Mankind.* New York: Universe Books.

Appendix 3

Institutional Sources of Sustainability Indicators

Entity	Type of indicators	Website URL
United Nations	full range, organized by division (e.g. UNCHS, WHO)	www.un.org www.unhabitat.org
International Standards Organization (ISO)	full range (ISO 14000, e.g.)	www.iso.org
International Council for Local Environmental Initiatives (ICLEI)	full range of local indicators	www.iclei.org
World Bank	development and infrastructure	www.worldbank.org
World Resources Institute	full range	www.wri.org
Worldwatch Institute	full range	www.worldwatch.org
Organization for Economic Cooperation and Development (OECD)	full range	www.oecd.org
Green Building Institute	buildings and structures	greenbuilding.org
Wuppertal Institute	energy, materials, economies	www.wuppertal.de
Rocky Mountain Institute	energy, materials, transport	www.rmi.org
Center for Maximum Potential Building Systems	energy, materials, buildings, land planning	www.cmpbs.org
National Institute of Standards and Technology	energy, materials, buildings	www.nist.gov
United States Environmental Protection Agency (EPA)	environment	www.epa.gov

(*Continued*)

Entity	Type of indicators	Website URL
United States National Laboratories (Berkeley, Livermore, Oak Ridge, Sandia)	energy, materials, transport, environment	www.lbl.gov www.llnl.gov www.ornl.gov www.sandia.gov
National Academy of Science	energy, environment, sustainability, green accounting	www.nas.edu
Institute for Local Self Reliance	energy, waste, local indicators	www.ilsr.org
Society of Environmental Toxicology and Chemistry	energy and materials	www.setac.org

Index

Note: Bold page numbers refer to tables; *italic* page numbers refer to figures.

Abercrombie, P. 205
Adams, T. 97, 102
adaptability and flexibility 179–180
Alberti, M. 9
American Civic Association (ACA) 97
American Society of Civil Engineers (ASCE) 10
Anaud, G. 6, 7
Angelides, P. 159
Annan, K. 66
Anthropocene 11
anticipatory planning 181–182
architects 97, 98, 101
Armitt, Sir J. 10
atmospheric carbon dioxide 3–4; and fossil fuel divestments 32–33; and global surface temperatures 6; and transport 63
Australia 8, 94

backlog expenditures 158
Bank for International Settlements: *The Green Swan* report 201
Barcelona 37, 91, 95–96, 98, 183
Bashroush, R. 73
"beautility" 98
Bellah, R. et al. 169
beneficiary charges 197
Bennett, E. 99
Bettman, A. 205
biomimicry 75
bonds as financing mechanism 194
Boston 90; Central Artery/Tunnel Project (CA/T) 111–112
Botswana: Okavango River Delta project 178
Bourdon, D. 67
Braudel, F. 167
British Rail: Hatfield crash (1999) investigation 173–174

Brooklyn Bridge 38
Brunner, A. 98
budgeting *see* financing and budgeting
Burnham, D. 97, 99

California 13, 132, 159, 177, 192; Budget Act: definition of "capital outlay" 55; Resource Renewal Institute: Fish in the Fields initiative 201–202
Canada 94
capital costs *see* sunk capital/costs
capital facilities 55
capital investments 55; coordination 177; innovative 32–33
capitalism: climate crisis and inequality 11–12; disciplined 32–33
carbon dioxide *see* atmospheric carbon dioxide
carrying capacity analysis 150–152
Castell, M. 12, 57, 164
centralized *vs.* decentralized institutional designs 170–172
Cerdá, I. 37, 77, 91
Chadwick, E. 88–89, 91
Chapin, S. 103
Chicago 21, 57, 188; Columbian Exposition (1893), Great White City 97–98, 99
China 65, 87, 96, 136; river delta mega-agglomerations 47; Three Gorges Dam project 145–146
Choay, F. 91, 172
Churchill, S. 69, 70
circular economy 17–18, 24, 64, 204
circular finance 20–22
citizens movements 105
City Beautiful movement 54–55, 97, 98
city planning and infrastructure 85–87; cause of estrangement 106–107; changes to mode

221

of planning 98–101; grassrooted 104–105; infrastructure-led planning 95–96; new realities of city-region 102–104; origins 88, 90–92; public health 88–90; reciprocal relations 36–38; reform movements, Europe 98; reform movements, US 96–98; 20th century estrangement 92–95
civic art movement 96–97
civic centers 97
civic improvements 54–55
civil/municipal engineers 10, 101, 106
climate change 4; capitalism and inequality 11–12; and pandemics 30–31
coastal infrastructures 7–8; grey and green 14–16
Coffee, J. 191
collaboration 177–178; and financing 191
community capacity calculation 150–151
community facilities 55
community service areas 152
compact city movement 101, 106, 107
comprehensive planning 94, 98–100, 101; *vs.* needs assessments 159
conservation of resources 157
coordination 165–166, 176–177
Covid-19 pandemic 3, 58, 73
crises and institutional governance 163–164
critical infrastructures 58–59
Cronon, W. 21, 57, 188
culture and nature 66–67

Davidoff, P. 104
decentralized *vs.* centralized institutional designs 170–172
Delta Works, Netherlands 7
demand-capacity management 147–150; and demand management 155–157; infrastructure demand assessment 157–160; steps 149, 150–155
developer extractions/impact fees 196–197
Dowall, D. 155–156
Dupuy, G. 57

economic activity level 156
economic growth 65
ecosystem resilience 76
employment, population and housing projections 153–154
empowerment through infrastructure 46–47
energy, embodied 75
energy conservation programs 157
energy consumption 63, **64**, 72–73
enframing, concept of 47
engineers 10, 101, 106
environmental harm 65, 66

environmental movement 105
environs capacity calculation 151–152
equality/inequality issues 40; access to services 66, 68, 78; capitalism and climate crisis 11–12; grassrooted planning 104–105; zoning 100
estrangement 92–95; cause of 106–107
EU High-Level Expert Group in Sustainable Finance 188
Europe: city planning and infrastructure 90–92, 95; grassrooted planning 105; reform movements 98
evolution and ecology 33–34, 71
existing capacity and future demand 154, 163–164
existing and new community capacity calculation 150–151
existing and new infrastructure 158, 202–203
expositions 98

failed/poorly planned projects 40–41, 117, 176; hubris 7–8
financial sector deregulation 21
financing and budgeting 187–189; challenges 197–198; as Cinderella of governance 189–190; coordination 177; financing mechanisms 194–197; issues 190–191; life cycle funding/financing 13, 32, 187, 190, 192–193; private sector benefits and costs 191–192
flexibility and adaptability 179–180
flows/flux 44, 46, 68–69, 71; power of 3–7, 12–14
Flyvbjerg, B. et al. 176, 190
forests/trees 16–17, 18–19, 71
fossil fuel divestments 32–33
Franklin, S. 182
Fuerth, L. 164–165
future demand 154, 163–164
future directions 201–206

Garden City 37–38
Geddes, P. 88, 102
general obligation bonds 194
general taxes 196
GIS 14, 16, 150, 152
global cities 35, 36, 57; and mega-agglomerations/urban megaregions 5, 47
global condition 65
globalization 165–166
governance *see* financing and budgeting; governing institutions
governing institutions 168–170; challenges 163–167; institutional design 170–175; institutional networks 167–168, 171–172; leadership 182–184; principles 176–182

government: decline of public sector 203; funding and planning 9–10, 13–14; lack of confidence in 163–164; and private sector 54; *vs.* governance 169; *see also* public–private partnerships
Graham, S. and Marvin, S. 6, 92, 100
grassrooted planning 104–105
green and grey infrastructure 14–16
green/smart infrastructure 16–18
greenhouse gases 3–4, 6; *see also* atmospheric carbon dioxide
Griscom, J. 89
growth: economic and urban 65; progress and sustainability 32–33; *see also* population growth
growth management *see* demand-capacity management

Hall, P. 88, 92, 102, 117, 176
Hammarby Sjöstad, Stockholm 179
Haussmann, G. 37, 90–91
Heidegger, M. 46–47
high-speed rail (HSR) projects 190–191
history: atmospheric carbon dioxide 4; human population, production and consumption 11; infrastructure development 34, 35, 36–38; pre-industrial societies 5–6; public works and civic improvements 54–56; *see also* city planning and infrastructure
horizontal and vertical integration 178–179
housing: population and employment projections 153–154; reforms 37
Howard, E. 37–38, 77
Hughes, E. C. 169
Hughes, T. 55–57, 59
Hunt, R. M. 97
Hurricanes Katrina and Rita, US 15

impact fees/developer extractions 196–197
income rises and infrastructure demand 156
indispensable infrastructure 33–34
infrastructure: central role of cities for 8–9; characteristics *19*, **49**, **50–51**, 59–60; definitions and evolution of term 52–59, 60; keeping pace with 9–10; scale and modularity 18–20; and sustainability of cities 11–12; types, categories and role in society 48–52
infrastructure demand assessment 157–160
infrastructure hubris 7–8
infrastructure networks 17–18, 35–36, 38–39, 44–45, 57–58, 68; and network theory 43–46
infrastructure renewal priority 77
infrastructure resilience 76
"infrasystem" 59
institutional change *see* governing institutions

institutional design 170–175
integration: and coordination 165–166, 178–179; of systems and settlements 77–78
Intergovernmental Panel on Climate Change (IPCC) 32–33, 63
International City Management Association (ICMA): "Green Book" 93
International Energy Agency (IEA) 63, 73
international reports 10
interstate highway system, US 103–104; and "freeway revolts" 92–93, 104
investments (public and private gains) 29–32; failed/poorly planned projects 40–41; growth, progress and sustainability 32–33; indispensable infrastructure 33–34; multiple values of infrastructure 38–40; reciprocal relations 34–38

Jack, I. 173–174
Jackson, J. B. 85
Jacobs, J. 104
Johnson, S. 4–5
joint development 195

Klein, E. 201
Klein, N. 165
knowledge infrastructure 58
Konvitz, J. 46, 98
Korea: Saemangeum Seawall 7
Kostof, S. 71
Kulp, S. and Strauss, B. 7
Kunkel, B. 11, 12
Kunzmann, K. 95

Lancet Commission on Pollution and Health 31
land use zoning 37, 100, 101, 103; multifunctional intensive land use (MILU) 150–151
landscape architects 97, 101
large institutional networks (MSLINs) 167, 170
large technological systems 55–57
leadership 182–184
Levi Strauss, C. 35
life cycle: anticipatory planning using 181–182; financing/funding 13, 32, 187, 190, 192–193; of infrastructure 13, 31–32; of institutional transformation 175; planning 64, 115
London 20–21, 187; Crystal Palace Exhibition 98; Greater London Plan (1944) 95, 102; London Plan 24; Metropolitan Sewers Commission (1849) 89; Thames Barrier 7

McHarg, I. 67, 105, 150
McMillan Plan, US 99

McNamara, R. 105
McNeill, J. R. 39, 65, 68
McNeill, W. H. 39, 65, 68
McPhee, J. 8, 67
Maintenance, Repair, Rehabilitation, and Replacement (MRRR) programs 177
Maragall, P. 183
van Maren, D. 157
Marshall, G. C. (Marshall Plan) 182
mega-cities/mega-city regions 47, 202
Meier, R. 34
Melosi, M. 88–89, 105, 106
methane 4
Metropolitan Planning Organizations, US 104
Mississippi River and "Mr. GO" Gulf Outlet 15
Mitchell, W. 68
MOSE project, Venice 7
Moses, R. 183
multifunctional intensive land use (MILU) strategy 150–151
multiple values of infrastructure 38–40
Multi-Scalar Large Institutional Networks (MSLINs) 167, 170
municipal art movement 96–97
Municipal Arts Societies, US 97
municipal/civil engineers 10, 101, 106

National Infrastructure Commission, UK 10
National Intelligence Council, US 163–164
National Oceanic and Atmospheric Administration (NOAA) report (2021), US 3, *4*
National Planning Board/National Resources Planning Board, US 102–103
national subventions and transfers 195–196
nature 30; and culture 66–67; evolution and ecology 33–34, 71; smart/green infrastructure 16–18; and technology 47
nature services 45, 90; priority 74–75
needs assessment *see* infrastructure demand assessment
neoliberalism 21, 22, 23, 94
Netherlands 136; Delta Works 7
networks 57; institutional 167–168, 171–172; *see also* infrastructure networks
Neuman, M. 10, 29, 91, 96, 103, 167, *172*, 175, 183, 190, 198; and Bright, E. 14; and Gavinha, J. 163; and Hull, A. 5; and Whittington, J. 13, **48**, 157, 158–159, 169–170, 192
Neutra, R. 66–67
New Jersey State Plan 178, 179
New Jersey State Planning Commission 14
New Orleans and Southern Louisiana 15–16

new urbanism movement 106–107
New York 21, 35, 90, 188; Brooklyn Bridge 38; Municipal Arts Society 97; 19th century sanitary conditions reports 89; Regional Planning Association (RPA) 102; Zoning Code (1916) 100
Nolen, J. 99–100
norms, institutional 163, 164, 169, 172
Northern European Enclosure Dam (NEED) 7

Okavango River Delta project, Botswana 178
Olmsted, F. L. 89–90, 97, 99
organizations *vs.* institutions 168–169

pandemics 4–5, 30–31; Covid-19 3, 58, 73
Paris 37, 90–91, 98
partnership *see* public–private partnerships
Peterson, J. 89, 90
planning and design principles 74–78
politics and finance 191, 198
pollution 31
poorly planned projects *see* failed/poorly planned projects
population growth: and composition 156; and consumption 11, 29; employment and housing projections 153–154
power of flows/flows of power 3–7, 12–14
President's Commission on Critical Infrastructures Protection 58–59
private sector benefits and costs 191–192
private sector funding 21–22
private services 157
privatization 180, 181; and financing 188
process(es): structures and norms in institutional design 171–174; sustainable 68–71
Pryor, L. 8
public and private gains *see* investments
public good 22–23
public health 88–90
public–private partnerships 21, 32, 180, 195, 203; and joint development 195
public spaces 23–24, 90, 97, 98, 106, 107
public trust 23–24
public works 54

railways: British Rail: Hatfield crash (1999) investigation 173–174; high-speed rail (HSR) projects 190–191
rate process(es): theory of sustainability 69–71; and thermodynamics 64, 70–71
reciprocal relations 34–38
recycling and reusing 76
regional planning 102–104
rehabilitation of existing infrastructure 158

relational *vs.* technocratic leadership 184
reliability of critical infrastructures 59
renewable resource priority 74
resource regeneration rates 75
Resource Renewal Institute: Fish in the Fields initiative 201–202
resource substitution rates 75
revenue bonds 194
revolving/sinking funds 194–195
Roosevelt, F. D. 102–103

Saemangeum Seawall, Korea 7
Sagan, D. 203–204
sanitary reforms 37, 88–90
Sanzillo, T. 33
Sassen, S. 57
scale and modularity of infrastructure 18–20; matching to use 77
Schneider, E. 203–204
sea level rises *see* coastal infrastructures
security: and critical infrastructures 58–59; and surveillance 40
service standards levels 152–153
shared rights-of-way 77
sharing economy 24–25, 204
Shattuck, L. 89
Shiva, V. 66
sinking/revolving funds 194–195
Sitte, C. 98
smart/green infrastructure 16–18
social justice *see* equality/inequality issues
sources/generators and receivers/users 44–45
Spain: Barcelona 37, 91, 95–96, 98, 183; citizens movements 105
special assessments 196
special taxes 196
Star, S. 68
Stein, T. 4
Stockholm: Hammarby Sjöstad 179
subsidiarity 172, 179, 190–191, 203
subsidies and indirect financing mechanisms 194
sunk capital/costs 22–23, 31, 198; and fixed facilities 189; and institutional governance 163, 164
supply- *vs.* demand-driven consumption 159–160
systems theory 56–57

tastes/preferences and social groups 157
taxes 196
technocratic *vs.* relational leadership 184
technology 46–47, 202; capital and information flows 12; changes in 157, 203; energy consumption 72–73; ICT platforms and coordination 177; large technological systems 55–57; virtual/wireless 53
telecommunication: private sector 94; and transport 35–36, 72–73, 86–87
Tennessee Valley Authority (TVA) 102
Texas Urban Triangle 14–15
Thames Barrier 7
Thatcher, M. 23
thermodynamics 204; evolution and ecology 33–34, 71; and rate processes 64, 70–71
transformational power of infrastructure 46–47
transport: atmospheric carbon dioxide 63; telecommunication and 35–36, 72–73, 86–87; US 92–93; *see also* railways
trees/forests 16–17, 18–19, 71
trust: in financial governance 190–191; in governing institutions 164, 168

UK 94; British Rail: Hatfield crash (1999) investigation 173–174; high-speed rail (HSR) project 190–191; megaprojects 18; public health 88–89; reports 10; *see also* London
UN 68; Brundtland Report 33; Department of Economic and Social Affairs 203; Environment Programme (2016) report 11; Habitat 3, 63; URBAN 21 world congress, Berlin 66
urban network 57
urbanization 63
US 99–101, 106; estrangement of city planning and infrastructure 92–93, 94; grassrooted planning 104–105; grey and green infrastructures 14–16; President's Commission on Critical Infrastructures Protection 58–59; public health 89–90; reform movements 96–98; reports 10; Tennessee Valley Authority (TVA) 102; *see also* Boston; California; Chicago; New Jersey; New York; *specific organizations*
user fees 156, 197
users/receivers and sources/generators 44–45
utilities 54

Venice: MOSE project 7
vertical and horizontal integration 178–179
virtual infrastructure 53

Wilson, W. 90, 97, 98, 99, 101, 106
wireless infrastructure 53
Wolfensohn, J. 170
World Bank 21, 52, 94, 96, 105, 170, 180, 181, 182

zoning *see* land use zoning

For Product Safety Concerns and Information please contact our EU
representative GPSR@taylorandfrancis.com
Taylor & Francis Verlag GmbH, Kaufingerstraße 24, 80331 München, Germany

www.ingramcontent.com/pod-product-compliance
Lightning Source LLC
Chambersburg PA
CBHW061346300426
44116CB00011B/2017